Behind the Scenes at the Science Museum

MATERIALIZING CULTURE

Series editors: Paul Gilroy, Michael Herzfeld and Danny Miller

Barbara Bender, *Stonehenge: Making Space*

Gen Doy, *Materializing Art History*

Laura Rival (ed.), *The Social Life of Trees: Anthropological Perspectives on Tree Symbolism*

Victor Buchli, *An Archaeology of Socialism*

Marius Kwint, Christopher Breward and Jeremy Aynsley (eds), *Material Memories: Design and Evocation*

Penny van Esterik, *Materializing Thailand*

Michael Bull, *Sounding Out the City: Personal Stereos and the Management of Everyday Life*

Anne Massey, *Hollywood beyond the Screen: Design and Material Culture*

Judy Attfield, *Wild Things*

Daniel Miller (ed.), *Car Cultures*

Elizabeth Edwards, *Raw Histories: Photographs, Anthropology and Museums*

David E. Sutton, *Remembrance of Repasts: An Anthropology of Food and Memory*

Eleana Yalouri, *The Acropolis: Global Fame, Local Claim*

Elizabeth Hallam and Jeremy Hockey, *Death, Memory and Material Culture*

Behind the Scenes at the Science Museum

Sharon Macdonald

BERG

Oxford • New York

First published in 2002 by
Berg
Editorial offices:
150 Cowley Road, Oxford, OX4 1JJ, UK
838 Broadway, Third Floor, New York, NY 10003-4812, USA

Berg is the imprint of Oxford International Publishers Ltd.

Library of Congress Cataloging-in-Publication Data

Macdonald, Sharon.
Behind the scenes at the Science Museum / Sharon Macdonald.
p. cm. — (Materializing culture, ISSN 1460-3349)
Includes bibliographical references and index.
ISBN 1-85973-566-5 (cloth) — ISBN 1-85973-571-1 (paper)
1. Science Museum (Great Britain)—Juvenile literature. 2. Science museums—Educational aspects—England—London—Juvenile literature. 3. Science—England—London—Exhibitions—Juvenile literature. [1. Science Museum (Great Britain) 2. Museums.] I. Title. II. Series.
Q105.G72 L6835 2002
507.4'09421'34—dc21

2001006856

British Library Cataloguing-in-Publication Data

A catalogue record for this book is available from the British Library.

ISBN 1 85973 566 5 (Cloth)
1 85973 571 1 (Paper)

Typeset by JS Typesetting, Wellingborough, Northants.
Printed in the United Kingdom by Antony Rowe Ltd, Chippenham Wiltshire.

For Thomas

Contents

List of Figures

All photographs are by Sharon Macdonald unless otherwise stated.

Thanks and Credits

One of the things that I learned in the Science Museum was that authorship is distributed: behind any supposed 'author' are all kinds of others whose participation, sometimes unwittingly, shapes what is produced, though in the end, it is the acknowledged 'author' who, rightly, bears responsibility. I also learned that credits and acknowledgements are difficult and inevitably selective matters. Here is my undoubtedly inadequate attempt to offer my very sincere thanks to all of those who helped me in writing this book and carrying out the research on which it is based.

Numerous staff in the Science Museum made the research possible and enjoyable: thank you all. I would particularly like to acknowledge the extraordinary generosity, openness, intelligence, good humour and encouragement of the Foodies: Jane Bywaters, Ann Carter, Heather Mayfield, Jan Metcalfe, Sue Mossmann and Cathy Needham, and (demi-Foodies) John Hall and John Redman. Thanks too for invaluable reflective feedback on the manuscript. Robert Bud deserves especial gratitude for his role in making the research possible and for giving support and intellectual insight. Thanks are also due to Sir Neil Cossons, then Director of the Science Museum, for allowing the research to go ahead when directors of many other museums surely would not, for his willingness to explain his own vision and for his comments on the manuscript; and to Terry Suthers, then Head of Public Services, for so generously assisting me to gain access to many different corners of the Museum organisation. John Durant, Assistant Director at the Museum and Professor of Public Understanding of Science, also played a vital role at times as a go-between and provider of encouragement. I would also like to thank my neighbours in the Design office and the following who went more than usually out of their way to help me with the research: Robert Anderson, Sandra Bicknell, Roger Bridgman, Sue Cackett, Robert Fox, Jane Insley, Ghislaine Lawrence, Peter Mann, Alan

Morton, Derek Robinson, Doron Swade, Anthony Wilson, Tom Wright. Perhaps here is the right place to say that I have tremendous respect and admiration for Science Museum and for those who work in it. I would also like to express my gratitude to those many others whom I met on my museum travels and who took time to talk with me and show me around their institutions.

I was not the original 'author' of this research. The idea of carrying out an ethnography of a science exhibition was Roger Silverstone's and he did all of the difficult business of setting up the research, only to have it appropriated by its ethnographer. For not only accepting this with good grace but also helping me to cope with, think through and write (sometimes jointly) about the research, and for offering support and critical insight on my work, I am extremely grateful. I also thank Gilly Heron who carried out most of the visitor interviews discussed in chapter eight. Financial support for the research was provided by the Economic and Social Research Council and Brunel University.

I have been very fortunate in the academic homes which I have had since beginning this research: the Centre for Research into Innovation, Culture and Technology at Brunel University, the Department of Sociology and Social Anthropology at Keele University and the Department of Sociological Studies, Sheffield University. In all of these I have had great colleagues, thoroughly committed to understanding the social world even while the scope for doing so sometimes seemed to be increasingly institutionally fraught. I would particularly like to acknowledge the following fellow researchers of science, organisations, museums and culture whose ideas and conversations have helped me work out where I stood: Andrew Barry, Georgina Born, Jeanette Edwards, Gordon Fyfe, Penny Harvey, Kevin Hetherington, Eric Hirsch, Richard Jenkins, Adam Kuper, John Law, Maurice Roche, Ursula Sharma, Nick Stevenson, Pnina Werbner and Steve Woolgar. Jeanette Edwards, Gordon Fyfe and Andrew Barry also gave me fantastically encouraging and helpful comments on my book manuscript. I am also grateful to Bob Franklin, Pete Marsh and Alan Walker for support, to Gillian Brown and Jesrine Clarke for help with some technical matters, and to Barbara Carey for lending me Kate Atkinson's *Behind the Scenes at the Museum.*

I have also had the opportunity to work out my ideas in seminars and in previous publications. Thanks are due to audiences and seminar organisers in the Association of Social Anthropologists conferences at the Universities of Hull and Oxford, the Anthropology and Archaeology section of the British Association for the Advancement of Science in Leeds, Brunel University Department of Human Sciences and CRICT, the Johann Wolfgang Goethe University of Frankfurt Institute of Cultural Anthropology and European Ethnology, Goldsmith's College Joint Anthropology, Sociology, Communications and English seminar, Keele University Department of Sociology and Social Anthropology, Lancaster University Department of Sociology, Leeds University Museums Forum, Manchester University Department of Social Anthropology, Oxford University Institute of Social and Cultural Anthropology, Reading University Department of Sociology, the Science Museum, Sheffield University Department of Geography, and the Women Heritage and Museums/Social History Curators Group workshop on Women and Science Museums. In their capacity as editors (and sometimes more) of my work, the following have also provided me with valuable feedback: Mary Bouquet, John Durant, Sara Franklin, David Gellner, Eric Hirsch, Alan Irwin, Allison James, Les Levidow, Joelle LeMarec, Philip Schlesinger, Brian Wynne and Robert Young. A version of chapter three was previously published in *focaal. tidschrift voor antropologie* (number 34, 1999) and in Mary Bouquet (ed.) *Academic Anthropology and the Museum: Back to the Future* (Berghahn 2001). I am grateful to the editors and publishers for permission to use this chapter here.

After so many years had elapsed, I probably would not have decided to write this book had it not been for encouragement from Michael Herzfeld, Simon Holdaway, Danny Miller and, especially, Kathryn Earle. They probably didn't know until now just how important their comments were. The interest of Michael, Danny and Kathryn made Berg's Materializing Culture series a natural home for the book; early comments from Michael were crucial in shaping the way in which I wrote it and Danny's enthusiastic reading gave me the energy for the final polishing. I also thank the other, still anonymous, reader for their helpful suggestions. Roger Hall's meticulous copy-editing helped to domesticate the manuscript. To find one of my best former students, Emma Farley, charged with the task of looking after my manuscript at Berg and doing so with such care, cemented my sense that this was the right publishing home.

My 'real' home has been vital to sustaining me during the original research and the subsequent writing of this book. Mike, Tara, Thomas and Harriet have not only put up with my interest in museums but have also (sometimes at least) let themselves be coerced into visiting them with me. Their often forthright views on different museums, their comments on parts of this manuscript, and their support have been sustaining sources of food for thought, and for life, for which I am indebted.

Taster

'The nation's museums and galleries are under the spotlight as never before. Changes in funding and management are clearly inevitable and an increasing number of directors now argue that these must be radical and rapid. . . In the heartland of the traditional museum business the vision of tomorrow is still obscure. The battlefield will be the marketplace and the casualties will be those museums that fail to appreciate the public no longer lives in the 19th century. . . the culture must change' (Director of the Science Museum, *The Times*, 1.5.1988).

'The Science Museum is in the grip of a cultural revolution' (Science Museum curator, *Science Museum Annual Review* 1989).

'I detect with appreciation [the Science Museum's] first steps to becoming not only the nation's showplace for the best in contemporary science and technology but its expanding role in promoting a broader public understanding of these important issues. . . Industrial success depends on national attitudes to science, engineering and manufacturing' (the then Prime Minister, letter to the Science Museum Trustees, published in *Science Museum Review*, 1987).

'Just because it's the first exhibition to be really carried out since the new Director, yes, that does mean that all eyes are upon us. We're the guinea pigs! . . .' (Project Manager of Food exhibition, 1988).

'So the assumption was that just because we were an all female team all we would be doing was showing a bit of cookery' (Member of the Food team, 1990).

'It's not as lively as I'd expected', 'It doesn't look so very different from everywhere else', 'It's a bit flat' (Discussion, Food team, after opening of gallery 1989).

'This gallery has a supermarket logic' (*The Food Programme*, Radio 4, 1989).

'It's so refreshing to see something where people can interact with the exhibits, take part and actually touch things. It's so different to, for instance, the Science Museum of my childhood when everything was in glass cases and you had to read a lot of very small print to know anything', 'I didn't think food was very – was *science*. . . Well, it has to be – it's in the Science Museum', '. . .being cynical, I was a bit suspicious of how much McDonald's and Sainsbury's and so forth is pushed at you - but then, there you are.' 'But, you know, I would imagine they would use experts' (Science Museum visitors, 1990).

Admission: Going In

The aim of carrying out ethnographic research in the Science Museum was to study the construction of science in museum exhibitions, exploring the agendas and assumptions involved in creating science for the public. On 3 October 1988, the day that I began fieldwork, admission charges were introduced at the Science Museum. This was one of the first national museums in Britain to initiate what was later to become a much more widespread practice of charging for admission, a practice which was, and continues to be, highly controversial.[1] There were pickets and media reporters at the main entrance to the Museum and many (though not all) of the Museum staff were wearing 'Stop Charges at the Science Museum!' stickers.[2]

Although I had read about debates over the possible 'commodification' or 'Disneyization' of museums, and had read articles about charging which had appeared in the press in the preceding months, I had not fully appreciated the passion that the introduction of charging would generate, the national and historical significance with which it would be imbued, or the many other changes in museums – and national culture more broadly – with which it would be associated. Neither had I anticipated the degree of contention which it, and its associated changes, would arouse within the Museum itself. This seemed to be an important moment in the history of public culture, one which was bound up with more widespread shifts in the relationships between national institutions and their publics and the government. Debates, many of which had been long simmering, were thrown into particularly sharp relief: debates over public accountability, consumerism, the role of national cultural institutions, knowledge, authority and authorship. To be permitted to do fieldwork in an institution so much engaged with these dilemmas, and whose actions were seen as so symbolically significant, was a great privilege. It was exciting, absorbing, demanding and, sometimes, a political nightmare.

At the time, although fascinating and ethnographically irresistible, the debates over museums and their changes sometimes felt like a distraction from the main stated aim of the ethnographic research – to investigate the construction of science for the public. Like other researchers working on 'the public understanding of science', I sometimes worried that 'science' was disappearing from the study.[3] However, as I was to find, these debates and changes in the Science Museum were thoroughly enmeshed with (though not simply determinative of) the ways in which 'science' was imagined into public display.

On day one of fieldwork, a delay on the Circle Line (something with which I was to become all too familiar) had made me late for a meeting with Mr Suthers, the head of the Museum's newly created Division of Public Services. So, instead of rushing to join the commotion at the Museum's main entrance, I followed the instructions that Mr Suthers had given me by phone the previous week and slipped into the Post Office next door where there was an entrance leading to some of the Museum offices. The warder checked that the divisional head was still available to see me and I was given directions – up what felt like 'secret' staircases behind the scenes of the Museum – to his office. Mr Suthers, a bearded and very amiable Yorkshireman, was not wearing a 'Stop charges at the Science Museum!' sticker. He was dressed smartly and arose to shake my hand. As I apologised for my lateness and sat down, my eyes fell upon the capacious glass bowl of fruit and bottles of Perrier on his wide and tidy desk. 'Very healthy,' I remarked. He grinned: 'Well, we like to try to give the right impression.'

As Head of Public Services, Mr Suthers was responsible for those aspects of the Museum which were defined as dealing with 'the public'. Its tasks, which ranged from educational services and mounting exhibitions to managing the restaurants and toilets, could to some extent be defined as 'impression management'.[4] Public Services was concerned with managing and maintaining the Museum's 'front stage'. The Museum's other main division, 'Collections Management', dealt, as its name implies, with the Museum's collections of artefacts. It was focused on work which for the public was mostly 'back-stage': the acquisition, conservation, restoration, storage, researching and cataloguing of artefacts. To have named these sections of Museum organisation 'divisions' was highly appropriate, for, as I was to learn, the division between 'the objects' and 'the visitors' was one which ran through much of Museum discourse. Objects and visitors made different demands – demands which could not always be easily reconciled.

Mr Suthers explained the role of Public Services and outlined the recent managerial restructuring in the Museum for me. At the time I could not really grasp quite what had been collapsed into what, or appreciate its significance. 'Don't worry', he told me, 'You'll hear plenty more about it and you'll soon get the hang of it.' He was right. The restructuring was a recurrent topic of conversation in the Museum and usually one of the first things, especially in my early days, that Museum staff explained to me. It was regarded as crucial for understanding other things going on in the Museum, and, indeed, what was happening in 'the museum world' more generally. In particular, it was regarded as crucial for understanding exhibitions, the making of which was to be the focus of my study.

On my first day in the Museum I also met several other curators, most of whom seemed to walk and talk very fast, to joke a lot, to work in offices piled high with books, papers, intriguing-looking objects and coffee cups, and to be full of ideas and of a sense of 'living in interesting times' (as one put it). There was lots of talk of 'the Director', of 'before' and 'after', of 'the old guard', of the 'public understanding of science'. One curator told me that I would 'end up with a model of factional warfare', another that 'curators are stubborn buggers – the most opinionated people that you could ever meet – we are all convinced that we are right', and Mr Suthers described his job as '90 per cent firefighting'. This was a world behind the scenes that I had not quite expected. It seemed almost like the world of David Mamet's play, *The Museum of Science and Industry Story* (1988), in which Chicago's Museum of Science and Industry comes alive at night with skirmishing groups – railroad workers living in the transport exhibits, miners in a display of coal mining, 'Potowatamies' in an area devoted to 'primitive technologies' – seeking to stake out and protect their own territories and interests while commenting ironically on the museum's subject matter and its role. My task was to enter the behind-the-scenes world of the Science Museum, to find out how it works, what kinds of passions and ideas motivate practice, and whether and how this percolates into the science that is put on public display.

Framing and Following

This research was part of a broader programme of research on the 'public understanding of science', research which sought to investigate understandings of science in diverse public settings.[5] Studying the makers and consumers of a science exhibition was a means of following the processes involved in 'translating' expert scientific knowledge into knowledge for a lay public. One of the particular interests of the research was to consider how the specific demands of museum exhibition would shape what was presented to the public and also what visitors would make of it. In an earlier study of the making of a science television programme, Roger Silverstone (who devised the Science Museum research) had shown how televisual demands (such as, the need for a good story and dramatic pictures) 'framed' and shaped the representation of science.[6] What kinds of demands would a three-dimensional exhibition, a representation which would remain in place for a decade or more, make on the representation and understanding of science? By observing the day-to-day activities and negotiations involved in producing an exhibition, the hope was that such demands would become evident – as indeed they did.

As I have already noted, and as will be described more fully in the chapters which follow, the museum study also spread beyond these concerns with the nature of the medium to consider the nature of the broader cultural 'moment'. Given that the changes under way within the Science Museum were of such pervasive local concern, given that the exhibition whose making I was following in detail was explicitly framed in terms of such changes, and given the echoes that I heard at so many museum conferences and other museums that I visited, this I felt to be inevitable. What this means for the account which follows is that this is a story about a particular time as well as a particular place. This specificity is important. It is important not only because specificity matters but also because it throws some of the more long-standing features and ambivalences of museum ambition and practice into relief. Like the 'social dramas' of which Victor Turner has written, this 'time-place' seems to me to be worth speaking from, in order to speak of and to broader political-cultural concerns.[7]

Edging beyond original research aims and reformulating some of the models initially used is often a consequence of ethnographic research as the ethnographer struggles to make sense of local priorities and ways of seeing. As well as spreading wider, this ethnography also shows that the 'communication model' with which the research began – a model in which science was taken from the world of science and translated by the museum into something to be 'responded to' by the public – is far too neat in practice. By participant-observing messy actuality, it becomes clear that scientists sometimes intervene later than this model would imply and visitors earlier. Moreover, the process itself, while in some respects a matter of translation, is more multi-faceted and did not straightforwardly 'begin' – or indeed 'end' – with 'the science'. Neither, indeed, are 'science', 'scientists', 'the public' or 'museum staff' necessarily homogeneous groups or categories. Carrying out ethnography highlights some of the important differences within each of these – differences which have significant consequences for the kinds of displays, and forms of knowledge, constructed.

Following the local players and trying to understand their concerns and their ways of seeing and doing, was, then, a principal and in many ways traditional aim of this ethnography. While ethnographic research often has the useful capacity to redefine itself and move beyond its original remit, it does nevertheless inevitably begin somewhere and with particular players. Most often these are human players. An important strand of social research on science and technology, which has come to be called actor network theory, has, however, argued that we should not accord agency only to humans.[8] Instead, we should recognise that non-humans (particular technologies or objects for example) may also be actors and exercise agency. While this perspective sometimes seems to me to pay too little attention to language and classification, taking into account the actions of the non-human as well as the human does more empirical justice to the case here than would considering only human actions. Moreover, one of the problems that an ethnographer working in a relatively 'unexotic' setting may face is how to defamiliarise the familiar.[9] Trying to overcome my own original presuppositions about agency, and the discreteness of the social and the technical, was a useful defamiliarising strategy which helped me to see, or frame, things in new ways. In the story below, my own beginning point was 'the exhibition' – an exhibition about food which came to be called 'Food for Thought. The Sainsbury Gallery'. In terms of primary actors, this led me to pay particular day-to-day attention to a group of Museum staff charged with the task of creating the exhibition; but beyond this I attempted to follow a myriad of different kinds of actors who came to be involved as the exhibition was negotiated into being.[10]

Writing in and Reading off

As Handler and Gable point out in their superb study of Colonial Williamsburg, 'most research on museums has proceeded by ignoring much of what happens in them.'[11] Instead, it is generally based on the finished exhibition, with a tendency to assume that researcher interpretations somehow map onto meanings 'written in' by the culture producers. Moreover, just who (or what) is 'the culture producer' is also rather unproblematically assigned. Sometimes it is the particular individuals who have been directly involved who are so assigned, at others it is institutions in general, 'the state', 'dominant ideology' or 'corporate capitalism' (with these sometimes being elided with one another). What an ethnography, especially one coupled with historical and political-economic analysis, can provide is a fuller account of the nature and complexities of production: of the disjunctions, disagreements and 'surprise outcomes' involved in cultural production. It can highlight what did not survive into finished form as well as what did, and also some of the reasons for particular angles or gaps. As the ethnography here shows, agency and authorship – the social allocation of agency – are contested and negotiated in ways which have consequences for the nature of the cultural product and for some of the ways in which it will be interpreted.

In chapter four I set out in more detail an 'authorial puzzle' which constitutes a main plot of this book. In brief, this was the fact that the food exhibition turned out differently in some significant respects from the Museum exhibition team's expectations. For the exhibition team, it was an opportunity to create a democratising, empowering exhibition. Yet, the final product also came to be interpreted as a representation of a rather less than democratising free-market enterprise culture in which the public is expected to make choices but denied some of the means to make them. How an exhibition can end up different from original intentions in politically significant respects is one of the stories that this ethnography tells. It shows us that the process which is sometimes called 'encoding' in cultural studies can be just as multifaceted and disjunctive with cultural texts as 'decoding' by audiences.[12]

As we shall see below, exhibition team members themselves give accounts for the disparity between their original aims and the finished exhibition. My account differs from these, however. This is not because their accounts are dishonest (though given the importance of impression management in an institution like the Science Museum it is likely that any account will be carefully constructed). Rather, it is because events are understood, described and even perceived according to particular conventions and circumstances. The ethnographer tries to understand these and also to draw attention to assumptions and details that participants may have taken for granted or not noticed.[13]

My account here has also benefited from being able to move backwards and forwards across time to use insights derived from visitors to revisit the material on exhibitionary production and *vice-versa*. I should also note that, while I am critical of analyses of cultural products which simply 'read off' production and intention (or, indeed, consumption) from 'texts', I also think that theoretically-informed critical readings of cultural products are a valid and often insightful contribution to understanding. Such analyses seek to explore the possible significations of specific representations through an understanding of broader cultural practices of meaning construction.[14] Sometimes, in discussion in the Museum and at museum conferences, I have heard comments to the effect that such analyses are redundant and that all that matters is 'what the visitors think'. While I agree that it is important to research visitors (chapter eight discusses this in detail), this is ideally coupled with consideration of more critically-informed accounts. The task of any audience research is not simply to celebrate whatever visitors, viewers or readers do or say but also to consider what they do not and the reasons for both. Moreover, the move towards rather uncritical celebration of visitor or viewer 'readings', plus the dismissal of what might be called 'deep expertise', chimes with a particular cultural constellation (explored in this book) in which there is a privileging of the consumer ('the customer is always right') and a distrust of certain forms of expertise and complexity. This cultural perspective – which in various areas of public life is becoming secured as a kind of moral principle – is not without its problems, and one aim of this ethnography is to highlight some of its easily unnoticed side effects.

Exoticism, Parallels and Overlaps

When I began this research, the Science Museum was already both familiar and unfamiliar to me. Like many members of the British public, especially the middle-classes, I had visited the Museum before. One Museum wisdom has it that most visitors come three times – at the age of nine, then with a child of nine, and finally with a grandchild of nine. In fact, this was usually related with reference to masculine gender: 'He comes at nine, then as a father. . .' Perhaps this is why I had missed out on my own visit at nine (or at any other years during my childhood), and had to wait until the next stage (though my children were younger than nine at the time). Nevertheless, when I began the research, the Museum was already in some senses familiar to me as a place which I had visited, and more broadly as part of a genre, of museums, which were part of my own cultural landscape. It was also, however, deeply unfamiliar both in the sense that there was much – especially about its workings – that I had never encountered before, and also in that it remained an exotic and even magical place for me. I loved the immensity of the Science Museum and its almost surreal internal diversity, and the possibility of going behind the scenes of this world felt like – and was – a great adventure.

I can still almost viscerally feel the excitement that I first felt on being able to go from the front-stage of the Museum displays through doors, often hidden at the back of galleries, into what initially seemed to be a maze of footfall-echoey staircases and doors to mysterious offices. I liked having my own key to be able to use these doors, and being able to move, unchallenged by the security warders who manned the boundary, from visitor space to curator space. However, although the Museum retained its magic for me and although I continue to find the workings of museums fascinating, much of the day-to-day activity in that world behind the scenes was familiar and even mundane office life: writing (mostly at computers), reading, 'shuffling paper' (as routine administration is referred to), making telephone calls, photocopying, picking up and sending faxes, having coffee, holding meetings, chatting, and leaving and arriving for other meetings or conferences, or perhaps for a spot of shopping. Much of this, and its everyday tribulations and celebrations – someone going off sick, the photocopier breaking down, misplacing an urgently needed file, a promotion, a birthday, a piece accepted for publication – was very much like the routine academic milieu.

The parallels with my own university world ran deeper, however. National museums and universities are both public institutions in receipt of state funding; both have an educational and public service remit. Museum staff, like university staff, are concerned with issues of knowledge, communication and research. At the time of my fieldwork, museums and universities were pursuing sponsorship and their publics (visitors or students) more actively than previously; and in both there were claims that research was under threat. There was talk, and evidence, of 'cutbacks', 'efficiency savings', 'managerial restructurings' and 'down-sizing'. Moreover, new forms of audit, with an accompanying tide of bureaucracy, were being introduced, and yet more – especially performance indicators – were looming on the horizon.[15] There was also a level of concern, that we have now come to take for granted but which then felt new in its intensity, with PR (the management and creation of good public relations) and its accoutrements of corporate images and logos, and careful use of the media.

The Museum was not, however, identical with the university. Museum staff also had particular concerns – with objects and conservation, with gallery space, with the national status of the institution, with their own specific promotion practices – which, while analogous in some respects, were also important to understand in themselves. In the account which follows my primary aim is to describe the museum context and allow the reader to contemplate any analogies. Nevertheless, one of my motives for returning to this Science Museum material is my own continued awareness of parallels between the dilemmas and debates which I witnessed in the Museum and those in other areas of public life, especially, though not exclusively, in universities. In trying to make sense of how the best of intentions from very capable people can end up by having ramifications which they do not expect, I have returned again and again in my thoughts to the case described here. What was going on in the Science Museum illustrates well some of the issues raised by changes underway in many public institutions. I have myself welcomed some of these changes – trying to find less arrogant and more attractive and interactive ways of engaging with visitors, students or audiences, for example – but I am also deeply concerned about some of the consequences for our conceptions of knowledge and for our cultural ambitions more generally. I will return to this in the final chapter.

The Museum context also overlapped with the university world. Museum staff sometimes attended the same conferences as myself; we shared common academic acquaintances; some Museum staff worked on similar topics to academics I knew and had work published in the same edited volumes. In the Museum I was as likely to find people willing to discuss with me, say, actor network theory, as I was in the university. One senior member of the Museum staff was working on a project that was funded under the same programme as mine, the Economic and Social Research Council's 'Public Understanding of Science' programme, which provided us with the opportunity for some most illuminating conversations. He also held a visiting chair at a neighbouring university. Another Museum employee, who had published on matters of museological representation, helped to negotiate access for the research. He sat on the interview board at which I was appointed and acted to some extent as an unofficial local research supervisor as well as being a tremendous source of insight and intellectual discussion.

Some Museum staff knew a lot about anthropology. We sometimes discussed it, Museum staff joking about being 'my tribe' and about my observation of their 'savage customs'. One curator wrote a wonderful illuminating short spoof called 'The Museum People: an interactive ethnographic experience' – heavily influenced by Colin Turnbull's study of the Ik – which she presented to me as a foretaste of my observations of the 'bizarre behaviours' of museum staff to which she was looking forward. Some others in the Museum configured my work through the less exoticised frames of management consultancy and organisational expertise (on which others at my university were, at the time, collaborating with the Museum). For them, I was there to 'look at how we make decisions' (as several staff put it) and to come up with a plan of action to improve this. As a recently completed management consultancy exercise by a private company was widely believed to have led to restructuring and redundancies in the Museum, there was also, naturally enough, some initial suspicion about what I might be doing there.

Many Museum staff were reflexive, and often ironic, droll and self-critical, about their work and about museums more generally. Insightful though this was, it sometimes led me to worry about whether I would have any 'extra' layers of analysis to add to those already offered by my 'subjects'. Nevertheless, the bringing together of different strands of Museum life, and attention to a fast-moving process on which it is not always easy for the participants to reflect at the time, makes an ethnographic portrayal by a participant-observer different from *in situ* accounts. So too does the way in which an anthropologist might choose to frame and explore the material. I hope, then, that what follows may offer some new ways of seeing for those involved as well as restating what they already know.

In producing this account I have over the years benefited enormously from the opportunity to discuss my work with Museum staff and to present it at a number of seminars and conferences in the Museum. Such dialogue with those we seek to write about is not necessarily unproblematic but, culturally shaped as it inevitably is, it undoubtedly helps further understanding, especially in the context of highlighting misunderstanding.[16] In formal terms, the Science Museum did not have any rights of censorship over what I produced. I have, however, sought comments on draft material and have tried as far as possible, where this did not infringe upon the integrity of my analysis, to take these into account. What is described here was in many ways a learning process for all involved. It is being published many years after the events it describes and the participants' lives have moved on. All members of the exhibition team with whom I worked, for example, have had their then temporary promotions confirmed. All have gone on to make significant and impressive contributions to museums and exhibitions.

Names and Identities

Carrying out research in a large public institution raises certain particular problems. I could not, I believe, conceal the identity of the place in which I worked. The Science Museum is important for being Britain's National Museum of Science and Industry. Its national (and international) status is a key aspect of its particular public and institutional dynamic. Neither could identities of some of those working in it easily be disguised. For example, the Museum had one Director – Dr (now Sir) Neil Cossons – a well-known public figure. While I do not use pseudonyms, however, I do quote members of the Museum without giving their names where this is not relevant; also, of course, when they spoke to me on the understanding that I would not reveal their identities.

There was a complex politics of naming in the Museum. Staff of higher rank, especially those at the level of Keeper, were mostly referred to by a title and surname (at least to their face) by those junior to them, and by first names by those of equal or higher status, though there were notable exceptions of individuals who preferred to be addressed by their first name by all staff of whatever rank. The names that I use here are those which I generally used at the time to address Museum staff. Thus, I use first names for members of the exhibition team with whom I worked, but use a title and surname for the Museum's Director. Only very senior staff (and only some of those) used the Director's first name when they spoke to him, and I was surprised to find that many addressed him simply as 'Director'. The Head of Public Services, Mr Suthers, would, I am sure, have been happy to be 'Terry', and this is how he was widely addressed. Younger staff, however, were more likely to call him 'Mr Suthers' and as I perceived myself as rather junior at the time, I do so too.

Following the Exhibition

In practical terms, much of my ethnographic following of the making of an exhibition was carried out in the two neighbouring offices where the exhibition team was located. The smaller office was the base of the Project Leader and the Project Manager; the larger was occupied by the four other members of the Team. I generally spent more time in the latter, partly because it was less cramped, and also because, with more occupants, there tended to be more discussion. The Leader and Manager frequently popped in with the latest 'developments' and for coffee and biscuits (to which there was an 'ode' on one of the cupboard doors). In addition to office-based work, however, Team members would frequently go on visits outside the Museum (to other museums for ideas or to borrow artefacts, to food companies, to nutritional advisors, to designers, to auctions) and inside it – on 'recs' or 'reccies' (requisitions – chasing up things which they wished to use in the exhibition),[17] to collect faxes,[18] or to the Museum workshops and other services to check on how certain reconstructions or interactive exhibits were getting on. They also crossed the boundary into the main Museum to carry out visitor research, and, once the exhibition was actually being built, to watch and participate in its construction and 'shop-fitting' (as the furnishing stage of the gallery creation was called).

With six different members of staff often going off in different directions I had to make decisions, often on the spur of the moment, about whom to accompany. Sometimes this was limited by the fact that they had not asked for prior permission from those they were visiting for me to join them and felt it might be awkward (as to a food company concerned about industrial espionage). Mostly, though, I simply opted for whatever sounded the most interesting. Despite the fact that it was impossible directly to observe everything involved in exhibition-construction, Team members would report on their excursions at regular Team meetings (as well as sometimes discussing them informally in the office) which acted in some ways as an 'obligatory passage point',[19] in this case, in the movement of results of excursions into the exhibition itself.

In addition to following the Team members, I also carried out semi-structured interviews with many other Museum staff, especially those involved in exhibition-making. There were also two other new exhibitions being planned during the period of my fieldwork – Flight Pad (an interactive exhibition linked to the Aeronautics Gallery) and Information Age (a new computing gallery) – and I attended some of the meetings for these exhibitions. I interviewed some of the staff involved, partly to try to get a sense of similarities with, and differences from, the Food exhibition. Another development which I tracked, discussed in chapter three, was an ambitious attempt to 'rewrite' the whole Museum, known as the Gallery Plan. I attended meetings for this and also interviewed many of the staff involved. There was also plenty of opportunity for more informal discussion with Museum staff – over lunch (which was often at Imperial College next door), in corridors, at social events such as the Christmas parties and in the Design Studio up at the top of the Museum where I had been given a desk (well away from the Food team so that I could 'escape' if necessary). The Museum's 'in-house' designers, who occupied this large open-plan office, were not working on the Food exhibition. In a new development, there had been a decision to use outside designers. Not surprisingly, this was regarded with some annoyance, and created a starting point for much informal discussion of changes under way in the Museum.

My research was not, however, bound by the physical boundaries of the Museum. In addition to following the Food team to meetings outside (to a 'Retreat' in Lancashire, to visit designers in Chester, or to film-editing studios in Soho, for example), I also sought to locate the Science Museum experience within the broader museum world (a phrase used by those with whom I worked) by visiting other museums and heritage sites (especially those which were discussed in the Science Museum) and interviewing staff there. These included the National Museum of Photography, Film and Television in Bradford and The National Railway Museum at York, which, together with the Science Museum, constitute the National Museum of Science and Industry (sharing financial and managerial arrangements to a large extent). It also included other science museums and science centres, such as the Manchester Museum of Science and Industry, the Birmingham Museum of Science and Industry, and Xperiment! in Liverpool. I also went to influential new sites such as Jorvik, Ironbridge Gorge Museum, Green's Mill, the Design Museum and the Museum of the Moving Image, and also other museums in London, especially in the South Kensington area (the Natural History Museum and the Victoria and Albert). I was able to attend a number of conferences dedicated to discussing museums' developments (including the large international 'Museums 2000' conference),[20] and also a course which involved visiting innovative museums in the north west of England with other museum personnel and hearing about examples from other parts of the world, including the United States, Canada and Finland. All of this gave me an understanding of some of the likely background knowledge of those with whom I was dealing (many museum staff making visits to other museums in order to develop their ideas about exhibition) as well as both alternative ways of doing things, plus the web of institutions and concerns within which the exhibition was likely to be interpreted.

Following the exhibition's life after opening – its life with visitors – was also an important aspect of the research design. This allowed exploration of the extent to which the 'actual' visitors to the Food exhibition corresponded to those imagined by the Team and designers, and of the ways in which they appropriated the exhibition more generally. The methodology as well as some of the results of this research are discussed in more detail in chapter eight.

Book Structure

In this book I bring together an account of exhibitionary production with analysis of the finished exhibition and visitor study of it. In doing so, I have struggled over two particular presentational difficulties: (1) Whether to keep these three dimensions – production, text, consumption – separate (as to some extent they were in the real time of the research) or to allow them to overlap (which helps to throw some of the issues into relief and make the analytic point that they are interrelated); (2) Whether to give a narrative rendering of exhibition-production or to focus on themes. In the end, I have tried to do something of all of these. The book mainly keeps production, text and consumption separate, partly because there is a narrative development following the time-plotted process built into the structuring of my account, but also because it allows the finished exhibition and visitors to intrude into production where this helps throw questions into relief. Similarly, while I focus mainly on particular themes – otherwise I feared that the narrative would read too much like a set of details (complexity can overwhelm) – I also try to convey a sense of the narrative. To some extent here I have been stimulated by the textual freedoms of novels such as Kate Atkinson's *Behind the Scenes at the Museum* (1995) (which also provided inspiration for my title), which use movement between different time-frames in the unravelling of their plots. My account uses changes of tense for similar reasons.[21]

Related to this presentational difficulty, I have also found myself somewhat torn between producing a 'messy text' in the sense used by George Marcus – a text which resists closure and the evocation of totality – and the narrative compulsion to tell a story, which seems to invoke a move towards closure as Janet Hoskins has noted.[22] Messiness had resonance for the complexity and ethical fuzziness of much that I wanted to say about the Museum; but it also seemed to me that there were certain stories that needed telling and that without some tidying up (which is, of course, inevitable) these would be submerged. So, again, rather than try to make an either or selection I have tried to work with this tension and to produce a narrative account, with a sense of direction which results from following a process, but which also tries not to lose the sense of what was in many respects a messy business.

Museum staff, during the time that I worked with them, were being urged, in increasingly forceful terms, to consider and define their 'target audience'. In writing this book it occurred to me that I should do the same and I struggled to try to decide which, of those various possible audiences jostling in my head (Museum staff, anthropologists, academics, people working in museums more generally, myself. . . .), should really be my 'target'. As I did so, however, I came to the view that this 'aim and fire' model was rather impoverishing. If I kept only one audience in mind my task would certainly have been simpler, but it seems to me that the process of mentally negotiating between different audiences and struggling to find ways that can talk across boundaries is a key part of thinking and writing. Some of my hopes are that those who work in museums and related cultural institutions will find that my account of the Science Museum illuminates aspects of their own practice, assumptions and dilemmas, as well as other ways of doing things. I have thought about the issues which I discuss in relation to debates in anthropology, sociology, cultural, media, museum, science and organisational studies, and I hope that the book highlights the relevance of the museum as a subject of study to these (and perhaps other) disciplinary areas, at the same time showing the worth of these debates and an ethnographic perspective to those already interested in museums and science.

The Chapters

Chapter two, 'Cultural Revolution in South Kensington', is an account, told primarily through a focus on the national museums in London and on the Science Museum in particular, of the changes – sometimes described in the press and in the Museum as 'revolutionary' – under way in museums and related institutions at the time of my fieldwork. As well as giving an account of what seems to me to be an important period in public culture and in the development of public understanding of science initiatives, this chapter also provides a broader context, taking us further behind the historical facades of London's museum quarter.

Chapter three explores some of the cultural changes under way and how they were organisationally negotiated by telling the story of an attempt to revise thematically the whole Science Museum and reorganise its exhibition spaces. This is a chapter about the search for 'vision' and the struggle with revision. The processes and debates involved highlight the ways in which possibilities were culturally framed within the Museum: what was sacrosanct, what was repugnant, what felt compelling, what seemed dangerous, what looked irreconcilable. The chapter also shows something of the workings of the Museum: who and what mattered, who and what could make a difference, who and what could make it happen – or not.

Chapters four to seven delve further into these matters. They ethnographically follow the making of a particular exhibition, Food for Thought, which was at the time regarded as something of a 'flagship'. These chapters tell the story of the multiple hopes and ambitions of those involved in making the exhibition, their labours to 'get science across' to the public, their assumptions about the nature of 'science', of 'the public' and of how these might be brought together. These are chapters about struggles with authorship and materialising dreams, about conflicting demands and desires (between 'object love' and 'clear messages', for example), about how a final exhibition may be subtly and unexpectedly shaped along the way by matters which may have seemed trivial or been taken for granted at the time.

Chapter eight moves to the exhibition's reception by visitors. Here my aim is to explore not only congruencies with and differences from the virtual visitor imagined during the construction of the exhibition but also the frameworks within which visitors 'read', and physically engage with the exhibition, and to some extent, as I argue, with exhibitions (especially those of science) more generally. As we will see in the production of the exhibition, critical discussion of the politics of display tends to be foreclosed, and as in previous chapters I am concerned to understand why this is so.

Chapter nine moves beyond the ethnographic account to a broader discussion of the cultural changes described, and of the politics of the production and consumption of science for the public. The chapter, and the book, ends with a consideration of some of the implications of this for more recent – and possible future – developments in museums and public culture.

Notes

1. In 1997 the new Labour Secretary of State at the new Department of Culture, Media and Sport announced, as one of his first ambitions, that he would abolish admission charges at national museums. However, it was only in the run-up to a general election in 2001 that measures to achieve this were put in place and while some national museums welcomed the decision, others were more reluctant, arguing that it failed to recognise the nature of the new consumer. The Science Museum announced that it would abolish charges by late 2001. For a useful review of arguments see *Museums and Galleries Commission* 1997; and for current government policy: http://www.culture.gov.uk. Also see chapter nine below.

2. Where I use Museum with a capital M, I am referring to the Science Museum.

3. Similar worries were shared by researchers on some of the other Public Understanding of Science projects ongoing at the time. As we came to realise, however, this apparent 'disappearance' of science was an important feature of the ways in which it was locally contextualised. Alan Irwin and Brian Wynne, in a volume bringing together some of the work on the Public Understanding of Science programme, observe that: 'the "disappearance" of science does not mean that it serves an unimportant role in such situations – it is more that "science" as a category blurs into other areas of social practice and contestation' (Irwin and Wynne 1996a: 13).

4. This term is from Goffman 1969. The theatrical terms 'front-stage' and 'back-stage' which I use below are from Goffman's dramaturgical model. See also Law 1994.

5. The programme was funded by the Economic and Social Research Council. I discuss some further aspects of this programme, and the wider emphasis on The Public Understanding of Science, in chapter two. See Irwin and Wynne 1996 for some of the work of the programme.

6. See Silverstone 1985. The term 'framing', which indicates the concerns within which science is located, is used in the title of this detailed narrative of the creation of a BBC *Horizon* programme about the Green Revolution. In chapter nine I discuss the concept further. Silverstone 1988, 1989, 1991 and 1992 contain discussion of museums as media and consideration of some of their differences from other media, especially television.

7. See chapter one of Turner 1974 for a discussion of social dramas; and also chapter nine below.

8. Some of the classic works making this argument are Callon 1986, Callon, Law and Rip 1986 and Latour 1987. John Law's ethnographic study (1994) of a science organisation is a sustained example of the use of this perspective

which also contains reflective criticisms of it (as well as reflections on parallels with management in universities); and Latour's semi-ethnographic account of the plans for a 'guided-transportation' scheme for Paris engagingly follows an ultimately doomed process using actor network ideas (1996). For discussion of some of the shortcomings as well as further potential of this perspective see the contributions to Law and Hassard 1999.

9. Strathern's discussion of what she calls 'auto-anthropology' (1987) highlights some of the particular difficulties which may be involved where the anthropologist shares cultural presuppositions with the people being studied. I have discussed this and 'parallel context ethnography' further with reference to my work in the Science Museum in Macdonald 1997.

10. The notion of 'following' the actors is used by Latour (1987) in his account of how to study science and technology; and Marcus (1998: ch.3) discusses different modes of 'following' (e.g. of persons, things or metaphors) as a means of avoiding predefining the boundaries of what is being studied.

11. Handler and Gable 1997: 9. Their own study is one of the notable exceptions; so too, though less extensively, are O'Hanlon 1993, Sabbagh 2000 and Schneider 1998. Others commenting on the paucity of research on what goes on in museums, and calling for ethnographic study, include Karp 1991: 24, Clifford 1997: 166, González, Nader and Ou 1999: 111 and Shelton (forthcoming). The same is much the case for cultural and media studies generally: see, for example, Howell 1997, Silverstone 1994, Thomas 1999 and Willis 1997.

12. The influential model of 'encoding' and 'decoding' in relation to cultural texts was devised by Stuart Hall (1980). David Morley notes that part of the significance of this model was that it moved analytical emphasis from the meaning of a text to 'the conditions of a practice' (Morley 1995: 302). See also McGuigan 1992: ch.4; and Stevenson 1995: ch.1.

13. I have discussed strengths of an ethnographic perspective in relation to the Science Museum in particular and organisations more generally in Macdonald 2001. Other chapters in the collection by Gellner and Hirsch 2001 also highlight reasons for an anthropological perspective on organisations, as do chapters in Wright 1994. Book-length ethnographic accounts of organisations which I have found illuminating include: on museums and museum-like institutions – Davis 1997 and Handler and Gable 1997; on culture producers – Becker 1982, Born 1995, Miller 1997, Wulff 1998; and on science and technology – Downey 1998; Gusterson 1996, Kidder 1982, Latour and Woolgar 1979, Law 1994, Rabinow 1996, Traweek 1988, and Zabusky 1995.

14. For a useful discussion of different strands in such analyses as well as a set of illustrative examples – including one on museums by Henrietta Lidchi 1997 – see Hall 1997. Some particularly illuminating examples in relation to

museums include Bal 1996, Bennett 1995, Duncan 1995, Haraway 1992, and Kirschenblatt-Gimblett 1998.

15. See chapter two.

16. One misunderstanding concerned my use of inverted commas. It is worth noting here as an example of a particular problem of fieldwork conducted in the same language in which it is written about. In addition to using inverted commas in ways common to many kinds of writing (to indicate a quote, a term or a technical concept), I also use inverted commas to indicate (especially on the first instance or where this is not necessarily clear from the context) terms which were used in the local case. In other words, these are 'indigenous terms', even though they may be very familiar to the reader. Were the study of people whose native language was not English, the originals of these terms would probably be given. This is a common ethnographic convention which implies no value judgment about what is being described.

17. A requisition is the paperwork required to get things done, especially to move objects from one part of the museum to another (or from one site to another). Without this authorisation many tasks cannot be accomplished and therefore 'recs' are a frequent subject of curatorial concern.

18. At this time fax machines were relatively novel and the Science Museum had just one central fax machine. Exhibition team members had to collect faxes from this, several floors and corridors – and sometimes a queue – away.

19. This term is from Latour (1987: 150) in his account of how to follow scientists and study 'science in action'.

20. Boylan 1992 is the proceedings of this conference (complete with audience discussion) and gives a good sense of some of the debates under way at the time. It includes a contribution by the Director of the Science Museum, Neil Cossons, which provoked a good deal of debate (Cossons 1992).

21. I use changes of tense to remind of the fact that the action that I describe is located in the past, to convey a sense of engagement and lived present, and to unsettle. See Davis 1992 for insightful discussions of the complexities of tense in ethnography.

22. See Marcus 1998, especially chapter eight; and Hoskins 1998, especially pp.4–7.

Cultural Revolution in South Kensington

The Science Museum is located in the affluent London area of South Kensington. Here, in one of the world's most famous museum quarters, national achievement, history, culture and educational excellence line the wide streets. The buildings exude authority, solidity and the weight of history. Despite the bustle of tourists – more than ten million visiting the area each year – the general impression is one of permanence and imperturbability. Yet in the late 1980s the press was widely reporting 'culture clash', 'crisis' and even 'cultural revolution' behind the monumental facades.

In this chapter, I provide some historical information about the Science Museum as a means both of situating this ethnography and also of highlighting some of the continuities and discontinuities in the Museum's conceptualisation of its role. I also outline changes which were under way at the time of my fieldwork in the Science Museum. In doing so, I pay attention both to the detail of innovations in the Museum – including managerial structures and marketing strategies – as well as to ongoing transformations in museums and public culture more generally. In addition to providing a portrait of some of the apparent cultural shifts, and of perceptions of what was going on, my aim is to highlight influences coming to bear upon the Science Museum (and other museums in South Kensington) and the very detailed (and sometimes apparently trivial) forms in which these could be realised, as well as the ways (also detailed and also sometimes apparently trivial) in which it acted in relation to them.[1]

About South Kensington

Much of South Kensington was developed in the Victorian period, and much of the funding (as well as some of the objects) for establishing the museums came from profits raised by the Great Exhibition of 1851.[2] Like the Great Exhibition, the development of the area was enthusiastically supported by Prince Albert and has for that reason sometimes been referred to as 'Albertopolis'. From its beginnings, when the indefatigable Henry Cole (later Sir Henry, Director of the South Kensington Museum from which both the Science and the Victoria and Albert Museums evolved and the inventor of Christmas cards and much else) petitioned for its name to be changed from Brompton to South Kensington, the area has manifested concern with its public image.

The Science Museum is situated on the west side of Exhibition Road which runs on a north-south axis through the centre of South Ken (as Londoners call it). It is flanked on its south side by the relatively inconspicuous Geological Museum and beyond that the splendid red-brick gothic edifice of the Natural History Museum. Science lies on its northern side too, in this case Imperial College, London University's distinguished college of science and technology, and the Science Museum Library, which is shared with that of Imperial College; at one time, the Royal College of Mines occupied the building next to this. Across Exhibition Road, arts and sciences now divided, roosts the vast Victoria and Albert Museum, the V&A. It is only a few minutes walk up Exhibition Road to more Victorian majesty, the Royal Albert Hall, to Hyde Park, with the rather ugly memorial that Victoria had built for her Prince Consort, and beyond that to Kensington Gardens and Kensington Palace. The Royal College of Music is sandwiched between Imperial College and the Royal Albert Hall, and one block to the west lies the Royal College of Art.

There are plenty of expensive hotels and rather good, if pricey, sandwich shops in the area too, as well as some excellent restaurants, with several ice-cream vans laying in wait for museum visitors. The coachloads of excited schoolchildren, and the families emerging from the tube station exits, are probably making for the Science Museum or the Natural History Museum; the women with hats and arty ear-rings are on their way to the V&A, as are the art-students with their portfolios; the men wearing tweed jackets, air-soled shoes and taking long strides are probably curatorial staff from the Science or Natural History; and those with dark suits and shiny shoes could well be the new breed of marketing staff.

The Science Museum Building

The Science Museum building fronting onto Exhibition Road is of a classical design, impressive and elegant in white stone with tall Ionic columns, capturing the traditional and modern dimensions of the Museum's role [Figure 2.1]. As the *Architects Journal* described it at its opening in 1928: 'It is modern, but soberly British; post-war but not fantastic; or "cranky" like certain science institutes on the Continent'.[3] The set of collections, however, which formed the basis of what was displayed, had officially been known as 'the Science Museum' since 1885. Many of these collections had their origins in the Great Exhibition of 1851 (the Crystal Palace exhibition), and were subsequently housed, along with the arts and crafts collections that would subsequently make up the V&A, in the South Kensington Museum, established in 1857. This Museum was located on the present site of the V&A, on the east side of Exhibition Road, originally in temporary corrugated-iron buildings nicknamed the 'Brompton Boilers'. Then, in the 1860s, the 'non-art' collections (as they were often known) were moved to a set of long thin buildings on the west side of Exhibition Road, which had served as refreshment rooms for the 1862 International Exhibition.

Figure 2.1 'Modern but soberly British': the Science Museum. Courtesy of the Science Museum/Science and Society Picture Library.

The opening of the more spacious East Block, as the new building was called, was the result of many years of discussions and set-backs, in which arguments about the need to do something to try to match what the French and Germans were doing with their science and technology collections were often voiced.[4] France's *Conservatoire des Arts et Métiers*, a national collection of technological artefacts, had been opened as early as 1797; the *Deutsches Museum*, Germany's national museum of science and technology in Munich, was ready to open in 1913, although it did not actually do so until 1925 due to the First World War. That Britain, while claiming to be the birthplace of the Industrial Revolution and a leading nation in technological development, had no similar permanent national museum for exhibiting its achievements was described as a 'scandal' in a document presented to the government in 1911. Due to difficulties over securing a site and the interruption to all plans on account of the First World War, it was to be more than a decade before the East Hall was finally opened; even then, all of the projected buildings had not been completed. With these, said Viscount Peel at the opening in 1928, 'the country will have a Science Museum which need fear no comparison with any in the world'.[5] It took until 1961, however, for the Central Block to be completed, and more than thirty more years for a projected West Block to be even started. International comparisons since have continued to be one impetus in the Science Museum's self-conception, as they are for all national museums.

'Incalculable Benefit to Intellectual Progress'

In addition to national exhibitionism, demonstrating the achievements and worth of Britain, the Science Museum has also been regarded as having a public educational remit since its earliest days. Indeed, the Great Exhibition (like other international exhibitions), of which the Science Museum was partly an offspring, was also intended to have this dual function. On the one hand, such world exhibitions were acknowledged as international competitive arenas: nations were awarded with medals as at the Olympic games.[6] On the other, it was also argued that they provided the public with the opportunity to see the best in current international developments, and thus helped to educate craftsmen and workers in particular. Such an argument was also used with regard to the value of the Science Museum collections and for the establishment of a national museum of science and industry. A Catalogue of the Machinery and Inventions collection (c.1910), for example, noted that one role of such a collection was 'to offer to the engineer suggestions or ideas from other branches of his profession that may prove fruitful in the work upon which he may be engaged'.[7] The Bell Report of 1911–12, which was influential in presenting arguments for a permanent Science Museum, argued that such a museum would not only 'be a worthy and suitable house for the preservation of appliances which hold an honoured place in the progress of Science or in the history of invention' but also that it could 'promote an intelligent appreciation of the leading facts and principles of Science and of the ways in which invention has applied these to the furtherance of the industrial welfare of the World'.[8] The first part of the report concluded that such a museum would be 'of incalculable benefit alike to intellectual progress and to industrial developments, and will be recognised as an institution of which the country may well be proud'.[9]

Although those who came to work in the Science Museum were not for the most part scientists researching particular collections and hoping to make scientific advances by doing so, as was the case in the Natural History Museum, they included individuals with practical experience in engineering and industry who emphasised the importance of the careful research of the collections and 'scientific' modes of display. This principally meant typological and evolutionary modes of arranging objects, locating them alongside similar objects with the same function and putting them into a time-series from the most primitive to the most advanced (these two principles not always being easy to combine, and one was sometimes prioritised over the other). As Steven Conn has observed, these modes of display were the physical manifestation of 'the assumption that objects could tell stories'; more specifically, arranged properly, a museum exhibition could highlight underlying 'general principles' (as both the Catalogue of Machinery and Inventions and the Bell Report put it).[10]

In the late-nineteenth and early-twentieth century, there was generally little conflict over the idea that such 'general principles' could be both permanent and the latest discoveries. Museums were as important as universities in engaging with 'cutting edge' science, and more important in displaying it to a broad audience.[11] By the 1920s, however, this idea had been superseded in most scientific disciplines, as had the centrality of both collections and museums to much of the more prestigious scientific research. Science was now more likely to require sophisticated laboratory equipment and deal with processes and phenomena not so readily visible to the human eye.[12] This was to present difficulties for museums of science, and later – as technologies also became more miniaturised and intricate – for museums of technology. The strategy adopted in the Science Museum from the day that it opened, of accompanying some machines by working models – using handles outside cases or compressed gas – to demonstrate how they worked was not so straightforward in the case of, say, computer chips (to take a case that was under much discussion in the Information Age project which I observed in the Museum). This growing invisibility of science has been one of the problems with which all museums of science and technology have had to contend.[13] By the time that the new impressive facades of the Science Museum on Exhibition Road were completed, the role of the Museum as a research institution and as one of the most epistemologically apt sites for representing contemporary science was already in question. The Museum still had, however, an important role *vis-à-vis* the public, though this too was not static.

Visions of Visitors

One consequence of the demise of the idea that museums were material manifestations of the latest scientific principles, argues Conn, was a shift in orientation towards less knowledgeable visitors – especially children – which in many places was under way by the 1920s.[14] We see something of this in arguments about modes of display in the Science Museum in its early years. Thus, where the Bell report (1910) listed 'the ordinary visitor' last in its list of types of visitor, with 'the student', 'the technical visitor' and 'the specialist visitor' coming first, Henry Lyons (Director of the Museum) in 1922 put 'the ordinary visitor' first and 'the specialist' last. He also laid down new guidelines for the writing of labels which were intended to make them more accessible to non-specialists. In his suggestion that there should be a main part of the text in bold type and a longer sub-text in a different type, what he was pioneering was later to be called 'multi-level' text. This, with further subtle but significant refinements, would be claimed as fairly innovative when I carried out my fieldwork. However, even what seems like an outrageously modest proposal now – that labels should not contain more than 400 words – met with objections from those he referred to as 'the older ones' on his curatorial staff.[15] More generally, as subsequent Science Museum director David Follett comments:

> In placing "the ordinary visitor" first Lyons was much ahead of his time: many years, decades in fact, were to elapse before the museum world

> generally accepted that museums were as much for the "ordinary visitor" as for those already knowledgeable in their fields, and began to apply the modern arts of display with him in mind. Certainly in 1920 the staff of the Museum thought only of the presentation of the Collections to the technically minded – the ordinary visitor just had to make the best he could of the exhibits.[16]

Nevertheless, Henry Lyons won one particularly notable battle, and one which fits Conn's argument perfectly: the establishment of a 'Children's Gallery' in 1931. Not only did the Children's Gallery contain many working models, it was also 'the first realisation of the principle that the presentation of the Museum Collections should not stop at the exposition of technical development'.[17] Showing the role of the technologies in everyday life, albeit within a very clear narrative of technological improvement, was at the time considered a daring new dimension to Science Museum display. Although the Children's Gallery contained some objects from the Museum collections, there were by no means as many of them as in other galleries in the Museum. To this extent it was a portent of what was to become much more widespread – though never ubiquitous and never uncontested – in the Museum as styles of presentation intended to convey more 'context', such as dioramas, were increasingly introduced over the following years. The demonstrative dimension also continued and could be said to have culminated in the opening of Launch Pad, an area containing only 'hands-on' interactive exhibits and no objects from the collections, in 1986.

To say that museums were in part an expression of an 'object-based epistemology', and that they reflected, and tried to cope with, changing ideas in science, is not necessarily to deny their roles also as 'instruments of liberal government'. The latter perspective has been explored especially by Tony Bennett in his work on the birth of the public museum.[18] Drawing on Foucault and Gramsci, Bennett is concerned to highlight the ways in which the development of the public museum was bound up with attempts to transform a populace 'into a people, a citizenry'.[19] To this end he pays particular attention to features of museum architecture and display techniques, as well as comments made about visitors, which illustrate concern with the public. His argument is not that this is a simple matter of control of visitors by the dominant classes as a way of the latter maintaining their class position. Rather, the public museum is a product of a liberal urge to 'civilise' or 'educate' the masses in order to produce 'a voluntarily self-regulating citizenry'.

'As such, the public museum is concerned not only to impress the visitor with a message of power, but also to induct her or him into new forms of programming the self-aimed at producing new types of conduct and self-shaping'.[20] Progress, a preoccupation of nineteenth and early twentieth-century liberals, was to be effected not by keeping the masses as they were, but by giving them 'an opportunity to civilize themselves'.[21] Museums, as part of the informal sector of education, were important to this in that they embodied the spirit of voluntarism which was central to the liberal idea.

Museums, then, can be explored as agencies for imagining and attempting to construct particular kinds of public without being necessarily conceived of as an attempt at class dominance (though there might be such attempts and it might nevertheless result) or as unidimensional.[22] Rather, debates about visitors, and attempts to shape their behaviour in the museum (to prevent them eating sandwiches in the lobbies or to try to get them to read labels, for example), might reveal ambivalent visions of visitors (as unruly hordes or as self-motivated learners) and contradictory impulses (to keep them out or to pull them in). In addition, changing scientific ideas and perceptions of the scientific and research role of museums were inevitably inflected on the workings of museums and their exhibitions. The attempt to cope with multiple demands, and what must sometimes have felt like irreconcilable dilemmas, has surely been a characteristic of the public museum from its inception and museums like the Science Museum have been shaped by multiple impulses rather than the unproblematic 'writing in' of any single narrative.

Moreover, as we shall see further below, museums may also have to labour against their own physicality:[23] the objects and architecture of museums do not always lend themselves unproblematically to the visions of either science or of the visitors that museum staff wish to materialise. This was perhaps less the case in the nineteenth and early-twentieth century when new museums, embodying the latest ideas, were constructed, and especially when science and liberal ideals could both be expressed in evolutionary narratives. Particularly for those working in existing and long-standing museum buildings, however, the architecture of earlier visions can prove an impediment to implementing their own, and objects can behave obdurately, as we shall see in some of the ethnography below.

Crisis and Accountability

Museums have, perhaps, always perceived themselves to be in crisis as Conn suggests.[24] Given the multifaceted and potentially conflictual nature of their task this is not surprising. At the cusp of the 1980s and 1990s, however, this came very publicly to the fore and was repeatedly voiced in the media, with headlines such as 'Museums facing financial disaster: Britain's heritage in crisis'.[25] This particular article in The Observer focused on the financial problems facing national museums, problems which arose from a combination of changed arrangements for funding museums and declining money available to them. Other articles described 'culture clash' and even 'cultural revolution' as being under way not just in South Kensington but also in museums and public culture more generally. Although there were in these accounts many echoes of previous dilemmas – over relative orientation to research or to the public – they took on new inflections in the late-twentieth century.

The 'cash crisis' which national museums faced, in what was, ironically, 'Museums Year' in 1989, was in part an outcome of a transfer of responsibility for the maintenance of buildings from a central government agency – the Property Services Agency (PSA) – to the museums themselves. This was part of a much more extensive governmental strategy at the time of 'devolving financial responsibility' as part of a 'rolling back of the state' which was intended to tackle what the Prime Minister, Margaret Thatcher, described as a 'dependency culture'.[26] Although national museums received state funding, and this was meant to enable them to take over the functions of the PSA, they all agreed that this was woefully inadequate, particularly in the face of what they claimed were years of neglect and accumulating structural problems left behind by the PSA. There were reports of leaking roofs at almost all of the national museums, the Tate Gallery, for example, catching the rainwater in buckets alongside some of its masterpieces.[27] The financial squeeze was compounded by rising costs of conservation and display, both of which – like salaries – were rising faster than the funding received by the museums. A report on the national museums by the Museums and Galleries Commission in 1988 described a troubling state of affairs even before this latest financial 'crisis':

> The funding gap is serious, and has had adverse consequences in all the national museums, which have had to leave unfilled varying numbers of posts in their complements (though these were determined after

> Government staff inspections). The effects are lamentably to be seen in terms of closed galleries, reduced security, curtailed opening hours or days. . ., backlogs of work (e.g. on conservation and the production of catalogues and other scholarly publications), less ability to help schools . . ., inefficient use of staff time (word-processors can hardly be afforded), and less good service to the public. . . Most serious is the danger of a cumulative, long-term decline in curatorial standards, as reduced staff are increasingly stretched and often unable to maintain contact with other international scholars, find time to attend international gatherings, take necessary study leave or publish accumulated experience.[28]

At the same time, as in all other areas of the public sector, museums were being called on by the government to demonstrate 'public accountability': that is, to justify their entitlement to spend what was referred to in government rhetoric as 'taxpayers' money'. The use of this expression, in place of what had been more commonly termed 'public' or 'state' 'funding', was part of the 'new-think' which the Conservative Government was attempting to promote: a way of thinking in which previous state functions were all to be questioned and individuals were to exhibit 'self-sufficiency'.[29]

Quite how to assess 'accountability' – how to make it visible and how to quantify it – was itself the subject of a fast-growing industry of consultants and experts. 'Performance indicators' was the term used for the characteristics used to 'measure' so-called 'effectiveness' or what was termed 'value for money'.[30] The quest, in other words, was for readily countable signs which could be used as currency equivalents to decide on whether 'value for money' (greater output for reduced input) was being rendered. There was extensive debate about what would constitute suitable performance indicators for museums but, within the ethos of the time, it was clear that 'the public' (alias, with slightly differing connotations, 'visitors', 'customers', 'consumers', 'the tax-payer') was considered by government to be one of the, or *the,* most important judges of performance. As the number of visitors attending was a neatly countable 'output' it was widely believed that this would become one of the main indicators of museum performance in 'spending taxpayers' money'. This too created additional pressures, for if museums were to be judged on the number of visitors they received they had to create displays and other facilities which would attract visitors; in the vicious circles of the time, this entailed spending money. The problems were perceived as potentially still more viciously self-perpetuating. Many working in the museum world believed that if they were to follow the government's encouragement to find other ways of raising revenue (by charging for admission, for example) this would mean only that the amount of state grant-in-aid (as public funding was called) they received would be cut further. Not surprisingly, there were disagreements about what to do, and while some museum directors argued that the only way out of this predicament was to become more independent of government by generating a greater proportion of their own income, others saw this as a longer term road to ruin.

In order to prompt national museums into taking greater charge of their own finances, the government required for the first time that the museums should draw up five-year corporate plans, setting out their objectives in relation to 'strategic plans, ideas, and finance'. These were to be presented to government as part of museums' bids for funding (which was no longer to be assumed) and were to be revised each year. There were also significant changes in the management of national museums. Legislation in 1983 established so-called 'independent Boards of Trustees' – appointed almost exclusively by government – at the majority of them, transforming them into 'independent public bodies'.[31] Previously, most nationals had been managed within government departments: the Science Museum had been part of the Office of Arts and Libraries. Trustees are persons drawn from those in Britain known as 'the great and the good' – individuals who collectively would bring to bear expertise deemed relevant to the running of a museum. In the case of the Science Museum (or, more properly, the National Museum of Science and Industry),[32] there was in 1988 a thirteen-strong all-male board consisting of a mix of industrialists, such as Sir Austin Pearce CBE (who was the Chair of the board), Sir John Harvey-Jones (famous for his success at ICI and for his management ideas) and public worthies (including His Royal Highness the Duke of Kent). There were only two professors on the board, an indication, perhaps, of the general anti-academic stance of the government at that time and its endeavour to make public institutions 'think like industry'. Officially, the Trustees 'own the collections and have the statutory duty of caring for them and ensuring public access' as well as responsibility for the buildings.[33] As the Museums and Galleries Commission explains, 'though the Trustees have the final responsibility, they have no executive role (it could hardly be otherwise, since they are unpaid and often have other commitments which preclude their devoting even one day a month to the museum). The Director is the Trustees' executive arm'.[34] In practice, then, the establishing of independent Boards of Trustees did not diminish the role and significance of the Director. However, despite the small amount of time they were able to devote to their task, Trustees were capable of having a significant effect, both of limiting the autonomy of directors (as we will see in the next chapter) and of opposing the government. In 1989, Trustees of National Museums (including the Science Museum) made an announcement that they would collectively resign if the funding crisis of museums was not ameliorated by the greater input of state funds, which contributed to an (albeit smaller than requested) increase in the overall budget.

Introducing admission charges was one of the means by which museums attempted to reduce the funding gap which they faced. The V&A introduced a 'voluntary charge' in 1985 and the Natural History Museum began compulsory charging in 1987. The latter led to a 40 per cent drop in attendance and it was widely believed that the loss was particularly of poorer visitors. The voluntary charges at the V&A led to a drop of about 30 per cent and also failed to raise much revenue, partly, perhaps, due to a counter-charges campaign which produced badges stating, 'I didn't pay at the V&A'. In 1987, prior to the introduction of charging, 3.4 million visitors were recorded at the Science Museum, a figure superseded only by the British Museum and the National Portrait Gallery. The National Museum of Science and Industry (NMSI) as a whole, of which the Science Museum is a part, could claim to be the most visited of all with nearly five million visitors in total.[35] After the introduction of charges at the Science Museum, however, the visitor figure for the NMSI – which the Science Museum delayed in producing – was down by 60 per cent. Despite the bullish statements in the press that this was only to be expected shortly after introducing charges and that figures would soon return to their previous levels, there was undoubtedly concern among the museum management. If charging was partly a response to calls for greater public accountability, the decision of the public to stay away was clearly not a desirable message for the museums.

Marketing, Image Management and Contest

In response, museums went to new lengths to try to market themselves and make themselves attractive to visitors. All of the South Kensington museums employed consultancy agencies to help them with 'identity makeovers' which resulted in new corporate logos and advertising campaigns.[36] Seventeen staff at the Natural History Museum were sent to Disneyworld, Florida, to study customer care and corporate image techniques; and the museum management angered some staff by trying to distinguish between 'curators' and 'scientists', and handing the creation of exhibitions over to a unit which pioneered visitor studies (research on visitors) and mainly 'objectless' interactive exhibitions.[37] At the V&A too there was conflict over the role of 'research' or 'scholarship' as Elizabeth Esteve-Coll, who became director in 1987, introduced a new institutional structure which 'effectively separates the scholars from direct contact with the exhibitions'.[38] As at the Natural History Museum, Mrs Esteve-Coll's attempt was to create more 'visitor-friendly' exhibitions and she regarded this as only achievable if the input of scholars was curbed. As she explained: 'We must make our collections more accessible to people who have not had a higher education or and who do not have much knowledge of the classics or the Bible. . . We know from research that most people can only take in two or three ideas so rather than have a mass of objects we will concentrate on a few major themes. . . and show objects related to these activities'.[39] The V&A also launched a controversial advertising campaign (designed by Saatchi and Saatchi – the advertising company employed by the Conservative Party during their successful 1983 General Election campaign) which for many people came to symbolise the changes under way at the time. The advertisements featured the caption: 'An ace caff with quite a nice museum attached' [Figure 2.2]. For those V&A staff who publicly called for Mrs Esteve-Coll's resignation, this advertisement was a blatant admission of the debasement of scholarship and the proper functions of the museum, and their subsumption to mere commercial and leisure interests.

For others, however, some of the changes in museums were rather welcome. The V&A advertisement could be seen as a witty and honest recognition of the fact that many people go to the V&A for its good restaurant. The attempts by Mrs Esteve-Coll to deal with the 'snobbery' of the 'arts mafia' or 'those reactionary museum people sitting in their ivory towers' was applauded by some as a championing of 'the ordinary visitor'.[40] Likewise, the new emphasis at the V&A, the Natural History Museum and the Science Museum on making museums more attractive to visitors through improving general facilities such as restaurants and shops, and trying to increase the 'accessibility' and 'fun-content' of exhibitions (on topics such as designer tights at the V&A) were seen by many as a rather welcome breath of fresh air.[41] Even admission charges were sometimes claimed as democratising: the director of a metropolitan science and technology museum explained to me that people liked to feel that they were deciding how to spend their own

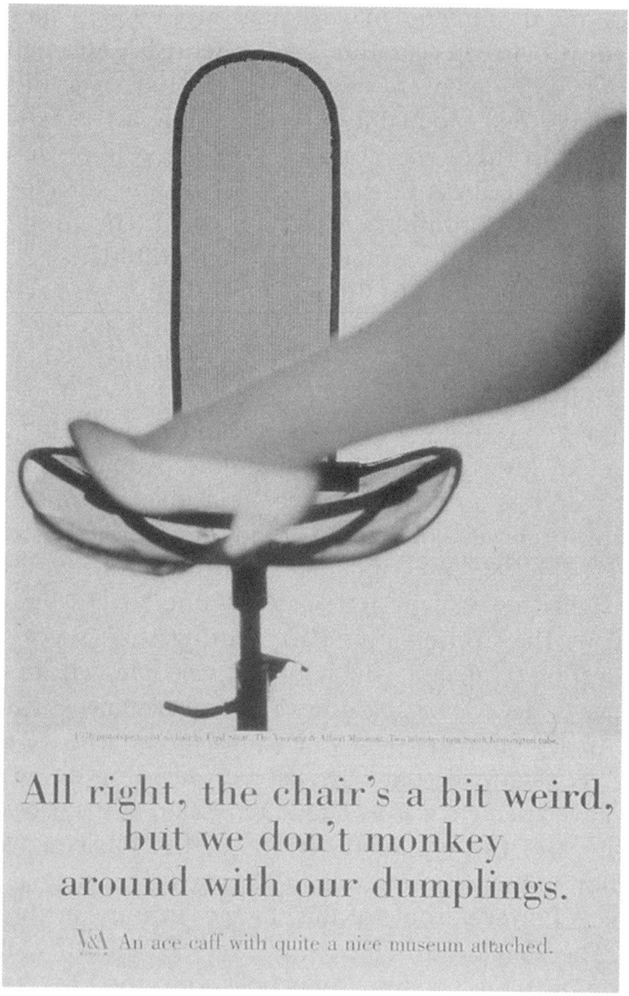

Figure 2.2 'An ace caff with quite a nice museum attached': V&A advertising campaign. Courtesy of the V&A.

money and, not only was it perfectly valid that museums be one of the possible leisure possibilities in which they could do this, but they would also value the experience more if they had made that active choice to spend money on it. Being a consumer – one of the key notions of this period and one which felt new in its ubiquitous use – was clearly being cast as an active and liberating subjectivity rather than as some kind of dupe to market forces. Conceptualising visitors not as a public but as consumers was seen as important for the museum by this director at least. If the nineteenth century museum had sought to transform a populace into a public, and had seen that as a major political advance, it now seemed a time to transform that public into more active and plural subjects: consumers.[42]

The V&A was far from alone in its experimenting with exhibitions of popular culture: other museums did so too, or used techniques of popular cultural representation in their displays. In London, for example, the late 1980s saw the opening of the Museum of the Moving Image, a museum of television and film which catered to popular nostalgia in its inclusion of favourite children's television characters, and the Design Museum, which exhibited not only new design innovations but also familiar everyday items referred to as 'design classics'. Many museums in the late 1980s and 1990s also staged what were called 'People's Shows'. These involved 'ordinary people' throughout the country exhibiting their own collections of mostly rather everyday items – beer mats, teddy bears, egg cups, for example.[43] This entailed not only a representation of popular culture but also allowed exhibition space to be used by those not normally able to do so (or who perhaps did not even visit museums). As such, this too was part of a broader and much discussed development: the attempt to open up museums to previously absent or only passively represented groups. Involving 'the community' or 'giving voice' to, say, ethnic groups who had had no say in the display of 'their' artefacts, was much discussed in both Britain and elsewhere).[44] Feminist, post-colonial and social history perspectives were also increasingly in evidence at museum conferences and in articles and reviews in professional museum literature such as the *Museums Journal*. Other developments included exhibitions questioning and reflecting upon the authority of the museum itself or, as in the much-discussed case of 'Science in American Life' at the National Museum of American History, upon social dimensions of science.[45]

Alongside the intimations of 'crisis' and 'disaster', then, there was also a lively sense of change, of 'opening up', of provocative challenge to the *status quo*. At the same time, rather than smoothly superseding earlier certainties and practices, many of the 'new developments' were the focus of debate and sometimes resistance. The museum became, very publicly, 'a contested terrain'.[46] It became not just a site, but one of the most significant of sites, in which broader battles over the fraught relationships between culture and truth were fought out. The great expansion of interest in 'museology' since the mid-1980s from academics in diverse cultural and social disciplines is itself an indication of this.[47]

Challenge and the Museum Renaissance

In the 1980s there was also a massive increase in the overall number of museums. This increase was paradoxical if what museums stood for (history, stability, fixed identities) was really coming to an end, as various social theorists suggested, unless explained as symptomatic of an attempt to keep hold of such anchor points at a time of identity turbulence.[48] The precise extent of this 'renaissance' of the museum or 'heritage boom' is difficult to determine due to a lack of data (and discrepancies over what should count as a museum).[49] Nevertheless, a survey in 1988 estimated that 57 per cent of all museums had opened since 1970.[50] Everybody in the museum world at that time was aware of, and many were fond of quoting, the finding that on average a new museum was opening every fortnight in the UK.[51] The Director of the Science Museum suggested that it was only a matter of time before the passenger arriving at Heathrow would find that the whole of Britain had become one vast heritage park.[52] This heritage boom was not restricted to the UK, however, though undoubtedly it was felt there particularly strongly and became bound up with debates about the nature of Britain as an 'old country'.[53] Similar escalations in numbers of museums were occurring across much of western Europe, in the United States and Japan, and increasingly in much of the rest of the globe. For the established museums, of which the Science Museum was one, this rash of mostly independently run museums was both encouraging in that it suggested that 'the museum idea' had not become as *passé* and defunct as some had thought, and worrying in that the new museums posed a challenge to the established museum idea through their use of unfamiliar display strategies and in the capacity of many of them to attract visitors who might otherwise have attended the established museums.

There were two main types of these new independent museums, with a variety of hybrids between the two including new local authority museums (such as the North of England Open Air Museum at Beamish, County Durham). There were those set up and run by enthusiastic volunteers, which were generally registered (if at all) as non profit-making charities.[54] Then there were attractions which involved paid staff and which were more commercially-orientated and made an admission charge. As both of these types of new museum had tourist potential, they sometimes also became eligible for funding as part of urban regeneration programmes. Interestingly, many of the new heritage attractions involved the salvage and display of industrial sites and technology – iron furnaces, textile mills, potteries and factories.[55] While this covered some of the same subject matter as museums of science and industry, the 'new heritage' tended to present a 'total environment' which the visitor entered and 'experienced' ('experience' being a key word in the advertising leaflets, and one that we shall meet again in the Science Museum). Such museums generally tried to convey something of the lives of 'ordinary folk' connected with these industries, perhaps employing actors to 'bring the past to life' as the promotional leaflets so frequently claimed. The popularity of these sites also challenged established museums such as the Science Museum to consider adopting some of their display and marketing techniques.

Another challenge to museums of science and technology was the development of science centres,[56] the first of which is generally said to be the Exploratorium which opened in San Francisco in 1969.[57] Those which emerged in Britain in the 1980s (The Exploratory in Bristol, 1987, Eureka! in Halifax, 1987, Techniquest in Cardiff, 1988) followed the same general pattern of collection-free interactive hands-on galleries. In their aim to show general scientific principles, and in their exclusion of any kind of context, these science centres (which did not use the term 'museum') were in some respects an inversion of the industrial heritage movement. They were nevertheless likewise very popular and were an encouraging development for museums of science and industry in that they seemed to indicate a popular interest in science. Several museums of science and industry also incorporated areas on the same principles, the Science Museum's Launch Pad, 1986, being the first; others included Xperiment! at the Manchester Museum of Science and Industry (1988) and Technology Testbed in the National Museums on Merseyside at Liverpool (1987).

Like other new developments, however, they were not unproblematic for established museums. In the case of the Science Museum, the success of Launch Pad in attracting visitors was regarded as counterbalanced by the fact that it contained no objects from the collections and by the disruption its visitors were sometimes described as bringing. (Many staff said they wished Launch Pad could be moved to the car park, and on my own numerous walks through the Museum I was often struck by the contrast between the noise, bustle and sheer number of visitors in Launch Pad and the quiet of much of the rest of the Museum.) As such, the very success of Launch Pad in terms of its popularity with visitors was in some respects deeply worrying for the Museum in that it seemed to signal that what remained the key to the Museum – in terms of the views of most of its staff, in terms of its expenditure, in terms of its use of floor space, and in terms of its claims to singularity – namely, the collections, appeared irrelevant to a large number of those visiting it. This took on an even more worrying complexion in the late 1980s as proposals were made for Battersea Power Station to become an enormous interactive science centre, a development which would, potentially, shrink the Science Museum audience still further.

In the late 1980s, in some ways surprisingly, 'there were more museums and more people going to them than ever before. . .; [and] never before had they attracted so much attention from the press'.[58] Museums had moved, noted the Director of the Science Museum, 'from the twilight to the spotlight'.[59] The time was one of considerable change and challenge for museums as such fundamental matters as museums' roles, the task of their staff, the place of collections, their relationship to research and to visitors were all thrown into question to an extent which those working in museums at the time described as unprecedented. The politics of those changes were far from clear-cut. On the one hand, there seemed to be a healthy challenging and democratisation of the museum with new levels of concern with a more plural public plus a willingness to question and reflect upon entrenched practices. On the other, the financial difficulties led to increasing problems in meeting the needs of the collections and of the public (as the Museums and Galleries Commission report quoted above suggested). There were widespread fears of a 'dumbing-down' and 'Disneyfication', with a resultant loss of scholarship and expertise, and that 'market values' would be all that would count.[60]

A New 'High Priest' and 'Cultural Revolution' in the Science Museum

Directors of National Museums, appointed by the government and now on fixed term five-year contracts, were vested with greater responsibilities and potentially greater powers in the new managerial arrangements. Dr Neil Cossons was appointed as Director of the Science Museum in April 1986. In contrast to his predecessor, Dame Margaret Weston, whom a former employee described as 'stout and hearty but seldom seen',[61] Dr Cossons was highly visible. A face and a name with which everybody in the museum world was familiar, he was widely regarded as an 'innovator'. Newspaper reports (and he seemed to be in the papers rather a lot in the late 1980s and early 1990s) used phrases like 'the High Priest of Museums' and 'museum guru'. He was featured as 'The Experts' Expert' of museum directors (selected by other museum directors) in one Sunday paper in 1989, though it was a close battle with Sir David Wilson of the British Museum, who had come to represent a rather different perspective.[62] The features selected by admirers of Dr Cossons were particularly his 'popular touch'. He was described as 'a populiser in the best sense of the word', having 'pioneered the path of museums as places of entertainment'. His 'use of management skills had enabled his museums to meet the challenges of the 1980s whilst working with virtually standstill budgets', so bringing, said the director of the National Maritime museum, 'a new spirit of enterprise and confidence to museums in an era of government cuts'.

Those selecting Sir David Wilson, by contrast, made comments such as the following: 'Some directors have a clearer vision than others of what is fundamentally important. Sir David Wilson. . . insists on first principles – putting research and curatorial work before anything else. He has strong views on public access and wants to retain free admission to the BM', 'Sir David Wilson. . . has managed to keep the British Museum an oasis of scholarly calm while the rest of us are rushing around embracing versions of Thatcherism'. Lined up here, then, were lines of opposition which were the subject of constant debate among museum staff at the time: traditional curatorial, scholarly and research functions of museums, coupled with free public admission on the one side, and popularisation, reorganisation, enterprise and charges on the other. Although Dr Cossons came from an academic and curatorial background, with degrees and publications in economic geography and industrial archaeology, and although he tried to challenge this polarisation, it was for initiating change and promoting popularization in the museum world that he had largely come to stand.

Dr Cossons was particularly well-known for having established the Blists Hill Open Air Museum, part of the Ironbridge Gorge Museum Trust, in Shropshire – a reconstructed village with actors 'living history' – which had become one of the most notable and popular developments in the heritage boom experienced by Britain since the 1970s. An independent museum, and therefore largely dependent upon money levied by admission charges, Blists Hill had opened full-time in 1973. After that, Dr Cossons moved to become director of the National Maritime Museum, where he introduced admission charges in 1984, making it the first national museum in Britain to do so.[63] To many this was a kind of heresy, which ran deeply against what they saw as the spirit of the public museum. He argued, however, that it was part of what he called a 'plural funding policy'; this also included government grant-in-aid, sponsorship, and income from other forms of marketing.

Such a strategy was needed for museums to become less dependent upon 'the arbitrary cycle of public spending policy'.[64] In other words, charging could enable museums to become more autonomous.

When Dr Cossons was appointed as Director of the Science Museum, then, there was considerable interest and some apprehension about what he would do. Even in late-1988, when I began fieldwork, staff seemed to talk endlessly about the Director, trying to second-guess his plans. There was a constant attempt to look for signs of what he might be contemplating. Thus, one day I found staff huddled over photocopiers passing round a draft copy of a right-wing policy group report on the national museums which was said to have been leaked to the trades union by one of the Trustees.[65] The wording in some parts, I was told, 'looks terribly familiar', the implication being that the Director had been one of the sources of what was said in the report. One copy which was passed to me, had scribbles on it in the margin by those sections which might have implications for the future of the Science Museum. As well as trying to detect future courses of action, there was concern over the Director due, as one curator described it to me, to the fact that he was the 'only provider of scarce resources'. In this respect the Museum was, he suggested, analogous to the court of Henry VIII with a constant 'positioning for power' among its members.

All had expected some kind of change to be brought in by the new Director; and change there was, enough to be referred to as a 'cultural revolution' by some staff.[66] Managerial restructuring, or 'rationalisation' as Dr Cossons sometimes called it, followed. He spelled out that what was also needed was a 'change of attitude' among museum staff, some of whom were 'dinosaurs', who were not facing up to the present.[67] By the time that I began fieldwork 'dinosaurs' had become a matter of everyday museum discourse, some staff choosing actively to refer to themselves as such, and others, possibly picking up on an off-the-cuff comment made by Dr Cossons, constructed an alternative museum-type called a 'bright young thing'. Where dinosaurs were stuck in the past, bright young things were ready to grasp the changes that were under way. While in more serious discussions museum staff would deny that they could be categorised into these two types, these labels served as abbreviations for the division between the stereotyped 'research/no change' and 'populist/entrepreneurial' distinction that was frequently invoked.

One curator colourfully described the change wrought in the Museum as follows:

> What had happened was that the Director had come in and basically thought that the place was run by a load of wallies and dinosaurs. What he thought was that he had to get rid of all of the Keeper Barons – he had to smash the system. So he set up his own marines to break the old hierarchical ranks. What we had was a new socially open system – for the first time we were actually being consulted about things. It was a real enfranchisement for all those guys in their thirties and early forties who, though we didn't realise it before, had been kept down, back in Margaret Weston's day. So the Director broke through all that. He was having nothing to do with the wallies and dinosaurs, with all that business about hierarchy and rank. He smashed all that. He smashed what had been throttling the Museum.

While not all staff were so positive about the changes, the sense of change conveyed here was widely shared.

Restructuring and Re-presenting

One of the changes which Dr Cossons introduced – after a management consultancy had been carried out – was an institutional restructuring of the Museum. It was this that Mr Suthers had outlined for me on my first day at the Museum and which so many staff described and discussed as one of the first topics when we were introduced. Figure 2.3 shows the institutional structure before and after this change. As was pointed out to me, whereas in the old scheme collections-based departments constituted the main organising principles and the bulk of the institutional structure, in the new one these were all contracted into a division of Collections Management. All those other services which had perhaps been a little peripheral in the old scheme were suddenly given equal weight by becoming a new division of Public Services. Still more significantly, according to Museum staff, was the fact that exhibitions were no longer to be organised within the collections departments but in the new Public Services division. In the old scheme, exhibitions had been seen as organically related to the collections (that is, specially designated groups of artefacts), with an exhibition generally having been devised by the curator of a particular collection (such as Space, Land Transport, Electricity) within a particular collections-based department (Transport, Physical Sciences, for example). In the new scheme, however, the directional link in which the collections were the primary impetus in defining what was exhibited was severed, a move which was also under way at the V&A and the Natural

Before

Physical Sciences   Wellcome (Medicine)   Transport   Engineering

Museum Services   Administration   Library

After

Collections Management

Public Services   Resource Management   Marketing

Research and Information Services

Figure 2.3 Managerial restructuring in the late 1980s.

History Museum. Instead, and as at the neighbouring national museums, the starting point and the main orientation of exhibitions was to be to the public.

To some extent it was surprising that this should have been regarded as such a significant change for the Science Museum as it had been concerned with 'the public' and education since its inception. It would be wrong equally to imply that visitors had been ignored in the previous scheme, or that the collections would be ignored in the new. The shift was more subtle; but from the point of view of those involved it was no less significant and controversial for that. This attempted shift in orientation of exhibitions was part of a whole raft of developments aimed at giving 'the public' – or 'consumers' or 'customers' as they were increasingly called – greater priority in the Museum's activities.

Other innovations included the Museum's newly adopted 'Mission Statement'. Mission statements were a relatively new concept in the Museum in the late 1980s and the subject of a good deal of mirth among some staff (who jokingly linked it to the television series *Star Trek* with comments like 'Beam me up, Scotty!' whenever the words were mentioned). This mission statement was: 'To promote the public understanding of science. . . .'. The Museum had, of course, long had a public remit and an acknowledged role in promoting public understanding. What was different in this new scheme, however, was the conceptualisation of 'the public' as made up of 'consumer-citizens' – 'choosing selves'[68] – and an attempt to provide not just what they 'ought to have' but what they might 'want'. In the Museum, this meant new emphasis on what were referred to as 'front of house' matters. These included the external appearance of the Museum, its promotion, its exhibitions and especially the entrance areas, its 'customer relations', and its 'customer services'. The consultancy agency, Peter Leonard Associates, was paid £425,000 to 'create a new identity' for the Museum. In doing so, Peter Leonard stated that he 'refused to look on it as a museum. Our job was to get people through the doors'; and, as such, it was more appropriate to create something which would draw 'people in from the street in the same way a high-street shop would do'.[69] Thus, the Museum came to sport banners, featuring the new modern logo (very different from the coat of arms) on its exterior; a spacious new entrance area (with cash tills) and large adjoining book and gift shop was constructed; the East Hall – the first area entered by visitors after entering – was redesigned with a base-lit steel drum information desk at its centre and enormous screens projecting scenes from different parts of the Museum hovering above [Figure 2.4][70]; Jean-Michel Jarre's music was piped into this area to help convey a sense of the dramatic mystery of science, the modern being emphasised in contrast to the great

Figure 2.4 Industrial age meets space age: Information desk in the refurbished East Hall. Courtesy of the Science Museum/Science and Society Picture Library.

nineteenth-century steam engines (which, because of their great weight and bulk, could not be located anywhere else). Museum 'warders' were officially renamed 'stewards' (though nobody outside the marketing department referred to them as such) and were clad in blazers instead of their previous rather militaristic uniforms. They were encouraged to chat with visitors as part of a new 'customer care' approach. A trading and mail order company was created, featuring products specially selected by the Museum and some Science Museum own lines, such as pencils and keyrings with the corporate logo; later this was expanded to a mail-order catalogue. Galleries were hired out (though only to companies deemed 'suitable') for parties and events. Actors were hired to 'interpret' displays – so Mr Gillette demonstrated his newly designed razor and Mr Hoover the remarkable invention of the vacuum cleaner. New toilets and lifts were installed and plans were being drawn up for improved restaurant facilities. The Museum set up a new marketing department and strove to project its new corporate image and logo further into the public arena through an advertising campaign which included advertisements on the London tube and the Museum's first ever television advertisement.[71]

In 1989 the Museum also set up a Department of Interpretation. This was part of a raft of policies concerned with 'visitors', this plural term being most often used in the Museum in preference to the singular 'the public'. Visitor research, while certainly not entirely absent, was a relatively new venture for many museums, particularly the nationals, and particularly in its more qualitative and investigative forms. The Natural History Museum was especially active in promoting such research, part of a world-wide boom in interest in museum visiting whose origins lay in the increased recognition of the potentially diverse nature of the audience.[72] With this new field came a new technical language and procedures such as 'formative evaluation', 'summative evaluation', 'meta-evaluation', 'customised random sample', 'stratified sample', 'focus groups'. Visitor research and procedures of evaluation and interpretation were increasingly professionalised. Staff went on specialised courses, and conferences and seminars were held. In the Science Museum it was at the end of the 1980s, during the period of my fieldwork, that consultants on 'visitor behaviour' were employed for the first time and training courses were run for members of staff to help them to evaluate the Museum's exhibits. These entailed looking at numerous 'bad examples', culled all too easily from the Museum's exhibitions, of labels and information panels which the consultant would denounce as 'appallingly long-winded and confusing', together with our own usually still ham-fisted attempts to write improved 'short, simple and snappy, please' ones.

Although Henry Lyons had tried in the 1920s to put 'the ordinary visitor' first, this was done from a somewhat different perspective and without all the paraphernalia of trying to find out what visitors might want. The difference can be characterised with reference to the broader new ethos in public service as neatly summed up in a catch-phrase of the 1980s, 'the customer is always right'. Museums, while not exactly operating on the principle that customers were always wrong, had tended to be run within a more paternalistic ethos. In many cases, particularly in museums such as the Science Museum with a more explicitly educative role (as opposed, say, to art museums where social distinction is more central), the public was conceptualised as a child which needed educating and bringing up properly. To take an analogy from school: it was rather like a mode of teaching in which the teacher stands at the front and imparts information compared to the so-called 'child-centred' pedagogical approaches in which children are encouraged to organise their own time and movement and follow up their own lines of inquiry, approaches in which 'education' and 'play' are regarded as inextricably linked.

To move from a model in which the museum sought to provide knowledge which the public lacked to one in which museums should begin from the point of view of what the public (the child) might want and desire, was undoubtedly a significant, if subtle, shift of emphasis. For some museum staff this felt rather like being told that they had to give in to whatever ridiculous demands an unruly brat might make of them. Others relished the idea that teachers should at long last come down from their lofty positions in front of the blackboard and get their hands into the sand-pit. The shift in task required of museum professionals was like that described by Zygmunt Bauman for intellectuals and cultural mediators more generally, a shift from acting as *legislators* to one as *interpreters*.[73] Rather than setting out knowledge which museum staff had, on the basis of their own scholarly pursuits, defined as that which the public should know, the emphasis was now on a type of translation in which the nature of the audience was to be taken much more fully into account. As part of what Macnaghten and Urry have called a 'polling culture' – a culture which they suggest became 'peculiarly powerful in late twentieth-century societies' and in which policy-making is justified through surveys of public opinion – the museum was being turned into an agency of social research in its own right.[74]

Public Understanding of Science

> We had been going along for years, not really sure of what we were about. We vaguely thought it was something to do with collecting objects or saving the nation's heritage. But he Dr Cossons came in and said that it was the *public understanding of science* [said dramatically]. Though what that means, I don't know. Here I am, supposed to be dealing with it – and you are too.

This partly ironic comment by a member of the Museum's Education Department at lunch one day received a good deal of agreement from others around the table. As one said: 'Yes, it has become a buzz-word but nobody really knows what it means'.

The prominence given to the notion of 'public understanding of science' at this time, and its specific history, is worth exploring briefly here, for it highlights the cultural constellations at play beyond the Museum with which it was in interaction. In asking about the term, I was sometimes directed towards a report produced in 1985 by the Royal Society – the independent scientific academy which represents the interests of science in Britain – entitled *The Public Understanding of Science.*[75] This published and widely distributed report made a strong argument for recognition of the importance of science which, it implied, was being underestimated by the general public and by a government which was giving insufficient financial support to 'British science'.[76] In effect, the report was a bid on behalf of the science community in Britain for a greater slice of support from public finances during a period when those finances were being squeezed and those in receipt of them were being called upon to justify the worth of their cases. Bruce Lewenstein has noted that the phrase 'public understanding of science' in the United States in the period just after the Second World War was generally used to mean 'public *appreciation* of science'. In many respects this was what the British science representatives in the mid-1980s were calling for.[77] 'British scientists' were represented as concerned that 'British science' would cease to be a player on the international stage if their funding was cut still further.

Representing science as national, effected partly through comparisons with other nations (especially the United States, West Germany and Japan which were seen as faring much better), was a strategy which could be repeatedly found in the arguments employed. This was not surprising given that state-funding was at stake and given the Prime Minister's own penchant for nationalist rhetoric. In its report, the Royal

Society made two main justifications for the national importance of science. One was economic: expressed in terms of 'national prosperity', the argument here was that the nation as a whole would reap economic benefits if 'British science' were more to the global forefront, but also that individual companies could prosper if their workforce were more positively inclined towards science and technology. ('Hostility, or even indifference, to science and technology, whether by shopfloor workers, by middle and senior industrial management or by investors, weakens the nation's industry'.)[78] The second was political: in order to make informed decisions within a democracy, citizens need to be 'scientifically literate'. There was here an implicit casting of the public as deficient and misguided in its present 'lack of uptake' of science – a 'deficit model' of the public, whose failing had to be repaired by getting more science 'out' or 'across' the boundary from a specialised and relatively bounded world into that of the largely ignorant masses.[79] Discovering better ways to 'package' and 'present' science, and of overcoming 'barriers to learning', were, in this way of thinking, the tasks of a 'public understanding of science project'. Moreover, there was also an assumption that better 'understanding of science' would surely bring a better 'appreciation' of, or public support for, science (though research within the Public Understanding of Science programme itself, as indeed elsewhere, has indicated that this is by no means necessarily the case and can, indeed, even be to the contrary).[80]

Harnessing its own concerns to those expressed in the Royal Society report was in part a recognition of the potential (and to some extent long-existing) role of the Science Museum in what was often seen as 'packaging' and 'presenting' contemporary and potentially 'useful' science to the public and to generally improving 'scientific literacy'. The Royal Society had specifically drawn attention to the educational potential of science museums and science centres, stating that 'recent initiatives in developing fully interactive exhibits and mounting temporary exhibitions on the scientific aspects of current affairs are of considerable value and deserve strong support'.[81] Moreover, 'public understanding of science' became a clear orienting idea for the Museum's tasks which would also, to an extent, demarcate it from the other kinds of museums competing for a share of the public funding. Dr Cossons, borrowing from marketing jargon, came to express this as 'the brand name of the public understanding of science'[82]: 'public understanding of science' was thus a label – even a kind of guarantee of quality and worthy intentions – under which a variety of 'products' could be 'sold' (to the public and to the government). The strategy, adopted in 1986, was one which did indeed win a degree of approval – though no special funding – from the Prime Minister who wrote to the Trustees in 1987 (quoted in full):

> Britain was the first industrial nation and it must always remain a source of great pride that it was from here that the new technologies which were to transform man's life spread throughout the world. We are very fortunate that in the collections of the Science Museum – the nation's museum of science and industry – we have the best record available anywhere of the vital steps to industrialisation.
>
> But industry does not stand still and countries which once learned their skills from Europe are themselves exemplars of high quality manufacture, design and marketing. Industry in Britain is facing up to this challenge and the current performance of our manufacturing sector, particularly in the fields of innovation and productivity, gives cause for optimism.
>
> However, industrial success depends on national attitudes to science, engineering and manufacturing. That is why I am delighted that the Science Museum also displays the most modern technologies – for example in the new galleries on the Chemical Industry, Plastics and Space Technology.
>
> Since 1983 the Science Museum has acquired the status of an independent national body, run by its own Board of Trustees. This marks a new era of self confidence and authority for the Museum and I detect with appreciation its first steps to becoming not only the nation's showplace for the best in contemporary science and technology but its expanding role in promoting a broader public understanding of these important issues.[83]

In addition to the wider network of public understanding of science interests within which the Science Museum could locate itself, there was, perhaps, another internal reason why public understanding of science was embraced by the Museum's Director in the late 1980s. This was the potential for public understanding of science research. This facilitated a linking of the term 'research' not just to the collections but to the public. It enabled the Director to steal some of the steam from his opponents' arguments by continuing to put emphasis on research. By establishing a Professorship of the Public Understanding of Science and launching a new journal and hosting and funding research on the subject, it was intended to make the undervalued public dimensions of the Museum's tasks more professional and scientifically respectable. This was also one reason why the research which I was doing, financed under a public understanding of science programme, was hosted by the Museum; though it was also a reason why some of my own work caused some in the Museum a degree of consternation.[84]

More broadly, however, the emphasis on public understanding of science was also a response to changes within science and its relationship with society. Nineteenth and early twentieth-century museums of science could confidently display scientific principles separate from social factors, and it was generally believed that museum displays could display those principles not just adequately but perhaps better than anywhere else. This was no longer the case. Science in the late twentieth century was widely conceived of as difficult and abstruse, a matter for very specialised expertise. As the Director of the Science Museum put it: 'We are the first society which actually enjoys the fruits of science and technology without having any understanding of it'.[85] Not only was understanding often 'lacking', so too was confidence: science was increasingly seen not as an unmitigated 'good', but often as a 'bad', a producer of environmental and other problems. What was needed, he explained, was public understanding of science, in which museums could play their most important role. A central plank of this confidence-giving public understanding was to illustrate the utility or 'use-value' of science – its relevance not so much to 'progress' but to society and the environment. This chimed also with 'public accountability', and was witnessed in some of the topics which the Museum chose to address, food being one of these. Perhaps one of the most striking examples of this shift from arguing the worth of science in terms of the generalised good and progress to more specific social and environmental interests, was at the Natural History Museum where, in 1989, it was announced that no longer would the museum continue its previous aim to catalogue all known species. This task, the museum's director declared, was much more enormous than taxonomists had ever imagined: there were simply too many insects in the world to make this grand ambition ever likely to be fulfilled. Instead, the museum would concentrate on 'environmental, human wealth and human health issues'.[86]

In the late 1980s and early 1990s, then, those working in museums perceived themselves to be in the midst of widespread and sometimes rather bewildering change. It was a period in which even the great nationals in South Kensington found themselves undergoing 'cultural revolution' and having to address such multifarious issues as 'market forces', 'consumers', 'context', 'feminism', and 'political correctness'. For the then new Director of the Science Museum the question was what to do, and how to translate some of his ideas into the practice of the Museum's workings and – especially importantly – into its exhibition space. Much of this book focuses on the first permanent exhibition to be begun and completed under Dr Cosson's directorship, an exhibition which was widely, though not unproblematically, seen as his flagship. First, however, we turn to a much more extensive attempt at rewriting the Museum which was intended to create a 'new vision' for the 21st century.

Notes

1. In other words, I am concerned with museums not merely as 'sites' of some of the ongoing changes but also as agencies actively engaged in coping with, instigating, reformulating and ignoring those changes (see Fyfe 1996, Macdonald 1996). Good illustrations of this include the historically sensitive work of Tony Bennett 1995, Steve Conn 1998, Annie Coombes 1994, Gordon Fyfe 2000, Donna Haraway 1989, Andrea Schneider 1998 and Daniel Sherman 1989.

2. For the history of South Kensington see Bennett 1995 *passim*; Butler 1992 (ch.2); Crook 1972 (on the British Museum), Greenhalgh 1988 (on the Great Exhibition), Outram 1996 (on the Natural History Museum), Physik 1982 (on the V&A), Stearn 1981 (on the Natural History Museum), Whitehead 1981 (on the Natural History Museum), Wilson 1989 (on the British Museum) and Yanni 1999 (on the Natural History Museum). I have also drawn on entries in the *Encylopaedia Britannica* CD 1999. Prior to 1989 the Natural History Museum was officially 'The British Museum (Natural History)', but for simplicity I use the name by which it was popularly and later officially known. The history of the Science Museum is discussed in Butler 1992; Day 1987 and Follett 1978.

3. Quoted in Follett 1978: 86. Most of the following account draws on Follett 1978.

4. Follett 1978: 84. This kind of international competition through the medium of museums is an important aspect of the global spread and development of museums. For relevant discussion see Prösler 1996; and, in relation to world exhibitions, Benedict 1983, Harvey 1996, Roche 2000 and Wallis 1994 . For historical accounts of the development and spread of science museums

see Bedini 1965, Butler 1992, Danilov 1991, Mayr *et al.* 1990, Schroeder-Gudehus 1993, Sheets-Pyenson 1989.

5. Quoted in Follett 1978: 85.

6. See Lindqvist 1993.

7. Quoted in Follett 1978: 12.

8. Quoted in Follett 1978: 21 and 23.

9. Quoted in Follett 1978: 27.

10. Conn 1998: 4.

11. See Conn 1998: 12ff; also Forgan 1994 and 1996; and Pickstone 1994.

12. See Pickstone 1994

13. For example, this is the subject of repeated consternation in a recent symposium on museums of modern science (Lindqvist 2000).

14. Conn 1998: 19

15. Quoted in Follett 1978: 99. In the 1980s, by contrast, a Science Museum curator was told that his labels should be about thirty-five words long (Bud 1988: 152).

16. Follett 1978: 98.

17. Follett 1978: 115.

18. See Bennett 1995, especially the essays in Part One.

19. Bennett 1995: 63.

20. Bennett 1995: 63, 46.

21. Bennett 1995: 47.

22. On the roles of museums in social distinction see Bourdieu 1984, Bourdieu and Darbel 1991, Duncan 1995, and Merriman 1989, 1991.

23. See Silverstone 1992. Saumerez Smith 1989 and Bud 1995 give interesting accounts of struggles over meanings of objects in museum display.

24. Conn 1998: 261.

25. *The Observer* 23 July 1989. Other headlines at the time included: 'Museum in crisis' (on the Natural History Museum, *The Observer* 17 September 1989), 'Museums' cash crisis. . .' (*The Daily Telegraph* 17 July 1989), 'Culture clash in Kensington' (on 'the row' at the V&A, *Financial Times* 23 Feb 1989), 'Museums beg Thatcher to ward off ruin' (*The Observer* 16 July 1989), 'Museums send SOS to Maggie' (*The Standard* 17 July 1989).

26. For accounts of cultural, economic, political and social changes under Thatcherism see Heelas and Morris 1992; and, in relation to heritage and museums, Corner and Harvey 1991 and 1991a, Kawashima 1997, and McGuigan 1996. Young 1992 is a statement of some of the key ideas involved by one of the 'architects' of the changes. For anthropological analyses of the ideas of the free-market see Carrier 1997 and 1998. As part of the 'drive for effectiveness', the Conservative Government appointed industrialist Derek Rayner to scrutinise national museums in the early 1980s. The report dealing with the Science

Museum, which was probably much more sympathetic than the government would have liked, was produced in 1982 (Burrett, unpublished).

27. In *The Observer* 23 July 1989, article by Martin Bailey.

28. Museums and Galleries Commission 1988: 12. The report also gives figures on the funding gap, other relevant statistics and commentary.

29. For anthropological accounts of the conceptualisation of personhood involved in this thinking see Cohen 1992 and Strathern 1992, 1992a *passim*.

30. For general discussion of 'audit culture' see Miller 1998, Power 1994, 1997 and Strathern 2000. On 'performance indicators' for museums see, for example, Ames 1991 and Office of Arts and Libraries 1991. Bud *et.al.* 1991 is a sophisticated attempt to formulate a performance measurement model which includes factors such as 'enlightenment' and 'scholarship' based specifically on the Science Museum. An article published in this period by the Science Museum's Director gives an illuminating account of various impulses towards, and possible ramifications of, the new accountability in museums (Cossons 1991).

31. This was the National Heritage Act of 1983. Overall about 80% of Trustees were appointed by government ministers (Museums and Galleries Commission 1988: 17). In the case of the Science Museum all were appointed by the Prime Minister. The Commission stated that the appointment of Trustees is 'political only in the sense that they are made by Ministers. The Trustees' terms of appointment (generally five or seven years) reflect the expectation that they are not chosen for their support of any particular party' (1988: 17). The requirement for the national museums to produce five-year corporate plans was introduced in 1988.

32. The Science Museum shares a Board of Trustees with the other museums which together constitute the National Museum of Science and Industry: the National Railway Museum (York, opened 1975), the National Museum of Photography, Film and Television (Bradford, opened 1983) and the Concorde Museum at Yeovilton (1980). These other museums have their own directors but the Director of the Science Museum is the overall director and accounting officer of the National Museum of Science and Industry.

33. Museums and Galleries Commission 1988: 17.

34. Museums and Galleries Commission 1988: 17. In the case of the Science Museum the Trustees generally meet four times per year and this is supplemented with meetings of a number of Trustee Committees.

35. Report by the Policy Studies Institute (edited by Feist and Hutchinson) 1989: 6-7. The following figures are from their 1990 report, pp.46–7.

36. Macdonald and Silverstone 1990 also contains discussion of the changes under way. Museums were not alone in putting a new emphasis on image management and corporate identity at this time. Various social commentators

have seen this as a recognition of, or response to, the increasing emphasis on culture and the circulation of signs or symbols in globalized late-capitalism. Lash and Urry 1994, for example, make a general argument to this effect, giving particular emphasis to what they call 'aesthetic reflexivity' – concern with 'sign value', 'image' and 'design'. For discussion in relation to the sociology of organizations see du Gay 1997, Law 1994, Parker 2000 and Salaman 1997.

37. Originally, the ethnographic research which I undertook in the Science Museum was planned for the Natural History Museum but the management of the latter decided against it due to 'sensitivities' about the ongoing changes.

38. Article in *Financial Times* 23 February 1989, 'Culture clash in Kensington' by Anthony Thorncroft.

39. Quoted in *Financial Times* above.

40. See, for example, the vote for Mrs Esteve-Coll from Colin Ford, then Director of the National Museum of Photography, Film and Television in *The Observer* 23 July 1989.

41. For example, article by Janet Daley, 'The Mr Crapper Approach to Art', *The Independent* 25 October 1989.

42. I discuss this further in chapter six. Other commentators have noted a broader reconfiguration of the conception of citizenship at this time. Nikolas Rose, for example, has written that: 'The primary image offered to the modern citizen is not that of the producer but of the consumer. Through consumption we are urged to shape our lives by the use of our purchasing power' (1990: 102).

43. See Pearce 1998.

44. In Britain, the forum for a good deal of discussion was the *Museums Journal* published by the Museums Association, the organisation of museum professionals. Edited collections discussing some of these approaches include Hooper-Greenhill 1999, Karp, Kreamer and Lavine 1992, Moore 1997 and Stone and Molyneaux 1994.

45. These developments, together with examples, are discussed in Macdonald 1998.

46. Lavine and Karp 1991: 1.

47. Commentary on this expansion can be found in Macdonald 1996 and Sherman and Rogoff 1994.

48. For arguments see Huyssen 1995, Macdonald 1996, Samuel 1995, Urry 1996, Walsh 1992.

49. These terms are from Lumley 1988: 1 and Walsh 1992: 94.

50. See Hanna 1989.

51. E.g. Hewison 1987, Lumley 1988. See also Feist and Hutchinson 1990 and Audit Commission 1991.

52. Cf. his comment in Cossons 1989: 16 that 'by the end of the century. . . Europe will have become one vast open-air museum'.

53. See Wright 1985, McGuigan 1996. For the growth of museums and heritage elsewhere see, for example, Hendry 2000, Huyssen 1995, Lowenthal 1998, Newhouse 1998, Walsh 1992.

54. Museum registration was a subject of considerable concern at the time and the Museums and Galleries Commission was busy drawing up more stringent procedures for registration.

55. See Alfrey and Putnam 1992, Butler 1992, Fowler 1992, Lowenthal 1998, Lumley 1988, Macdonald 2002.

56. For discussion of this, see Barry 1998 and 2001, Butler 1992, Caulton 1998, Danilov 1982, Durant 1992, Pizzey 1987, Simmons 1996.

57. See Hein 1990.

58. Tait 1989: 174.

59. Cossons 1991: 15, 1991a: 186.

60. These fears were reflected, for example, in a conference held in 1990 by the Royal Society for the encouragement of the Arts, Manufactures and Commerce, which sought to address the question of scholarship in museums raised by the Museums and Galleries Commission report (1988). Some of the participants, including the Director of the Science Museum, Neil Cossons, argued forcefully against the opposition made between populism and scholarship, as against the suggestion that scholarship was under threat or that there was a 'managerial take-over' under way in museums. See Cossons 1991a.

61. Kohn 1989: 46.

62. *The Observer* 23 July 1989.

63. The British Museum had made a three month experiment with charging in 1974 as part of an initiative by Education Secretary Margaret Thatcher. This saw a serious fall in visitor numbers and the experiment was dropped, as were hopes to introduce charging at all national museums. See Hewison 1991: 165, Kirby 1988: 91, and Wilson 1989: 100.

64. Cossons 1988. See also Cossons 1989 and 1991. In 1989 he makes a strong argument that: 'Money from government and money from sponsors inevitably carries strings. It is a peculiar paradox that money from the user is, in effect, some of the cleanest money on which museums can lay their hands' (1989: 21).

65. This report was usually referred to as the 'Bow Report' because it was produced by the Conservative group known as the Bow Group. Authored by Sir Philip Goodhardt M.P. the report is entitled *The Nation's Treasures. A Programme for our National Museums and Galleries*. As far as I am aware, the Director was not a member of this group but directors of national museums would probably have been consulted in the preparation of the report. The report contains a number of specific 'wishes' of the Science Museum (e.g. to expand the National Railway Museum and to establish a National Health

Museum). Overall it argues for the importance of the nationals, for the need for them to have greater autonomy in their operation (including that the pay and conditions of museum staff be no longer linked to the civil service) and for them to have a higher input of funds, possibly from increased taxation. The issue of pay and conditions was a sensitive one in the Museum and the civil service union of which many staff were members was opposed to this change.

66. Kohn 1989: 46, Swade 1989.

67. See, for example, Cossons 1987 and 1988.

68. Rose 1990: 103.

69. Quotes from article by Gaynor Williams 'Leonard's High Street Touch in Science Museum' in *Design Week* 10 January 1989. The shop as a model for the museum was widespread at that time, perhaps most notoriously in Sir Roy Strong's comment that he wished the V&A to become the Laura Ashley of the museum world. See Macdonald 1998a for a discussion of this metaphor.

70. See Cannon-Brooks 1989 for a discussion of the East Hall re-presentation.

71. Beginning 'Discover man's favourite achievements for yourself at the Science Museum', the advert showed a bespectacled boy in scenes featuring weapons, surgery, aircraft and space. I first watched it on video with a group of Museum staff, one woman among whom commented rhetorically, 'How more stereotypical can you get?'.

72. See Miles *et al* 1988 and Miles and Tout 1992 for accounts of some of the pioneering work at the Natural History Museum. Bicknell and Farmelo 1993, Hooper-Greenhill 1994, 1999 and Lawrence 1991, 1993 give accounts of the growth of visitor research and evaluation.

73. Bauman 1989. For Bauman this is symptomatic of postmodernity. See also Barry 2001 for the associated shifts from 'you must' to 'you may', and 'learn!' to 'discover!'.

74. Macnaghten and Urry 1998: 75. I am grateful to Jeanette Edwards for bringing this to my attention and to Gordon Fyfe for the formulation of museums as agencies of social research.

75. Royal Society 1985. The Royal Society was founded in 1645. Election to a fellowship of the Royal Society is regarded as the highest accolade in British science. The report was produced by an *ad hoc* committee of members of the Royal Society, headed by the acclaimed geneticist, Sir Walter Bodmer.

76. The report also led to the establishment of the Committee on the Public Understanding of Science, a body dedicated to the promotion of science in the media, government and education. Indirectly it also played a part in the Economic and Social Research Council funding a programme of research called 'The Public Understanding of Science', under which this Science Museum ethnography was funded.

77. Lewenstein 1992: 45. See also Claeson *et.al.* 1996, Edwards 2002, Irwin and Wynne 1996, Wynne 1995.

78. Royal Society 1985: 9.

79. See the following for some discussion of this model: Haraway 1997: 94–6, Irwin and Wynne 1996, Wynne 1991, Ziman 1991.

80. See Irwin and Wynne 1996, Wynne 1995, 1996.

81. Royal Society 1985: 4.

82. Comment made during the opening address to a conference on 'Museums and the Public Understanding of Science', April 1992, London, Science Museum.

83. Margaret Thatcher. Reproduced in *Science Museum Review* 1987.

84. I have discussed this in Macdonald 1997.

85. Cossons 1992: 132.

86. Natural History Museum Corporate Plan 1990: 2. I also heard the Director of the Natural History Museum, Dr Neil Chalmers, speak on this topic in the Science Museum in December 1989.

A New Vision for the 21st Century: Rewriting the Museum

'Vision' was a term much used in the Science Museum during the period of my fieldwork and was, perhaps, common to many institutions in the thick of the enterprising cultural changes described in the last chapter.[1] The search was on for new perspectives and for 'visionaries' – individuals possessed of a kind of second sight which would enable them to see ways out of current difficulties and dilemmas into better times ahead. Managing vision into existence was, however, a difficult matter. Managing (as adjective and verb) visionaries could be equally problematic. In this chapter, I focus on an ambitious plan to 'rewrite' the whole Science Museum, to provide, as the briefing document put it, 'a new vision for the Science Museum as it moves into the 21st century'.

In the end, the initial grand plans for wholesale thematised revision were replaced by a rather different idea, to allow a more piecemeal approach which was dubbed a 'multi-museum' or 'museum of museums'. Nevertheless, the process of trying to revise the whole Museum was an extremely illuminating one from my point of view as it highlighted so many of the issues faced by a national museum of science and industry. It also gave me the opportunity to witness a series of highly intellectual debates, in which passions sometimes ran high and in which there was a feeling of fundamentals being thrashed out. When I have talked of the Science Museum to academic audiences, there has sometimes been an expectation that Science Museum staff would hold scientistic, perhaps naively positivist, narrowly technological or even rather celebratory views about science. The Gallery Planning Group discussions made it abundantly obvious that staff were aware of, and deeply engaged in, cutting-edge debates about critical, social and cultural perspectives on science, and held a variety of views on these. Although some staff felt disgruntled about the outcome of the process, and despite a pernicious rumbling that perhaps it had all been engineered just to keep some of the more headstrong curators busy, many felt that the opportunity to participate in these debates was worthwhile. The curator who described his feeling of enfranchisement brought by the new director (see chapter two), told me after the process was officially over:

> The GPG [Gallery Planning Group] was the most valuable curatorial exercise that I have ever been through. It was the most valuable forum for curators that we have ever had. The sort of collaboration between groups that went on had never happened before – you had people there who never talked to each other usually. As a process it was invaluable. As a forum for locating one's own perceptions in the wider Museum it was extremely valuable. . . . GPG was very valuable as a process – both personally and professionally. It gave me my voice. We were enfranchised. We had been in the Dark Ages – we didn't know it then – but we could see it once we were enfranchised.

The attempt to rewrite the Museum was not only about visions of science and of the Museum's role, it was also about professional identities, about relations between staff and between staff and Trustees, about the relationship between the collections and the public, and between the past, the present and the future.

In this chapter, I begin by looking at the context in which the Plan was requested and carried out and the various recursions through which it went. In doing so, my aim is to focus especially on the sources of struggle: why was it so problematic? And why, ultimately, did it not happen in the same grand form as had been originally envisaged? Alongside, I also seek to pay particular attention to the culturing of science – the different and contested ways in which science was conceptualised, mobilised and produced during the struggles which constituted 'The Gallery Plan'.

Conception

The Plan had been initiated by the Director in 1987, the year following his appointment. It was an attempt by him to make his mark on the Museum, as visionary directors at many of the nationals were trying to do at that time. The intention was that the Plan would provide the detailed basis for a major reordering and re-colonisation of the Museum space, a total reorganisation and updating of the Museum galleries over the following fifteen years. In particular, it was hoped that the Plan would 'somehow tie the place together' (as one member of staff put it) or 'give it an overall logic' (briefing document). To try to achieve this the staff involved were exhorted to 'think the unthinkable' – 'be bold!' (as they sometimes reminded each other). The backdrop to this was the then current layout of the Museum [Figure 3.1] which a 'Science Museum Management Plan' (1987) had described as 'confusing without much logical relationship of themes to one another'. Moreover, the document declared: 'this great Museum. . . is increasingly out of line with current views on presentation and interpretation'. This was to be addressed and remedied.

Staff were first appointed to work on the Gallery Plan in 1987 and by the time I began fieldwork some initial ideas had been formulated and sub-groups appointed to work on different aspects of the emerging Plan.[2] Initially, eighteen members of staff, chaired by the Keeper of the Department of Physical Sciences (as it was then), were selected to work on it. The majority of these were curatorial, together with representatives from the education department, the Science Museum library and the design office. Staff selected were not, however, only the most senior. Indeed, to the contrary – and to some extent surprisingly given the importance of the task and the high degree of consciousness among Museum staff about seniority and appropriate tasks – the group contained a number of less senior staff. These were the younger staff who 'had been kept down' previously according to the curator quoted above. All of the Museum's staff are ranked on a civil service scheme, the highest being 'A' and the lowest being 'G'. These grades are a matter of a good deal of discussion among staff, who can always assign a grade to a colleague immediately ('he's a C', 'she was an E until she was promoted recently'). This was described to me as 'grade consciousness'. More than half of the members of the Gallery Planning Group were Cs, Ds and Es (one might have expected all of them to be Bs), and this spread was pointed out as noteworthy in the Museum's own documentation about the group. In addition, seven of the eighteen were women, a proportion described by a group member as fairly high (though in fact about 30 per cent of curatorial staff were women). As we will see with the flagship exhibition on food, there seemed here to be an attempt to think (if not the unthinkable) differently by involving more younger and female staff – those who were likely to be 'bright young things'. Age, seniority and gender were here articulated to

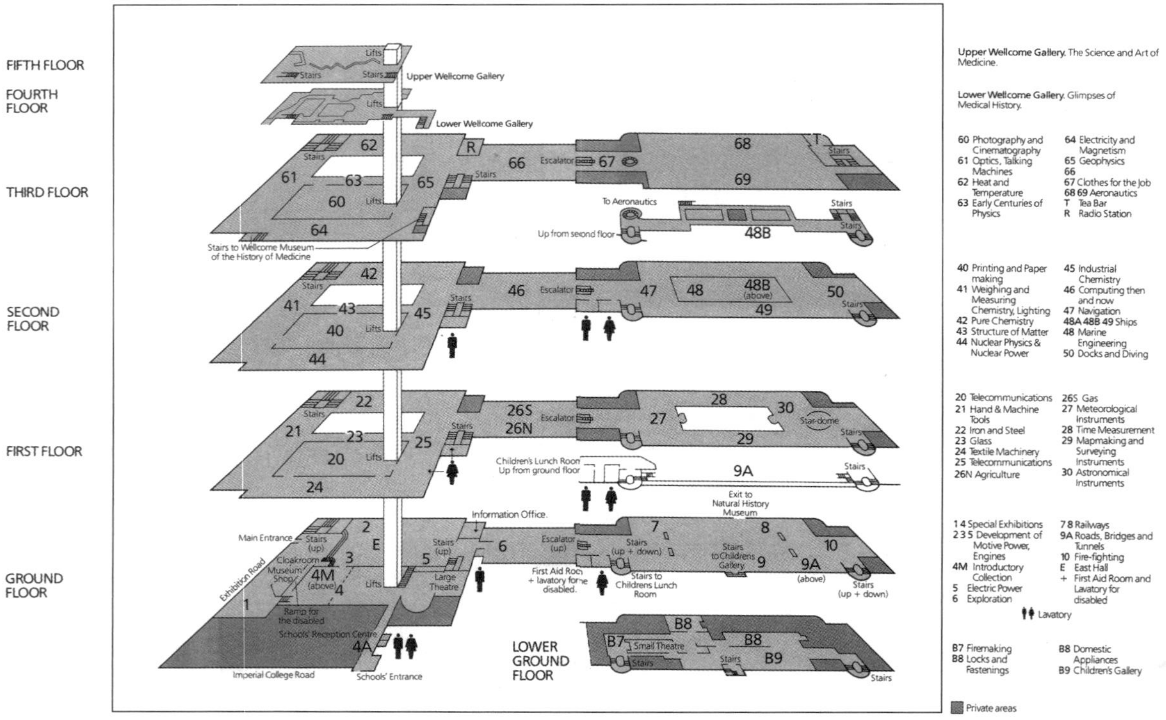

Figure 3.1 'Confusing and without much logical relationship of themes to one another': Science Museum layout in 1987. Courtesy of the Science Museum.

notions of 'flexibility', 'dynamism' and 'looking to the future'; youth, 'juniorness' and 'femaleness' being regarded as relatively 'flexible' and 'open to change'.[3] However, although those chosen to work on the Gallery Plan generally agreed that there was a need for a major revamp in order to create 'a new, exciting and attractive Science Museum' (briefing document, 1987), there were also plenty of areas of disagreement as I shall go on to discuss. First, however, I want to turn to the existing Museum and its perceived shortcomings.

How Things Were

As with many older and especially public museums (though not so much the newer themed attractions and science centres), the Science Museum was not created in one fell swoop on the basis of a 'vision' or 'blueprint', but was largely pieced together from collections inherited from elsewhere. These came not only from the Great Exhibition but also from the former Patent Museum, the Museum of Practical Geology, and from individual donors, as in the case of the Buckland Fish Collection (which was to prove something of burden for the Museum, the popularity of the sale of fish from its hatchery notwithstanding).[4] Over the years the galleries had continued to evolve in what the Gallery Planning Group regarded as a 'piecemeal' and 'illogical' fashion, leading to the current 'confusing' and 'dated' layout (as documents and discussions described). Discussions in the Group as to how to deal with this and rewrite the Museum suggested that there were three main interrelated problems in the then current organisation: (1) its taxonomic, collection-based form; (2) the lack of an overall organisation; (3) its presentational style.

Form

The layout of the Museum which the Gallery Planning Group sought to tackle was predominantly organised in terms of particular collections. That is, the Museum floor space was mainly chopped up into discrete areas on different subjects, relating to collections of artefacts that had been accumulated, generally over many decades. Such subjects included, for example, 'Glass', 'Optics', 'Aeronautics', 'Electricity and Magnetism'. Collections themselves were conceptually grouped into larger categories. So, for example, 'Transport' included 'Land Transport' and 'Aeronautics', the former having further subdivisions into 'Rail' and 'Road'. This kind of taxonomic subdividing is typical of a way of organising knowledge that the historian of science, John Pickstone, has called 'museological' or 'analytical', a form which he regards as particularly characteristic of science in the late nineteenth century.[5] It entailed a division of knowledge into specific 'domains' and an attempt to divide this into 'elements' which in theory would reveal a 'deeper level' of structure or process.

In the Science Museum, the categories themselves, however, were sometimes everyday classifications, such as 'Transport', and at other times were more scientific disciplinary ones, such as 'Earth Sciences'. As was characteristic of this epistemology, the larger taxonomy was not mapped onto the layout of the Museum: structuring was only to be found within discrete, generally disciplinary, domains. The overall layout did occasionally reveal some logically varied attempts to place related subjects near to one another: for example, 'Photography and Cinematography' next to 'Optics'; various instruments of measurement adjacent to one another on the first floor; and a selection of marine-related subjects occupying related gallery space on the second floor. This, however, was organisation by proximity without any incursion into the discrete bounded differentiation of the specific collections, where displays signal their individuality through different design styles and colours.

If there was a partial scientific and epistemological rationale for the organisation of the museum, there was also a strong local institutional one. This was a correlation of collections and persons. Each collection within the Museum was locally regarded as intimately linked to the curatorial staff who worked on it, headed by a keeper and, in a continuation of the taxonomic logic of specialism, each curator had their own area of expertise. The organisational identity and expertise of these staff, then, was concentrated around the collections, and despite the changes under way at the time of my fieldwork, this model was still firmly entrenched in everyday museum discourse. To talk of somebody as 'not really understanding the collections', as 'curatorially insensitive' or 'not having a good feel for objects' were serious criticisms. 'Object feel' was, perhaps, analogous to 'the good eye' of art historians, a construct which, Irit Rogoff hints, may also help to shore up a particular disciplinary approach and close off certain other perspectives.[6]

Many curators had worked on the same collections for the whole of their careers and had built up an immense detailed knowledge of *their* collections. The possessive pronoun is very appropriate here, it being typical in the Science Museum to describe curatorial personnel by the main collection on which they worked – 'She's Optics', 'He's Land

Transport'. This was accompanied by an affective relationship to the collections which I call 'object love' – a passion for the artefacts they curated. During my fieldwork I listened to many informative and impassioned accounts of the wonderful details of particular types of plastics, medical instruments or surveying equipment. There was no doubting the excitement of the curator whom I watched rummaging through a carrier bag full of plugs and sockets that somebody had donated to the Museum or of the curatorial thrill of seeing a 1920s fitted kitchen uncovered in one of the Museum's vast warehouses in Hayes. More than one curator, unhappy with some of the changes under way in the Museum, told me that they would have thought of moving elsewhere were it not for their deep attachment to their collections. 'Objects' themselves were variously defined for me as 'anything with an inventory number' – in other words, any artefact once it was part of the Museum's collections (and, therefore, 'harder to get rid of basically') – and as 'anything which you can put on a pedestal and worship'.

One member of the Museum staff (described as 'not really understanding the collections' by some others) was in favour of 'de-acquisition', a euphemism for 'getting rid of' museum objects. He tried to organise a seminar on the subject of 'objectness'; his intention was (as he described it to me) 'to get them [other curators] to see that we *make* something a part of our collections'. For him, it logically followed that 'we' could make them *cease* to be part of the collections. His view here, however, ran counter to the more widespread perception of objects as sacrosanct once they had become part of the collections. This definitional process was so powerful and so 'one-way' that even the contemplation of 'de-acquisition' was regarded as something of a sin.

Object love was also an important dimension of local notions shaping both exhibitions and the Museum more generally. Part of the local expectation was that curators would act as advocates for their collections. One dimension of this was attempting to have their collections on public display. (The majority of the Museum's holdings were not on public display in the Science Museum and some entire collections were in storage.) Having floor space for display, then, was part of a local battle for 'territory' – a key notion which Mr Suthers told me that I should list in a 'Museum glossary' along with 'objects', 'visitors' and 'tradition'. Territory, itself implicated in 'objects', 'visitors' and 'tradition', was necessarily also enmeshed with issues of professional status among Museum staff. Any attempt to do away with the assumption that exhibitions would be presentations of collections would, therefore, be a challenge to an important dimension of local professional identity. This was presumably another reason for the choice of many less senior staff on the Gallery Planning Group: they would be less likely to be thoroughly committed to particular collections and the collection-exhibition model.

Layout

The presentation of collections in an atomised fashion was also one reason for the lack of an overall plan to the Science Museum layout. So too was professional territorialism. Which collection had come to occupy which space was, in part at least, a consequence of the success of particular curators in preserving or acquiring gallery space. In some cases certain galleries had come to be regarded as the inalienable territories of certain collections and curators. Another factor was also involved in the evolution of particular subjects into particular spaces at particular times. This was the availability of sponsorship. In order to refurbish any gallery and to mount any major exhibition, the Science Museum had for many decades relied upon at least some (generally fairly substantial) input from external sponsors. Unlike exhibitions and performances in the arts, sponsorship of exhibitions of science, industry and technology almost always comes from companies with a direct interest in the subject matter.[7] Thus, an exhibition on gas is likely to receive sponsorship from a gas company, one on electricity from an electricity company. As one member of the Museum staff pointed out to me, an 'archaeology' of which exhibitions were produced when was, to some extent, a reflection of which industries were doing well at particular times. Thus, in the first example of the sponsorship of a 'permanent' gallery (as opposed to a temporary exhibition), the original Gas Gallery (sponsored by the Gas Council) opened in 1954, Electricity (sponsored by the Electricity Board) in 1975 and the Chemical Industry (sponsored by Imperial Chemical Industries) in 1986. Food (sponsored by the charitable trust of the supermarket chain, Sainsbury's), was a continuation of this trend. Moreover, perhaps partly because financial success brought companies into the public eye, this kind of archaeology also suggested that the timing of sponsorship could often be related to particular public relations concerns at those times: the opening of Nuclear Power (sponsored by the UK Atomic Energy Authority) and the Chemical Industry in the 1980s, as well as an exhibition on food at a time when food scares were becoming major public concerns, were examples which supported this suggestion.[8]

Other considerations were also involved in the organisation of space within the Museum. For example, large and heavy objects, such as beam engines, generally have to be kept on the ground floor because of their size and weight. There seemed to be – though this is not set out explicitly in any documents that I have seen – an idea of progress, of higher and more sophisticated technologies going upwards in the Museum; thus, land transport and steam power were on the ground floor and aeronautics and optics at the top. The basement was the location of the marginal: the children's gallery, domestic technologies (seen as especially the preserve of women) and 'fire-making' – one of the few exhibitions dealing with cultural 'others'.[9]

The contingency of available funding, allied with the fact that the expensive business of refurbishment had been carried out on a gallery by gallery basis over many years, meant that the Museum tended to evolve in a piecemeal fashion, highly constrained by its existing layout. The aim of the Gallery Plan, then, was to change this, and it was to do so while also challenging the atomised collection-based format. This was also to be coupled with an updating of the presentational style of many of the existing galleries.

Style

In the documents and discussions related to the Gallery Plan, the mode of presentation in much of the Museum was often commented upon negatively as 'unappealing to visitors'. The preliminary report stated that, in contradistinction to much of the current display, the revamp was to 'provide a lively, stimulating and easily digested insight into all aspects of science, technology, industry and medicine'; though, as we shall see below, there was a good deal of disagreement over how this should be done. In part, the perceived problems of the current Museum were simply that some exhibitions had been in place many years and had become 'tatty and dog-eared'; in addition to this many displays were condemned as too 'static', as 'patronising' or 'confusing'. Lengthy labels and 'poorly interpreted' object-based displays were singled out for criticism. As Tony Bennett has described, many museum staff in the nineteenth century were preoccupied with labelling as a means of making science, rather literally, 'legible' or 'visible'; objects, 'properly labelled', were seen as a better means of educating the working classes than the more abstract literary techniques.[10] Moreover, labels were seen as a further aspect of the 'analytical' scientific approach in which individual elements (in this case objects) were to be clearly indicated, the label providing an indication of an object's place within a taxonomic scheme. This was an approach which gave pre-eminence to 'sight' above other senses and to an object's relational place within its 'domain' (for example, the features of this particular engine in relation to others) above matters such as its mode of operation, social context or use. For the staff involved in the Gallery Plan, however, this kind of approach and information was generally regarded as 'outdated' and, as a mode of presentation defined by a curatorial/scientific logic, not sufficiently 'visitor-oriented'. The business of rewriting the Museum, then, was also a struggle to define new museological styles which would, among other things, connect to changing conceptions of science and to a shift in the relationship between scientific expertise and the public.

Re-visioning

> What the Director would really like is if we could rip it all out and start again, kind of beginning in the Stone Age and work through the Ages, Industrial Revolution and on, through the whole Museum, so that the visitor comes in the front door and follows a single route through the whole history of technology, and out again the other side. A bit like Jorvik on a grand scale – preferably with little cars to keep them moving too!

This half-joking account was voiced by one of the members of the Gallery Planning Group as I walked along to a meeting with him. Jorvik, a Viking exhibition in York which had opened in 1984, was the subject of a good deal of interest in museums in the late 1980s and early 1990s both because of its popularity and the fact that it achieved a very high throughput of paying customers (boasting over 500 paying-visitors per day and a higher rate of income per square metre in its shop than the local branch of Marks and Spencers), due partly to the fact that visitors take a twelve-minute ride in a 'time-car' through a brief history of the Viking settlement of 'Jorvik' (York's Viking name). The makers of Jorvik had visited Disneyland to learn about techniques of 'customer management'. As this was coupled with a potentially educational and scientifically respectable subject matter, Jorvik was a widespread subject of interest and discussion among staff in the Science Museum and other museums.[11] For some, Jorvik – with its recreated scenes and smells – was seen as a successful attempt to 'bring history alive', as it advertised itself; for others, however, it was regarded with disdain as a crudely commercial enterprise in which 'real, historical objects' had been replaced by 'mock-ups'.

As such, it was a focus for widespread debates in many museums at the time, about 'making museums more relevant' or 'dumbing-down', about 'democracy' or 'Disneyfication'. Jorvik was also often taken to exemplify what in the Science Museum was referred to as 'the historical' or 'the social' approach, which was contrasted with 'the technological'. The latter entailed an emphasis on mechanism and 'how it works' (as one member of the Gallery Planning Group who was an advocate of this perspective put it). These alternatives were also part of the negotiations involved in the Gallery Plan, reflected among other things in discussions about the nature of 'the visitor' and what he or she wanted or should be presented with.

The possibility of 'rip[ping] it all out and start[ing] again' was not, however, available: that would have entailed too much expense both in terms of lost revenue if the Museum were to close entirely during refurbishing and in capital costs over a short time period.[12] Instead, the Gallery Planning Group had to come up with a plan for a gradual programme of gallery replacement over 10–15 years which would attempt to both create a kind of overall plan to the Museum layout and at the same time might begin to break down the atomistic presentational style, as suggested by the idea of arranging the Museum into a narrative 'story of progress'. The Plan was, therefore, to be created in a struggle against what were dubbed 'practical considerations': the existing Museum layout, matters such as which floors could cope with heavy objects, which galleries were in need of most urgent refurbishment, and available funding. With regard to the last consideration, the Group was told that they had to create their Plan on the assumption that a budget of no more than £1.6 million per year at 1986 prices would be available (this being sufficient for no more than two major gallery refits per year). They were also not allowed to suggest extra building work (such as a new wing to the Museum). Their task was to 'be bold!' – one of the joking catch-phrases of the Group – but within tightly defined limits. Clearly, this was a tall order but it produced a good deal of creative thinking.

Before discussing the ideas that the Group came up with, I want briefly to reiterate that 'rewriting' the Museum was not just about reorganising the layout. Rewriting inevitably also entails inscribing certain cultural visions of, in particular, science, material culture (objects), professional expertise, and visitors. Of course, inscription is a messy, negotiated process and the 'visions' that it produces are likely to contain ambiguity and even contradiction. At the same time, however, the repertoire from which positions voiced in discussion are drawn, and the ways in which some of them are likely to become pre-eminent at certain times, is culturally located and not infinite (some suggestions could be, and sometimes were, defined out of existence as 'coming from another planet'). Likewise, to argue that certain visions were produced is not to assume that visitors would necessarily interpret the exhibition as the producers had intended; though what was produced would inform those interpretations. Below, I discuss first the general outline of the plans that the Group came up with before turning to some of the more specific areas of discussion and their implications in more detail.

Precepts: Visitors and Science

After the first meeting of the Gallery Planning Group – prior to my fieldwork – four 'working parties' were established to try to formulate some 'precepts' or 'ground rules' which would guide the more detailed discussions about the content of the exhibitions themselves. These groups and their remits were as follows:

1. *Function*: To look at the declared objectives of the Museum, how these are carried out in practice, the constraints which influence the efficient fulfilment of our role, and finally to assess the need for and, if necessary, suggest a redefinition of that role.
2. *Medium*: To try to reach a better understanding of the exhibition as a medium, what it can (and cannot) do for visitors of all kinds. How can we exploit our medium to its greatest advantage?
3. *Visitors*: Who are our visitors? Why do they come? What do they expect from a visit to the Science Museum? How do they use their time in the Museum and were they pleased they came? What competition do we face from other leisure activities and how should we respond to this competition?
4. *Building*: To look at this building, its shortcomings and potential and to recommend improvements in visitor access and facilities.[13]

As the report summarising the workings of the Gallery Planning Group notes, with the exception of the last group which reached its conclusions fairly uncontentiously, the other groups all 'enjoyed' 'philosophical debate... [which] stimulated heated discussion' and made evident that 'some firmly held and opposing views could not and should not attempt to be reconciled'. These views continued to be the subject of debate in subsequent meetings.

Nevertheless, out of this stage of meetings a governing 'ideal' and a number of 'objectives' were agreed. In relation to the former, the report states: 'The over-riding ideal of creating a new, exciting and attractive Science Museum with easily understood displays for our visitors to enjoy dominated the groups' thinking. Specific objectives to achieve this goal were identified. . . some representing a marked change from the entrenched attitudes we have inherited from the past.' What is particularly noticeable about this 'over-riding ideal', and the remit of the groups above, is the centrality which 'visitors' are given. Only the first group – 'Function' – does not explicitly mention 'visitors'; this is not so much because it is absent, but, on the contrary, as the more detailed notes show, 'visitors' were regarded as central to the Museum's 'function'. Some Museum staff commented on the way in which 'visitors' seemed to be the subject of so much talk at this time: '"Visitors" has become such a buzz word' commented one curator, and in one discussion one participant pointed out that it was important that 'we are now talking of visitor*s* – plural!'. No longer was 'the public' supposed to be regarded as a citizen-mass to be instructed.

Box 3.1 provides a list of the objectives that emerged from the first meetings and which provided the 'ground rules' for the more detailed plans. In addition to the centring of visitors, the list of objectives highlights some interesting shifts in the Museum's construction of science. The kinds of cultural work which museums do, and are perceived to do, in shaping science are not universal. In the nineteenth century, not only were museums regarded as exemplars of analytical techniques and as useful for scientific research as we saw in the previous chapter, they were also important sites for the legitimisation of scientific results. Prior to the eighteenth century, scientific legitimisation was principally effected by reference to the gentlemanly worthiness of the authors of the results; in the nineteenth, however, visibility to (at least some versions of) 'the public' came to be crucial as evidence of 'transparency' and 'objectivity'.[14] Museums of science became important spaces for this public presentation and therefore validation of objectivity and science.

During the twentieth century, however, alongside a growing bureaucratisation and professionalization of science, the validation of science became a more specialised process carried out largely outside the public domain.[15] If museums no longer had the same role as validators of scientific process, however, a new task came to be seen as more pressing

Gallery Planning Objectives

1. That the Science Museum as the world's pre-eminent museum devoted to the history of science, technology, industry and medicine has a duty to promote an understanding of the history of science and technology up to the present time.
2. Displays should be object-based to ensure that our rich and varied collections are made available to the public.
3. The traditional approach of a one-to-one relationship between collections and galleries should be relaxed. Objects from several collections would be employed together in a more thematic way.
4. The Museum cannot (and should not) attempt to be encyclopaedic, but should aim to be synoptic and cover all aspects of science, technology, industry and medicine as defined by the Management Plan.
5. Treatment must be exciting, stimulating and easily understood. The Museum should aim to create experiences beyond the mere showing of an object and to challenge the visitor to think about science and technology.
6. Major themes should be arranged logically in the building to enable visitors to select an area of interest from information points to follow it through.
7. The treatment should reflect historical, social, economic and cultural aspects of science and technology, although the extent of this broader treatment may vary according to the subject matter and target audience.
8. Where appropriate the Museum should make use of a wide range of supporting material, modern display techniques, reconstructions and live demonstrations.
9. It is vital to make it easier for visitors to find their way around. Improved signposting and the provision of multiple information points must be incorporated into the gallery plan.
10. The programme for gallery renewal must be carefully planned to ensure disruption and consequent inconvenience to visitors and staff is kept to a minimum.
11. The completion of exciting new ventures should be spread over the entire period of redevelopment so that there is a continuing awareness that the Science Museum is changing and that we hold our own against other leisure interests.

Box 3.1 Source: unpublished Science Museum Gallery document, 1987 in the face of increasingly 'hidden' scientific expertise. This was to inform the public about science, a task that, as science came to be regarded as increasingly complex and esoteric, was seen to require not just 'showing and telling' but more extensive processes of 'interpretation'. Number five of the Gallery Planning Objectives expresses this in terms of going beyond 'the mere showing of an object' and emphasising the harnessing of visitor agency by 'challeng[ing] the visitor to think'.[16] In many ways the Gallery Plan could be seen as a major attempt by the Science Museum to face up to this problem, and to the dated scientific legacy of its then current exhibitions and layout.

In the late 1980s, there were a number of other science-related changes which also pressed in upon the Science Museum's attempt to 'create a vision for the twenty-first century'. Objective four notes that the Museum should not attempt to be 'encyclopaedic'. This had been part of the collecting project of many types of nineteenth-century museum but, by the late twentieth century had come to be regarded as simply too ambitious and indeed impossible as we saw when the Natural History Museum revoked its aim of cataloguing the whole of the natural world.[17] The kinds of objects which the Science Museum dealt with were proving as prolific and troublesome as the insects with which the Natural History Museum had had such a problem. One member of the Gallery Planning Group calculated that the within the time-scale of the completion of the revision of the Museum, as many objects as were already possessed by the Museum would have been collected if current collection rates continued to accelerate as they had in the past. Already, the large proportion of objects in storage rather than on display was regarded as politically problematic: how could the Museum justify spending taxpayers' money on collecting objects which would never be on public display? The Science Museum was seen as having a particular problem here compared to many other sorts of museum, whose emphasis was on old or rare artefacts. (Comparison with other museums and types of museums was common in the discussions.) If the Museum was not to turn into a 'testament to the Industrial Revolution' or 'be fossilised in 1988', then this increase in the collections, together with a smaller proportion of older objects on display, was seemingly an unavoidable consequence. Moreover, though this was not much mentioned in the heady Group discussions, the fact that the Museum also showed 'the most modern technologies' – as the letter from the Prime Minister to the Trustees had put it (chapter two) – was also of significance for the Museum's claim to be important in the public understanding of science.

In the case of the Science Museum, being selective about what was collected had also to be done in the face of a dilemma which was the subject of a good deal of discussion in the Gallery Planning Group meetings as well as more broadly in the Museum. This was the dilemma over whether to try to collect *globally* or to build up a collection focused on *national* science, industry, technology and medicine. To some extent this had been less of a difficulty in the past because Britain was regarded as at the forefront of scientific, industrial, technological and medical developments. By collecting national products, therefore, curators were simultaneously covering globally important developments.[18] In the 1980s, however, it was increasingly clear that this was no longer the case and curators faced a problem over whether to try to collect globally – which could be very expensive – or to collect 'home-grown' artefacts which might be of little significance in the 'big global story' of scientific progress. Many curators could relate difficult cases of specific purchases of this type. In one of the Gallery Planning meetings one curator suggested that 'the nationality of objects is largely irrelevant'. This brought a good deal of protest, some members of the Group suggesting that it would not be irrelevant to museum visitors and others saying that it was not irrelevant from the curatorial point of view if 'you can't get hold of them!'. There was also much discussion of the prospect that the Science Museum might end up conveying a message not of progress, as the 'Jorvik solution' implied, but of national decline since the Industrial Revolution. 'If visitors can see the pre-eminence of Britain in the nineteenth century, then they'll get a different impression from 2000 or whatever' noted one member of staff. At one point, in discussion with the Director, the idea was mooted to reorganise the Museum explicitly around this contrast. The Industrial Revolution – in which Britain's pre-eminence would be evident – would be one major theme and the Information Revolution – which would be displayed as necessarily more international – would be the other.

Another science-related development that surfaced in Gallery Planning discussions, which is reflected in Objective seven, is the growth of social and cultural perspectives on science and technology. Many Museum staff were well read in these and saw in them interesting potential for challenging exhibitions which would 'make visitors think'. Others, however, were suspicious, regarding them as potentially too esoteric and intellectual for visitors to understand and as risking forgetting some of the Museum's traditional roles in showing objects and 'how things work'. They were also aware of the criticisms which could be made of some of the Museum's exhibitions from such perspectives, and this too fuelled the sense of need for revision. So how was this to be achieved?

Themes and variations

After coming up with the above objectives, the Gallery Planning Group split into three randomly mixed groups – X, Y and Z – to go away and try to work out just how the Museum could be reorganised in a way which would meet the challenges and objectives that they had formulated. As they had observed, there was a need to move away from the atomised and outdated collections-based model (Objective 5). Instead there was to be 'thematic' presentation (Objectives 5 and 6), which would not be necessarily based on themes drawn from 'science' itself (Objective 7). The difficulty, however, was that this had to be done while retaining an emphasis on objects from the Museum's collections (Objective 2), which were regarded as the Museum's 'unique selling point', and without 'ripping it all out and starting from scratch' in one go (Objectives 10 and 11).

Groups X and Y came up with the rather similar idea of dividing the Museum up into three main 'themes', though they varied in quite how they saw these as mapped onto the layout of the Museum. The themes were:

Group X

Science and Technology of Everyday Life
About Industry
About Science

Group Y

Industry
Investigative Science
Science and Technology of Everyday Life

As the document reporting this observes, 'Science and Technology of Everyday Life' 'represents the most radical innovation in the group's proposals'. It is this 'theme' which most closely relates to the attempt to focus the visitor in the Museum's exhibitions. The report explains: 'A large area of the Museum would be devoted to science and technology from the user's point of view. It is particularly aimed at the visitor with little or no prior understanding of the subject who will find the subject-matter readily accessible because it is related to everyday experiences.' While the Science Museum has long included exhibits which can be said to relate to 'everyday life', the idea of making 'everyday life' an orienting category is indeed 'radical' (as was locally perceived) in that it suggests that the categories of display will be based in 'everyday experiences' rather than on science or collections. Although this theme attempts to break down the barrier between science and the public it remains elsewhere with the retention of the categories 'Science' or 'Investigative Science'. Moreover, the traffic seems to be all one-way: from science to the public.

The ideas of Group Z, however, won the day. Their three thematic categories were the following:

Group Z

Knowing – science as a process for understanding the natural world
Making – technology as a process for transforming the natural world
Using – the use of technology in industrial, commercial and domestic settings

So why was this the most attractive option? To some extent it was simply that this proposal had, as the report notes, the most 'elegant simplicity' and its framework showed 'clarity and comprehensibility'. Expressed as verbs, these three categories nicely captured the attempt to move the emphasis away from static collections; moreover, they are fairly 'everyday', rather than specialised, words. Despite some similarity with the X and Y schemes, this does not work from already institutionalised domains and has what one participant described as 'the advantage of vagueness'. As such, it was more open to a more thoroughgoing blurring of boundaries ('Knowing' could be about both institutionalised science and also about 'common sense') and thus a more flexible and even experimental approach.

In the meetings at which the three proposals were discussed, and that of Group Z selected, it was decided that each theme should be represented on a particular floor of the Museum, with Using on the first floor, Making on floor two, and Knowing on the third. The rationale given for this ordering was, again, visitor-justified, the argument being that visitors would come first to floor one on which they would encounter the uses of technology which would be the most familiar of the three themes. Making would take them into the world 'behind' this, the creation of technologies; and Knowing would deal with the most potentially esoteric business of processes involved in the creation of scientific knowledge. Thus, built into the Museum would be a kind of hierarchy of different dimensions of the late twentieth-century techno-scientific complex on a continuum from the everyday and accessible to the relatively inaccessible and more specialised.

Three new groups were then formed – Knowing, Making and Using – each with the remit of 'fleshing out' the themes and deciding how they would be transformed into exhibitions in the Museum over a specified time period of ten to fifteen years. It was in trying to plan this transformation – a struggle against the legacy of the existing Museum, of timing, of space, of money, and of competing ideas – that some major difficulties emerged.

Definitional struggles

Each group convened a series of meetings with many individuals writing papers for discussion. Meetings were generally extremely lively and the debates highlighted just how thoroughly engaged Museum staff were with questions about museological display and about the nature of science. The negotiations also revealed, however, some very different perspectives on many of these matters, as well as different ideas about how they could be mapped out in practice.

Space, Objects and Professional Identity

To some extent space constraints were a source of disgruntlement for all of the groups. This was especially the case for the Knowing group as a large portion of the third floor, almost a third of it, was already occupied by a specially built gallery for the display of aircraft and it was made clear by the Museum management that this, together with a new exhibition of interactive flight-related exhibits, was to remain in place. Moreover, another new medical exhibition, at that time provisionally entitled 'Cutting Edge', was also scheduled to occupy the third floor. With nobody arguing that the aeronautical exhibitions could possibly be construed as part of the Knowing theme, and a very mixed response to the suggestion that the medical exhibition could, this severely threatened the integrity of the idea that the whole floor would be devoted to this theme. One Group member put it that 'the very thesis of a Knowing floor is undermined'.

Added to problems of what was already present, all groups identified a large number of collections which were (not uncontentiously) of potential relevance to their themes – or at least more appropriate to theirs than to the others. In the case of Knowing, for example, these included: Astronomy, Geophysics, Geomagnetism, Heat and Temperature, Electricity and Magnetism, George III (a collection of scientific instruments), Chemistry and Biochemistry, Meteorology, Surveying,

Nuclear Physics, Optics – far too many to fit in the space available. Many of these were 'object-rich' collections: that is, there were many artefacts which could potentially be shown and many of these were seen as historically important. Although there was general agreement that the Museum should retain objects as central in its displays (cf. Objective 2) and not go down what was described as the same road as the Natural History Museum, where many of the newer exhibitions consisted entirely of reconstructions and interactive exhibits, there was debate about how to show them. How many would there be and would they form the beginning point of the accounts or just fit into the 'stories' or 'messages' once these had been decided? In many ways, as the discussions acknowledged, the rationale of the thematic approach was the latter, which would almost certainly result in a relatively low number of objects. For some curators, this went against the grain of what they regarded as the important role of the Science Museum in showing objects relevant to the history of science and technology; an object-based approach was a significant strand of this discipline and one for which some Science Museum staff were internationally recognised.[19] Moreover, reducing the number of objects on display was also seen as politically dangerous both in terms of justifying the purchasing and storing of collections, many of which would never be on show, and in terms of attempts by curatorial staff to retain a major input into the creation of public display rather than have this undertaken primarily by non-curatorial education and design staff as was perceived as being the case in the Natural History Museum. The distaste for this model and the anxiety that it might be proposed in the Science Museum was palpable. As one curator put it:

> We have a deep fear of the way that they [the Natural History Museum] do their galleries. . . We feel very strongly that we're the ones with the ideas, we're the ones with the objects, we're the ones that dictate what happens and part of our great fear, which is also partly why we're keen to make sure the momentum of the planning for the themes goes on, is that we might go the same way.

In creating their plans, then, Museum staff were also inevitably engaged in a writing of their own professional identities. Yet, this did not mean that they were attempting simply to hold on to the *status quo*. As discussions in meetings showed, there were sometimes attempts by particular curators to try to argue for the display of their own collections (and occasionally the inclusion of certain other curators' collections as well because they might be piqued otherwise!) but on the whole the general principle of the thematic approach, with its refusal to acknowledge curatorial boundaries, was accepted. What these curators argued, however, was that the concept and practice of 'collection' should be retained through the idea of 'collector's collections'. These would be specialised collections, housed either elsewhere or on the premises in special 'visual storage', available as 'study collections' for those with a specific interest in the topic. To the extent that these would require conventional curatorial expertise and labour the curatorial role would be retained. However, rather than 'retreat' to this alone, which had previously been just one aspect of their job, they also argued for a broader remit in relation to display. One Group member suggested that what was needed was for curators to become 'curatorial GPs' (a GP being a 'General Practitioner', a medical doctor in the UK): 'generalist specialists – integrating, balancing and interpreting the findings of a broad spread of outside specialists – social historians, economic historians, political historians and others'. A similar idea was increasingly expressed and institutionalised in the then new concept of 'curator-interpreters', and the more widespread discourse in the Museum of 'interpretation' to characterise the changing role of the former 'curator'.[20]

If objects were to be retained, however, there remained differences about the role they should have and how they should be selected. One member of the Knowing group caused some controversy by arguing that many objects exhibited in the Museum were 'small, visually dull and virtually meaningless without a great deal of interpretation'. Given this, she argued, a main selection strategy should be to give priority to items with 'visual appeal', especially 'large and striking artefacts'. Others, however, felt that this was a renunciation of the role of interpretation: the point was to make even apparently 'dull' artefacts meaningful and interesting through museological techniques, such as placing them within narratives.

Visitors, Revelation and the Nature of Science

This debate over artefacts and the degree to which they could 'speak for themselves' was also linked to the nature of visitors – what could they be expected to grasp? – and to what was considered a particularly difficult problem for the Knowing theme, that of conveying ideas which might in many cases be rather abstract. Any museum or exhibition – and indeed any museum or exhibition plan – is inevitably a more or less implicit statement about its imagined audience. Members of the various groups differed sharply over the extent to which this potential audience should be imagined as entirely lacking in scientific knowledge or as reasonably well-educated. In some heated arguments about this various statistics were mobilised: 'One third of our visitors has a degree', 'Only one person per thousand in the population has a science degree'. Those arguing for constructing the visitor as relatively ignorant were accused of being 'patronising' and of 'dumbing down'; those who constructed the visitor as more educated faced charges of 'elitism' and of being potentially 'exclusionary'. One curator argued that to include the term 'ordinary people' in the documentation was condescending and a mistake because 'people aren't ordinary – they are all wonderful', and that trying to write for 'ordinary people' would create 'ordinary and mundane' exhibitions. The extent to which visitors would be interested in science and in certain specific topics (history of science was one source of contention) was also much debated and much disagreed over: 'Got to give them some romance', 'We need to grab them', 'They need something to get their teeth into – not just little snippets'. Of course, invocations of imaginary visitors were also a potentially effective rhetorical strategy for supporting one's own ideas or dismissing those of others: 'That's just not going to be interesting to visitors', 'Visitors will never get that', 'Visitors are not as stupid as you think: they're really going to like that'. The fact that little relevant visitor research was available made this kind of 'visitor hi-jacking' relatively easy, and many staff cast themselves as 'audience substitutes', staff without scientific backgrounds generally resorting more frequently to this.[21] This fed into a dynamic between an 'intellectual' and a 'lay' perspective in some of the groups (which I also observed in other contexts in the Museum), with some members employing a 'bringing down to earth' strategy of invoking the relatively 'scientifically illiterate' visitor when certain others were mobilising academic arguments. One curator in particular would often intervene in discussions with the opening phrase: 'I'd like to bring this discussion down to earth' – which became something of her hallmark.

This dynamic was particularly evident in debates about how to make visible the esoteric dimensions of scientific knowing. Insofar as Knowing was defined as about the 'practice' of science, some aspects were relatively unproblematic in terms of display: suggestions here included instruments of measurement and reconstructions of laboratories. Other matters were perceived as more difficult: in particular, demonstrating the social and economic dimensions of scientific practice, and providing a historical perspective without Whiggishly assuming a linear progressive development. One curator, for example, suggested that a section on physics might do this by incorporating social and economic dimensions through scientists' biographies. This, however, was dismissed by others as too 'conventional' and too much about 'individual scientists' or 'great white males'. A suggestion for conveying the amount of money involved in contemporary science was to exhibit a big pile of (reproduction) banknotes by a laboratory reconstruction; others argued that this 'would not get at the scale of it at all, or the international dimensions'. The problem, then, was that although there was general agreement that science should be regarded as social, just how to translate this into physical displays while keeping text to a minimum and objects to a maximum was far from easy.

The museological medium here seemed to run against the grain of the proposed 'message'. The nature of much modern science also contributed to this perceived 'visibility problem', with group members worrying about how they would be able to deal with the fact that many modern scientific processes are both so complex and on such a microscopic scale that they might be very difficult to represent without a very large amount of explanation. One Group member (a relatively senior curator) lamented in a discussion document that the danger was that matters would have to be expressed so simplistically as to tell the visitor very little indeed.

> [The curator's] best efforts will be bowdlerised until the visitor has to read, with dismay, that "super string theory is a sophisticated concept which allows physicists to organise their ideas on the forces of nature". If we can only tease our visitors, and not enlighten them, then let us not plunge blindfold into the quagmire. . . we must always ask ourselves whether museum display is the best medium for what we are trying to achieve.

This problem of displaying science and possibly abstract principles was repeatedly, and in different guises, discussed in the groups. In one discussion, a participant suggested that science could be regarded as 'objective knowledge' but this was roundly challenged by others; so too was another suggestion that science could be regarded as an accumulation of knowledge or progressively 'better' ways of knowing. In the majority was a characterisation of science as 'one type of knowing' (as one draft document put it). But if it was 'one type' what was specific about it? In a struggle over this, somebody suggested that it was 'one type of knowledge, based on objects' but others disagreed. 'Science is a kind of knowledge based on observations' suggested another, but mathematics was pointed out as an exception. Whether 'non-Western science' should be included was an especially difficult matter. Some members of the group argued that while the Museum had some artefacts in its collections which could relate to 'non-Western' traditions, these were rather few and so should not be included. There were also arguments that as these were part of a 'different tradition' it would be difficult to try to cover these as well as 'the Western tradition' – though whether the latter should also include Japan was a source of debate. In the end, it was decided that other 'ways of knowing' could be included as part of the overall theme of 'Knowing' but that 'science' should be restricted to the 'Western practice that has come to be called science'. Inclusive on the one hand, this strategy also risked creating a tier of 'ways of knowing', as some members suggested. Throughout, then, attempts to be more pluralist and to relativise science created difficulties for an institution which was in many respects premised on a conventional and progressivist viewpoint.

Fall-out

Despite the problems and continued worries about whether the Knowing, Making, Using division (or MUK as it came to be called) was such a helpful idea after all, the groups were pressed to work towards preparation of a document to be presented to the Trustees which would set out the case for approving the rewriting of the Museum – the Gallery Plan. At a briefing meeting about this, the Director called for more 'theology'. Each theme, he requested, should devise its own 'theology' – 'an intellectual justification. . . that makes sense. . . within the accepted canons of history and the aims of the Science Museum' – which would in turn fit into the 'total theology' (in 'a Trinitarian fashion', as the author of one report noted). The task of 'generating' this was identified as 'a creative work in its own right' and, therefore, one which 'requires a single person to be appointed to act as synthesiser'. This strategy was itself also a reaction to the despair of many staff at that time of getting anywhere given the differences of view within the Gallery Planning Group.

A fairly senior member of staff who had not been previously involved in the Gallery Planning Group was duly appointed as synthesiser and he produced a document called 'Planning for the Galleries'. Although the Director had requested a 'theological' document, he was not entirely satisfied with it, observing that 'this seems a bit abstract to me'. A member of the Gallery Planning Group also produced an alternative report, entitled 'Science Museum Gallery Plan', which he characterised as 'an intellectual manifesto' and in which he also sought to construct a 'theology' and 'synthesis'. On the basis of both of these, the Chair and Secretary of the Gallery Planning Group produced a draft report entitled 'Gallery Development Plan 1989 – 2004'. This was likewise not met with a good deal of enthusiasm by the Director, who commented: 'It lacks vision. There's a turgidity to it. . . . I'm beginning to wish I had never started this'. Nevertheless, the report was edited by the group as a whole and by the Director and retitled 'Gallery Development Plan: Thematic Principles'. This report, as its opening summary states, was 'concerned to capture the vision behind the planned transformation of the Museum's public exhibitions along three major themes – 'Knowing', 'Making' and 'Using'. In the very first paragraph, the report notes that 'increased emphasis is placed on relating the social and economic context of the collections', suggesting that this had come to be seen as the major failure of the Science Museum's current approach. The report goes on to provide a 'background' to the production of the Gallery Development Plan; an account of 'The Need for Change'; a description of the themes and an outline of what they will cover; and a proposed programme of the first years of implementing the Plan. This last section acknowledges that the programme would be extremely costly and notes that fund-raising efforts in recent years had proved disappointing. In a somewhat cryptic comment, which was to prove one of the stumbling blocks for the plan as it went to the Trustees, the report states: 'Realistically, if we are to be able to guarantee to deliver the new gallery plan within a reasonable period of years a fundamental new approach to the mechanisms by which the Trustees are enabled to fund major capital developments of this nature and magnitude may prove to be essential.'

This was then put to the Trustees in January 1989. I was not permitted to attend this meeting, one curator explaining to me that 'the Museum in general applies treacle to things. . . but the Trustees have especially sticky treacle'. Indeed, information about what went on at meetings of Trustees was not routinely available to Museum staff, which no doubt contributed to the 'treacly' impression. Even those who were present at the meetings (the heads of each of the groups in this case) did not always find it easy to interpret what was going on. In giving feed-back from the meeting, one remarked, for example, 'There was support for the "human element" approach I think – at any rate the chairman moved his body at that moment.' Mr Suthers, who also attended the meeting, provided a fuller memo on the objections raised by the trustees:

> (1) That they [the Trustees] did not fully understand the intellectual framework . . . and still had no vision of what the Museum would look like, (2) The plan is overwhelming, involving a complete redefinition of the Museum. Is it too rigid, might we come to regret it as the plan is implemented? (3) Is the plan deliverable anyway? Can the Museum sustain the initiative to attract sponsorship and implement the plan?

They also expressed concern over the disruption that implementation would cause, as well as over a number of more specific issues, such as the ousting of Shipping by a proposed Information Age gallery (a concern that was related to the presence of an admiral on the Board of Trustees by one curator). One member of staff irritably described the Trustees as 'imposing themselves on our professional expertise'. That they behaved as they did was perhaps a consequence of the new importance with which they had been vested: as noted in chapter two, they were now officially the owners of the collections and considerably more accountable than previously. Some Museum staff suggested that they were in part asserting their authority to make this felt and purposefully putting a brake on the ambitions of the still newish Director. Others, however, believed that because the Director himself had come to dislike the plan – and especially the fact that it was going to take so long before it could properly be put into effect – he had 'not pushed it'. Many of those who had been involved in drawing up the Plan were disappointed about the outcome. The curator who had been so positive about the experience of being part of the Gallery Planning process described himself as feeling 'suckered and exploited' and he blamed the failure of the Plan to be accepted on the fact that 'it wasn't sold properly – it was not marketed'. Somebody else commented that 'there is only one person in this institution who can grant life or death', so also putting the agency for the non-acceptance of the Plan firmly at the Director's door.

In response to what came to be characterised as 'the inflexible KMU scheme', more 'flexible' frameworks were suggested, in particular, what was called 'the multi-museum concept' or 'the museum within a museum idea'. Where the grand narrative of Knowing, Making and Using had sought to fit galleries into a pre-defined framework, the multi-museum concept involved acknowledging and working with the variety of galleries , topics and styles to try to create, as Mr Suthers's attempt to promote the idea put it, 'a varied and interesting menu of informational dietary fibre'. Instead of trying to weld everything together into one museum – with one overall logic – this new idea conceptualised the Museum more as a set of museums on one site, or, to quote Mr Suthers again, 'shops within a store':

> The "menu" we can then offer, and the manner and atmosphere in which we present it, will (as in a large shopping mall, department store, or hotel) vary in approach, enabling us to establish changes of pace, depth of information, and richness of objects displayed according to topic and perceived audience size and level of knowledge.

Throughout the documents discussing the multi-museum idea is the word 'flexible' – a concept which, as Emily Martin has shown, has come to be seen as ideal in many areas of late twentieth-century life, from business to the immune system.[22] 'Flexibility' has come to be the indicator of responsiveness to a fast-changing world, of the ability to adapt. This is, perhaps, the new form of progress. In the case of the Museum, flexibility was also seen to allow response to opportunities such as new sponsorship possibilities, or to incorporate a greater number of temporary exhibitions, perhaps on controversial or topical subjects. While for some Museum staff the multi-museum idea was an exciting prospect in its potential openness, others suggested that it was, perhaps, an outcome of a 'lack of direction and vision', and that it might mean that the Museum would be much more vulnerable to whatever 'pressures of sponsorship or fads and fashions that come along'. As such, perhaps, it would be an abnegation of the social role of the museum. In expressing these views Science Museum staff were locally articulating some of the more general arguments that could be levelled at notions of flexibility: on the one hand it seemed to promise openness, responsiveness and change; on the other, it potentially gave way to what Anthony Giddens has described as the 'juggernaut of modernity', a process careering away with little sense of any hand at the steering wheel.[23]

In either case, the multi-museum idea seemed to fit the times well in its celebration of multiplicity and fragmentation. Ironically, the lack of an overall layout in the Museum, which had been seen as one of the main problems at the beginning of the gallery planning process, came by the end to be seen as a forté. Instead of a fragmentation produced by a logic focused largely within disciplinary and collection-based boundaries and boosted by curatorial territorialism, the new think conceptualised the lack of an overall theme connecting the exhibitions to be an advantage, a creative space for maximising opportunities. This was, as theorists have argued for late-capitalism, a future-oriented disorganisation or de-differentiation: maximised variety offering maximum choice for operating in a tough market-place where, in the case of museums, sponsorship and visitor numbers were likely to be at a premium.[24]

The multi-museum idea, then, in many ways succeeded in doing what the plan put to the Trustees said any revision of the Museum must: 'resonate with the times'. It did so, however, not in the way initially attempted by those working on the Gallery Plan. Resonating with the present is a tall order for museums which inevitably – through their collections, their architecture and their role – carry a weight of the past. As the document presented to the Trustees elegantly explained: 'Exhibitions are historical signatures of their times.' As such, any large museum is like an autograph book whose pages have been filled over many years, perhaps containing signatures whose original significance and meaning is now faded or lost. What is involved, as Mieke Bal has observed, is a 'clash' of 'the past. . . with the present of which it is also part, from which it cannot be excised although it keeps nagging from within the present as a misfit'. This creates an 'unsettlement' within museums, themselves 'monuments to settlement'.[25] However, as the fate of the Gallery Plan highlights, re-visioning such a past-loaded space entails particular kinds of struggles and a redesign not just of space but also of entities which tend to be taken as fixed or as 'givens' for museum staff, such as science, objects, professional identities and visitors. In charting the unsettling business of trying to rewrite a national museum of science and industry, I have sought to highlight something of the cultural work and struggle that goes on 'behind the scenes', and to illuminate some of the locally important categories and divisions which motivate it. Those that I have particularly focused upon in this chapter are the contested and changing concepts of 'science', 'objects', 'professional identity' and 'visitors'. These are all central to the specificity of the Science Museum as a cultural agency, and indeed relationally contribute to its discursive formation. They do not, however, necessarily pull in the same direction: as the Gallery Plan discussions highlight, it is often tensions between them that fuel debate or drive ambitions to ground. A felt need to be 'object-based', for example, may run counter to more currently-resonant conceptions of science as social; or a 'visitor-orientation' may seem to threaten aspects of curatorial professional identity. Such tensions, however, need to be recognised; even 'readings off' from finished exhibitions need to be ready to recognise the potential ambivalence of production rather than reduce it to a set of predefined motivations.

In looking at staff and meetings in the Science Museum, and attempting to identify some of the key locally-motivating categories, my intention is not, however, to assume that all agency is local and that we can unproblematically understand museum staff as 'authors' of the Science Museum. On the contrary, my aim has been to show their struggle within a particular historical-cultural location, and thus to show how wider developments, such as increased competition from other leisure sites or the specialisation of science, are refracted within the particular problem of redesigning the Museum. By setting their ambitions against a cultural analysis of the then current museum layout, my intention was to highlight some of the often rather subtle transformations at work or attempted. At the same time, however, I also hope that an anthropological-ethnographic perspective helps to recover not just a degree of agency for museum staff but also local conceptions of agency and some of their critical and informed reflexivity. If exhibitions are 'historical signatures of their times', we should be ready to recognise that there may be more than one hand holding the pen – and, there may be more than one pen. Going 'behind the scenes' recovers some of that complexity. In the following chapters we continue this as we enter the world of exhibition making itself, joining a team busy with the exciting and fraught business of trying to create a new gallery in the Science Museum.

Notes

1. Cf. Law 1994.

2. Initially there was some reluctance to allow me to attend the Gallery Planning Group. As one of the members explained to me: 'This isn't an especially happy group at the moment and there are still some fairly strong protagonists and we're not sure that we've actually got sufficiently clear in our minds what out objectives are, so we're a bit floundering and only doing a bit of stop gap at the moment and we meet occasionally to mop up a crisis

and then we go into limbo again'. However, after some discussion I was allowed to attend, though (initially) not to tape-record. In allowing me to take notes but not to tape, it was said that I should be interested in the arguments rather than who made them. For this reason I do not attribute comments to particular individuals. I am very grateful to all members of the groups that I attended, and to the many staff who agreed to talk to me about it individually.

3. See Martin 1994 for an anthropological account of similar cultural constructions.

4. Follett 1978: 14.

5. Pickstone 1994. See also Conn 1998. This 'decompositional' conception of analysis also became widespread in areas other than science as Beaney (forthcoming) shows.

6. See Rogoff 1998: 17. She writes that 'teaching in art history departments, whenever I would complain about some student's lack of intellectual curiosity, about their overly literal perception of the field of study or their narrow understanding of culture as a series of radiant objects, someone else on the faculty would always respond by saying "Oh, but they have a good eye"'.

7. See Kirby 1988 for discussion at that time.

8. See Levidow and Young 1984 for a discussion of issues of sponsorship and bias in the production of the Science Museum's Nuclear Power exhibition which was subsidised by the UK Atomic Energy Authority. One curator at the Science Museum was reprimanded under the Official Secrets Act for having divulged information about the making of this gallery to the authors of this article. The memory of this experience made some staff in the Museum very aware of the problems of sponsorship – some were even campaigning for a sponsorship code. It also made some cautious about my presence: the curator who had been reprimanded pointed out at a meeting that staff members had not all been consulted. Perhaps because he also welcomed the idea of an outside observer, however, he also argued that I should be allowed to attend, which was agreed.

9. See Porter 1988 for an observation of the gendered nature of Science Museum space and a discussion of the representation of women in museums.

10. Bennett 1998. See also Dias 1998 on the privileging of the visual.

11. That Jorvik was 'scientifically respectable' and indeed 'scientifically authentic' was very important to its makers. When I interviewed one of them he was anxious to tell me about matters such as plans to make the heads on the models still more 'authentic' by basing them on computerised measurements taken from skulls that had been recovered in the Jorvik archaeological dig.

12. The changed nature of Museum financing, and in particular the introduction of admission charges, had made the possibility of shutting the

Museum for a year or two to undertake a major revision untenable. Thus, the demand to revise was coming at a time when it had been made less feasible to achieve it.

13. This is taken from an unpublished Science Museum Gallery Planning document of 1987.

14. See Shapin 1994 and Dias 1998.

15. Pickstone 1994; Shapin 1994.

16. See Bal 1996 chapter one for a discussion of the museological practice of 'showing and telling' and its representational ramifications.

17. On encyclopaedism in nineteenth-century museums see Prösler 1996 and Sheets-Pyenson 1989.

18. This is not to say that the Museum collected only national products in the past: it did not. The issue is one of proportions and focus.

19. See, for example, Fox 1992. Robert Fox was Assistant Director at the Science Museum until 1988 when he became Professor of History of Science at Oxford. It is worth noting that scholars could generally gain access for research purposes to stored collections. For an interesting discussion of the struggle to deal with different kinds of historical approaches in the Science Museum see Bud 1993.

20. This is broader museological phenomenon: see Gucht 1991. Mary Bouquet (1995) has also discussed it interestingly in terms of 'brokerage'; and in the context of the Science Museum Robert Bud also uses the term 'broker' and an analysis which draws profitably on Michel Callon's notions of translation and actor networks (Bud 1988; Callon 1986).

21. See Allison-Bunnell 1998 for a discussion of this process in the making of a film for a natural history museum exhibition.

22. See Martin 1994.

23. See Giddens 1990.

24. See, for example, Barry 2001; Harvey, David 1989; Held, McGrew, Goldblatt and Perraton 1999 (especially chapters 3, 4 and 5); Lash and Urry 1987, 1994.

25. Bal 1996: 15

'A Hot Potato' for a New Public: a 'Flagship' Exhibition on Food

Meet Jane, Jan, Sue, Heather, Cathy and Ann. They are the six members of what is informally known in the Science Museum as 'the Food Team' or the 'Foodies'. Permanent members of the Museum staff, they have been brought together into a 'team' to work specifically on the project of creating a new exhibition on the subject of what is, at first and only provisionally, called 'Food and Nutrition' (or, colloquially, 'Fruit and Nut' – this was a subject which invited lots of, sometimes half-baked, puns). This chapter looks at some of the heady early stages of exhibition-making, and at the nature of the context in which those involved worked. Because the Food exhibition was conceptualised in many respects as a 'departure' from previous ways of doing things, it is a good case through which to provide an account of an instance of, and response to, the ongoing 'cultural revolution'.

By 1988, when I began fieldwork in the Museum, some exhibitions that had been under way before the new Director's appointment had been opened, but none had been begun and completed within the new regime. 'Food', as the first exhibition to be carried out in the new Division of Public Services, thus acquired a special symbolic status in the Museum – and beyond it – as a 'hot potato', an indication of the 'new directions' that the Science Museum, and possibly other national museums, might take. As the Food Team leader, Jane, ruefully remarked one day: 'It is the Director's baby I suppose. But what does that make us?'. This brought peals of laughter from the other Team members and a cry of 'Don't ask!', followed by reflection on the way the exhibition had taken on this 'added significance'. Although Team members argued that they were the ones 'coming up with the ideas and doing the work' and generally shaping the exhibition, they acknowledged that Food and Nutrition had been permitted to go ahead because 'it fits the vision' and that if they were to 'do anything he really didn't like, we'd know about it'. A consequence of this 'added significance', however, was that 'everybody is watching and there are certainly some hoping that we'll fail'.

Later, during the planning of the exhibition, the Team experienced the Director not liking certain aspects of what they were doing; and this had major consequences for their work and the finished exhibition. They also lived with the sense of everybody watching to see how it would turn out. My presence, of course, contributed to this; when I first met Jane and discussed with her the possibility of participant-observing this exhibition, she said, 'Well, we're guinea pigs in everything else, so why not?'. Despite the sense of being the subjects of an experiment, however, members of the Food Team certainly did not see themselves as puppets. They had clear ideas about, and much enthusiasm for, what they were doing. In some ways they also enjoyed the fact that there was so much intrigue about their activities. They sometimes actively manipulated the intrigue, either by refusing to divulge many details about the content of the exhibition, (which contributed to another of their nicknames within the Museum: 'the coven'), or by promoting rumours about it. The latter included fabrications such as that they planned to install an enormous tea-cup and saucer, hovering over the Museum's central atrium, or that the exhibition would include a huge lump of cheese and animatronic mouse, or a vast 'Big Mac' (McDonald's burger). Amidst these fictitious exhibits they also released mention of others that were really to be included – a gigantic pot of chocolate mousse, an interactive exhibit in which the visitor would be able to experience what it is like to be a frozen pea, or a McDonald's fast-food outlet – so cleverly making it difficult for others in the Museum to know what was really going to be included and what was not. Active management of the information about exhibitions, whose making was generally fairly closed to those who were not directly involved, was characteristic of other exhibitions that I looked at. Those carried out in the 'old style', however, were much more liable to have information about them divulged by junior staff disgruntled with the approach or how things were being done. None, however, 'leaked' information in quite the same artful and playful way as the Food Team.

An Authorial Puzzle

In this chapter I also want to set the scene for a matter that I had not anticipated and which was to puzzle me a good deal. This was that when the exhibition finally opened, it did not 'feel' quite like the exhibition that those who had been making it had envisaged. I use the term 'feel' here because it was difficult, for the members of the Team as well as myself, to identify just what it was that created the sense of disjunction between the imagined new gallery and the one that materialised. As much as anything, the disjunction was a matter of 'atmosphere'. As members of the Food Team put it when we talked about the exhibition afterwards: 'It's a bit flat', 'Not as lively as I'd expected' (see chapter seven). Of course, this may have been part of a general emotional deflation – the 'coming down to earth' as one suggested – as an extraordinarily hectic, compelling and exhausting daily preoccupation came to an end.

Even so, the apparent 'flatness' and even 'seriousness' of the finished exhibition contrasted with the heady enthusiasm and joking which had characterised the early days. During the making of the exhibition there had been a marked sense of doing something different and perhaps even daring or subversive. The Foodies used adjectives like the following to describe the exhibition: 'exciting', 'busy', 'buzzy', 'lively', 'fun', 'interactive', 'hands-on and even body-in!', 'interesting'. They emphasised that it would be 'not boring', 'not your book-on-a-wall exhibition', 'not preachy', 'not trains'. Rather, it would contain humour and would tackle 'difficult' and politically sensitive subjects. Certainly, it was not entirely without these qualities and subjects, but for many reviewers and visitors, and to some extent for the Team themselves, these dimensions were not the ones that predominated, as we shall see later. Moreover, some of the 'before and after' contrasts were rather specific, particularly in the way that the exhibition seemed to be full of panels of writing ('too much reading' said some of the visitors; 'book-on-the-wall' said a curator) and much less 'busy' with 'interactives' and the 'market-stall atmosphere' that had been planned. Quite how there came to be this disjunction between 'encoding' (the production of the exhibition) and the 'text' (the finished exhibition) is one of the stories that I try to tell through this ethnography. It continues (with sub- and parallel-plots) in the following chapters, through the making of the exhibition to its final opening and viewing, or 'decoding', by visitors, critics and museum staff themselves.[1]

This puzzle is a theoretical as well as an ethnographic one. The great majority of analyses of museums and exhibitions read back from the finished product, the text, to assumed relations of production (generally 'dominant cultural interests', especially those of class, gender and race). Reading back does not allow for the kind of disjunction observed here. This is not to say that there is no relation between production and product or that 'readings back' are necessarily incorrect. It does, however, challenge us to acknowledge the complexity of the processes involved and to find ways of theorising the rather messy business of shaping cultural products. As we will see, there are aspects of the finished Food exhibition which can be seen as the product of dominant cultural interests, in this case those of food companies and market-led politics. Yet, as we shall also see, the plots and actors which lead to an exhibition which is legible in these terms, are more complex than a conscious 'writing in', and both more specific and more multifaceted than a nebulous notion such as 'false consciousness', or 'the institutional subconscious', would imply.

This puzzle, then, points to a more general question about the 'authorship' of cultural products and knowledge.[2] This, although it is often not thought of in these terms, includes science and the science that is presented to the public. Where, and by whom, we can ask, is that science constructed? By scientists? By 'society', 'the state' or by a particular set of social interests? By institutions with a public education remit? By particular individuals or even technologies and artefacts? Or is it by the members of the public themselves? In beginning with a team of museum staff involved in creating a science exhibition for the public, my intention is not to accord them sole authorship. On the contrary, by bringing a specific process (exhibition creation) and a specific group of people charged with that process (the Team) under my observational and analytical lens, my aim is not to presuppose a clear-cut authorial role but to focus on a visible site of intersection between science, state, materials, the public and other interest groups. Precisely because the Team have to mediate between diverse potential and actual players, we can try to track the negotiations (and sometimes, importantly, the lack of negotiations) involved in 'encoding'.

Thinking about authorship raises questions of actions and actors (as in actor-network theory) and of agency, this being a category which seems to have become rather naturalised in sociology and which surely cries out for further specification. Also, it takes us into issues of the attribution of 'credit' or authorship, of what Foucault calls 'the author function' and what we may also call 'the author effect'.[3] As a proprietorial discourse which seeks to bind particular agents to a particular text or product, 'authorship' concerns matters of authority, authenticity and 'the politics of signatures' (to use Derrida's phrase a little creatively).[4] As such, it also helps provide us with a conceptual link between debates in science studies, literary and anthropological theory (including anthropological writing debates). Here, however, as I introduce the Team and the task they faced, I merely want to highlight the idea that authorship is a more slippery and dispersed matter than might seem at first glance.

The Task

Creating an exhibition was a much more enormous, demanding and expensive task than I had ever imagined before I spent time behind the scenes in the Science Museum. Readers who are not experienced in museum work will, I think, share my initial surprise. Certainly, when I gave a first presentation about my ethnographic work to a group of other academics working on related public understanding of science topics, I was asked several times to clarify just how much the exhibition was expected to cost – '£1.22 million excluding staff costs,' I parroted, this being the way that its cost was always expressed in the Museum.[5] While this seemed an extraordinary amount of money to my colleagues (more than all of our research budgets put together), and while it was the most expensive exhibition in the Science Museum at that time, it was in no way out of line with the escalating exhibition costs in the late 1980s. What needs to be remembered is that although I use the term 'exhibition', as did those in the Museum, this was not just a temporary edifice expected to last for a short period, but the construction (including some – albeit fairly minor – structural alterations to the Museum building) of a large new gallery. It covered 810 square metres and was intended to be in place for at least ten years. At the time of writing it is still there, as are many considerably older galleries whose 'life' should have terminated according to original projections.

Responsible for the escalating costs, which were causing consternation among many museum directors during the eighties, was the increased use of new technologies of display, including audio-visual and computing technologies and 'hands-on' interactive exhibits, together with ever-more sophisticated forms of lighting, casing, photographic and three-dimensional reproduction and display panels. Although the Science Museum did not have to cope with the staggeringly high sums that were often paid for art works by the end of the

1980s, as a result of the major financial escalation in the art market at that time,[6] it thoroughly recognised the importance of exhibitions as 'style statements'. Having the latest technologies of display was a significant dimension of this. As one member of the Museum staff told me: 'We're a national museum and we can't get away with doing, you know, "on a shoe-string but inventive". We've got to be good. And if we're displaying cutting-edge stuff, we can hardly do so in some old cases or using yesterday's avs [audio-visual technologies]. We don't have that much choice when it comes down to it.' A glance through the *Museums Journal*, a glossy monthly which many museum staff receive as part of their membership of the Museums Association, shows the attention given to these matters in reviews of new exhibitions by museum professionals and reviewers as well as numerous advertisements for different types of lighting, cases and other technologies of display.

It was not only the scale of the costs of creating a new exhibition which surprised me. So too did the amount of time involved. The research project on which I was working had been designed and funded to last for two years. It quickly became evident, however, that this was nowhere near enough time to see an exhibition from its initial inception through to completion, and then to conduct visitor research on its reception. In Science Museum files that I read, for example, I came across memos written in 1981 suggesting an exhibition to open in 1988 but worrying that this was insufficient preparation time. As it happened, I was fortunate that Food was completed in what was regarded as an unusually – and to some people 'unseemly' or even 'ridiculously' – short period of time. This was twenty months from when a feasibility study was begun, at which point there was no commitment that the gallery would go ahead, and only fifteen months of production with all six team members in place. 'Inception' was, however, an extremely murky concept in practice. On the one hand, suggestions had been mooted for an exhibition on such a topic many years previously. On the other, the project had changed considerably and many, though not all, aspects of the previous plan had been discarded. Trying to identify 'inception' – that 'Eureka!' moment when it all began – was, then, rather like trying to say when a constantly and extensively repaired car actually became a 'new' car. By the time that I began fieldwork in the Museum, the full team had been in place for just over two months. This meant that I did not directly observe the early phase but had to rely upon discussing it with the Team, working through the available documents and each Team member talking me through her diaries. I was also able to attend some initial 'brainstorming' sessions of another exhibition, provisionally entitled 'The Information Age', then at an early stage of production. This, together with discussions with other Museum staff who had been involved in exhibition creation gave me contrasts and parallels through which to ask more of the Food case.

Below, I first briefly introduce to the members of the Food Team – those charged with the task of making this exhibition happen. I then discuss some of the 'departures' that Food was generally regarded as making from the usual ways of doing things – the 'traditional way' (features which were widely conceptualised as part of the 'cultural revolution' that was said to be under way in the Museum at the time). That Mr Suthers had listed 'tradition' as one of the key concepts which I would have to list in my Science Museum 'glossary' was not surprising for he, as head of the new way of doing exhibitions in the Division of Public Services, must have perceived himself to be in the front line of conflict with 'tradition'. The Foodies were, at that time, the main focus of his hopes and ambitions – and fears – in that battle.

The Foodies

There are various possible routes, and we can contrast two in particular, by which curatorial staff come to work in, and develop their careers within the Science Museum. One is the relatively specialist route: an individual with a particular topical expertise in which they have perhaps a higher degree or are undertaking one, joins the Museum at a fairly senior level (D or C, say), perhaps having worked previously at a more specialist museum (such as of shipping or the history of science). He or she then tends to concentrate upon a particular collection or set of collections and area of subject expertise. The other is a more generalist route characteristic of all members of the Food Team at that time (and indeed the way in which the majority of Science Museum curators begin). This entails joining a museum at a low grade and gradually working up. Generalists will also develop subject expertise and may choose to become specialists later but this is unlikely to be closely tied to their own subject-based educational background. Over the course of their careers they are likely to move from one subject area to another. The Foodies were all generalists in this sense and they argued that this helped them to be more flexible in their approach and better able to tune in to non-specialist expectations.

Below I list the grades of all Team members as they began the project. Although Mr Suthers was said to want Museum staff to be 'less grade conscious', issues of grading were deeply institutionalised. For example, as several staff pointed out to me, only curators of D and above were invited to what was referred to as the 'Science Museum Christmas Party' by some, and 'The Trustees Party' by others.[7] One member of staff described how 'Gs' in particular were looked down on by some 'higher' members of staff: 'It's like you've got G stamped on your forehead'. This could change rapidly with promotion and one curator told me that once she moved from G to F 'high ranks start talking to you where they hadn't before'. Promotions were managed as part of an annual review process, with certain targets being set. One strategy for being promoted was also to apply for a post within the Museum at a higher grade, as had some members of the Food Team. This promotion would be 'temporary' for the duration of the project, though staff obviously hoped that such promotions would be made permanent.

Jane Bywaters – Project Leader. Jane is in her mid-thirties. She was promoted to a D in the early stages of the exhibition-making; otherwise she would not have been allowed to sit on the appointments board for the other Team members. Jane has a degree in microbiology. In the Museum she has worked in a number of areas, including the Agriculture and Food Technology collections and the Wellcome medical collections,

Figure 4.1 Jane and the food pyramid on opening day.

where she had a particular responsibility for the ethnographic material. Shortly before working on the Food project, Jane had been a member of a 'visitor working group' and she attributes what she describes as her 'visitor-bias' to this and to the fact that she has 'worked my way up from being a G over the last ten years'. She once accused me of depicting her (in a draft of a paper) as a girl-guide, and I suppose it is true that I can easily imagine her leading us all on a successful camping expedition. But while the girl-guide image may capture her good-sense and skills of organisation, it does insufficient credit to her vision and sense of humour. All members of the Team agree – except during a few particularly difficult times – that Jane is a 'good leader' who successfully delegates and allows autonomy, while also providing support and a clear sense of direction. In the Museum more widely Jane is known as one of the 'bright young things' but also as somebody who is 'competent' and 'down-to-earth', rather than 'pushy' or 'just on the career ladder' (comments from various Museum staff). On the day of the opening of the gallery, after all the dignitaries have left, I ask each member of the Team to select an object in the finished gallery by which to have their photograph taken. Jane chooses an interactive exhibit – a 'food pyramid' – which she decides to refill with assistance as I take her picture [Figure 4.1]. She is clad in the stylish outfit in which she was introduced to the Duchess of York (patron of Museum's Year) who officially opened the exhibition.

Jan Metcalfe – Project Manager. An E when the project began, Jan is also in her thirties. Jan's degree was in Archaeology and she has a diploma in Museum Studies. Like Jane, she has been at the Science Museum for about ten years. Jan has been particularly developing her managerial expertise (though she tells me that she does not want to be confined to this as she enjoys curatorial work). Prior to joining the Food project she had been working (until the project stalled due to lack of funds) as a project coordinator on the Aeronautics project. One of Jan's main tasks is to liaise with the builders and workmen over the physical construction of the gallery; her forthright manner, ability to let people know clearly when things are not being done well, and readiness to joke and laugh make her especially well-suited to this task. Jan chooses to be photographed in the site office, from where the gallery construction was coordinated [Figure 4.2]. On the table in front of her is a deflated 'Mr Potato-Head' which she was given by a man from the Potato Marketing Board. Like various other more light-hearted aspects of the exhibition and personal favourites, Mr Potato-Head did not make it to the completed version.

Figure 4.2 Jan in the site office on opening day.

Heather Mayfield. Heather was temporarily promoted to an 'E' position when she joined the Food project. She had worked previously at the National Museum of Photography Film and Television, helping to get this under way. Hers was a pattern of moving between different sites of the National Museum of Science and Industry, which is fairly common among Museum staff. She also previously worked on the Wellcome collections. Heather often comes up with the most imaginative ideas and is also one of the members of the Team who most strongly voices the stance of representing lay people in the exhibition, sometimes teasing the others if she thinks their ideas are not sufficiently straightforward. Heather has amusing nicknames and descriptions of many other Museum staff, plus a rather wonderful subtle way of being subversive (as when she self-consciously and emphatically insists on only calling the food company 'Nestlé', 'Nestles' – pronounced 'Nessells'). She is the one who often promotes the false rumours about the exhibition; and is responsible for including the chocolate mousse pot and the McDonald's. I have chosen a picture of Heather (with Sue)

Figure 4.3 Heather (in foreground, with Sue in background) examines the Lyons Corner House exhibit about three weeks before opening.

admiring the installation of the Lyons Tea House which is part of the Eating Out section of the exhibition for which she is responsible [Figure 4.3].

Sue Mossman. Sue is also on a temporary promotion to E. Sue has worked in Physical Sciences and has developed a particular expertise in plastics, about which she later publishes a book; she has also worked as an assistant on both the Space and Industrial Chemistry exhibitions since she joined the Museum in 1983. Sue has a degree in Archaeology and at the time of creating Food is completing a PhD. She is active in trades union politics in the Museum and is generally the most vocal about political matters, including those concerning Museum organisation (such as sexism, redundancies and charging for admission) and those to do with the exhibition. She includes material on famine and originally wants to incorporate a section on the 'psychology of shopping' which would be, she says 'basically about how supermarkets con us into buying what we don't really want' – though this is one of those sections that falls by the wayside. Shopping, the global distribution of food, and processes of freezing and canning are areas that Sue covers in the gallery. She generally talks quickly and is sometimes described

Figure 4.4 Sue in front of the 1920s Sainsbury's reconstruction on opening day.

as 'sparky'; she doesn't suffer fools, criticism or what she views as political wimpishness gladly. Sue chooses to be photographed next to the 1920s Sainsbury's reconstruction [Figure 4.4].

Cathy Needham. Cathy is in her early twenties and is on a temporary promotion to an 'F', having worked at the Museum for about two years. Cathy has a degree in Geology. A talented artist, she is very inclined towards the aesthetic (and sports a great selection of hats). She often seems to think about her parts of the exhibition in terms of the attractiveness of particular artefacts (the others do this too, but it seems to be given even more predominance by Cathy). The elimination of some of her favourite sections during the process of exhibition-creation is something that causes her some unhappiness. Cathy's favourite exhibit is a model of a Victorian chestnut seller in a section on Snacks for which she has been responsible [Figure 4.5].

Ann Carter. The youngest member of the Team, Ann, has a History degree and is also on a temporary promotion to an 'F', having worked in the Museum for two years. Ann has worked on the Domestic Appliances collection, some of which at that time was displayed in the Museum's basement and in Engineering. During the making of Food

Figure 4.5 Cathy by the chestnut seller (part of 'Snacks') on opening day.

Ann is also carrying out a Diploma in Museum Studies, funded by the Division of Public Services. An open, no-nonsense and friendly person, Ann is often self-critical but always gets on with what she is doing very efficiently. She dislikes pretension and is often extremely to the point about shortcomings of some staff and Museum procedures, and has some very forthright language to describe people. Ann's areas of the exhibition are 'Bread' and 'Food in the Home', and she also assists Jane with a section on food poisoning. Here she is pictured at her desk in the Food offices [Figure 4.6].

Here I should, perhaps, also mention me. I have no areas of the exhibition to work on and my participation is mostly limited to fairly minor tasks such as helping to clean objects or cases, making tea and coffee, or running to the shops. Figure 4.7 shows me at the opening. This 'in-store bakery' is not my favourite exhibit but I somehow found myself roped in to standing behind this counter making bread rolls – partly because in the rush to get the gallery open, preparing rolls in

Figure 4.6 Ann at work in the Food offices about three weeks before opening.

Figure 4.7 Sharon in the in-store bakery on opening day. Photograph by Cathy on Sharon's camera.

advance had been forgotten (and nobody was sure that it would be evident that this was a bakery without them) and partly in an attempt to 'add a bit of life' to the exhibition which, as it finally came together, was perceived to need it. At the time, I was twenty-eight years old – somewhere in the middle of the ages of the Foodies – and had the kind of background that could easily have made me one of them, with a first degree in Human Sciences and a doctorate in Social Anthropology. To some in the Museum, especially on the non-curatorial side, I was regarded as a member of the Team, and the cheeky name used by some of the warders to describe the Team – 'the Magnificent Seven' – included me. I very much enjoyed the company of the Team and often found myself wondering whether I might not like to work in the more communal and practical world of the museum once my own fixed-term research contract came to an end. Trying to negotiate my way between empathetic support for the Team and critical distance is something that I found – and have continued to find – difficult.

In addition to those who are designated members of 'the Food Team', who are regarded as in front-line charge of the decisions involved in creating the new exhibition, are others also involved in the exhibition's creation. Probably the most important of these are the designers; indeed, at the royal opening of the new gallery, when the Director comments on this being an all-women team, a curator next to me mutters sardonically, 'So what about the designers then?'.

The Designers and other Participants

The designers – the 'Johns' – are based in Yorkshire and Cheshire but visit for meetings with different degrees of frequency depending on the stage in the process. They are also in regular communication by fax and, during the phases of drawing up the plans for the exhibition, realms of paper churn out of fax machines. The Johns are in their forties and present themselves as both 'northern' (with the friendly directness that this stereotypically involves) and stylish, with fashionable well-cut clothes. At the time, having mobile phones is fairly unusual and in the media it is regarded as a sign of being a 'yuppie' – a young upwardly mobile go-getter of the late 1980s and early 1990s, generally typified as more concerned with style than substance, and heavily into consumer goods. The Johns use their mobile phones to play along with the teasing that this brings from the Food Team, sometimes conspicuously walking around using them to each other when there is little need. The Johns choose to be pictured together next to a Juke Box

Figure 4.8 The Johns with the juke box on opening day.

[Figure 4.8] which they are very keen to have included in the exhibition. They say they love it as 'a beautiful object' and for its 'retro-chic'. While the Johns are the most visible face of their design company, and make the largest 'design input' to the Food exhibition, there are also others in their offices, such as graphic designers, who play more limited and specific, though significant, roles.

In addition to these individuals who are accorded a particular 'creative' input into the exhibition, there are many others whose work is also crucial to its completion. Many of these are not members of the Museum's staff: the Team consults numerous others such as academics working on nutrition and the history of food, industrialists, staff at specialist libraries, staff at other museums, organisations with particular skills (such as film editing, panel production or the creation of fake food), and representatives of diverse groups, such as the Friends of the Earth and the Good Housekeeping Institute. Other Museum staff who are involved include the 'line managers' of the Food Team – Mr Suthers and Dr Cossons; staff in the education department (who discuss educational aspects of the exhibition and prepare a teachers' pack to accompany it); the interactives team, who prepare hands-on exhibits; staff in audio-visuals, who work on electronic exhibits such as videos and computers; carpenters ('the Chippies') and others in the Museum workshops who create replica exhibits and prepare objects for exhibition

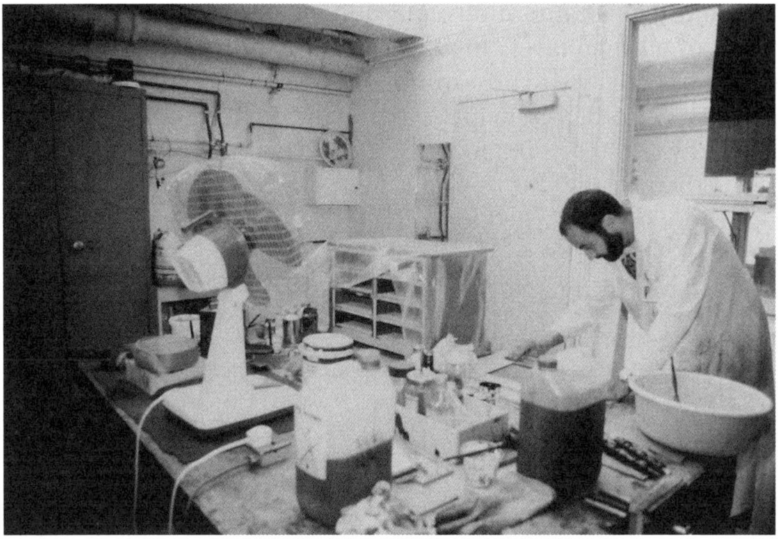

Figure 4.9 Hands-on preparations: working on an exhibit for food (a spice cabinet) in the wood workshops about ten weeks before opening.

[Figure 4.9]; photography; Construction and Building Works, which carry out the physical construction work necessary; and 'manatts' (manual attendants) who help to get things into place. Even from this truncated list, it is clear that an enormous number of people is involved in the process of creating an exhibition. And this, of course, does not include the multitude of non-human agents such as the sausage-machine [Figure 5.3], which caused Heather no end of headaches in its unwillingness, at first to be found, later to allow itself to be taken to the gallery, and still later to perform demonstrations of sausage-making to visitors quite as predictably as required; the oldest can in the world (which we feared might explode); the exercise bikes; and the artificial fruits and vegetables. Neither does it include those agents that caused unexpected disruptions such as the numerous train and London Underground strikes in 1989 which meant that many members of the Team could not get into work as usual; or the chicken-pox virus which afflicted several of us (including me), setting back the work on some areas unexpectedly. Of course, we should remember the numerous items used in the production of the exhibition such as the dratted fax-machine which always chose to malfunction at crucial moments, the personal computers on which exhibition text was revised and revised, and the kettle, without which the whole experience would have been much less pleasant.

It would take an enormous and quite unreadable book to give an account of all the players involved in the making of this exhibition. Instead, I begin with those human players who were in the local perspective accorded principal agency, and I outline the features that were locally selected as noteworthy and the intentions with which they began. I then follow this through, in the next chapter, to the ways in which those involved tried to realise these dreams, some of those they enlisted to help them, and some of the tribulations – and even nightmares – they encountered.

Gender and Team Structure

There were a number of things which were unusual – a departure from the then *status quo* – about the Food Team, as they, and other members of the Museum staff, pointed out to me. The first thing that was nearly always mentioned was the fact that they were all women. This, as the Museum's Director noted at the opening of the exhibition, was unprecedented in the history of the Museum. It was sufficiently distinctive for him to refer to the Team as 'the girls'. Women constituted about 30 per cent of the Museum's curatorial staff, though they were over-represented at 'lower grades' (of the civil service promotional ladder). Exhibition-making, which the Food Team told me was a 'jammy job' (no pun intended at the time I think), had been done mainly by staff on fairly high grades (generally a B or a C being responsible for content). As such, members of the Food Team were also relatively low-graded for the task they were doing. Other Museum staff also told me that creating exhibitions is 'what gives the buzz', building up and maintaining collections being seen as relatively routine by many, though not all, staff. The Team members themselves were somewhat ambivalent on why there were only women in the Team and of its possible consequences. Sometimes they wanted to dismiss it – 'it was just the way it turned out: best people for the job', 'it doesn't really make any difference I don't think'. They explained the circumstances in which members were appointed to the Team in terms which did not include gender: 'It was good to have somebody who had worked on domestic appliances, so Ann was a good choice'. At other times, however, they saw the all-woman team as a crucial – and encouraging – departure from previous Museum arrangements: 'It was an opportunity for a different way of doing things, and I think women are better at working in a team', 'We're more in touch with, like, ordinary people and women, who don't like the Science Museum and all the toys for boys stuff'. As such, although Team members were not selected because they were women, it was assumed that women would be most likely to agree with the perspective that was already defined by the time most of them were appointed. What we see here is the articulation of gender to a particular way of working and museological perspective as well as to a particular kind of positioning of these museum staff in relation to 'ordinary people' or 'the public' or 'visitors'. This self-designation by museum staff, which I have called 'visitor-hijacking' and have already noted in the Gallery Planning process, is probably fairly common in the everyday working of museums. It was certainly deployed in other exhibition groups which I observed in the Science Museum, though perhaps to a lesser extent and with different aspects of identity or experience being highlighted.

Another 'new' feature was the 'team structure'. As van Maanen has noted, team working became something of a 'buzz-word' in organisations in the 1990s. The Science Museum was utilising contemporary managerial ideas by moving towards this kind of structure, which was supposed to draw, in more egalitarian and collaborative fashion than in the more hierarchical working arrangements, on the diverse skills of its members.[8] Previously in the Museum, most of the content of an exhibition would be officially decided upon by one senior curator, generally a Keeper (that is, the head of a particular collection). In the course of a working lifetime a curator would expect to officiate over the creation of only two galleries on average, though there were some notable exceptions in the Science Museum who had been in charge of as many as six. He (or more occasionally she) would be responsible for writing what is called 'the story-line' of the exhibition – the outline account of what will be shown and of the main accompanying text, and, as part of that, selecting artefacts from the collections. In this, he would not work entirely alone but would be assisted by other members of staff (generally junior curators in his own department), whose tasks would probably include finding relevant pictures for the exhibition or arranging to borrow items from elsewhere. He would also work, with varying degrees of success, with the Museum's designers and might consult the Museum's education department for advice. The model, however, was very much one of a principal author – and, indeed, within the Museum, not only were curators often defined by their collections ('Sue is Plastics', as we have noted), but it was also typical to refer to galleries by the name of this 'author' – 'Tom's', or 'Robert's Chemicals'. This too was part of what Mr Suthers had meant by 'territory'. It existed, however, in interesting contrast with the absence of the curator's name on exhibitions themselves. There, names of sponsors and any external design companies would be listed but not those of Museum staff. This 'politics of signatures', as we will later see, had implications for the reading of the Museum. In it, the work of individual museum staff was subsumed to a signature which was both absent and present simultaneously – a 'floating signature' perhaps – the Science Museum itself.

Despite the model of senior curator as principal author, I heard numerous accounts from the designers with whom I shared an office and from staff who had taken a junior role in exhibition-making of the involvement of others in shaping the exhibition. In more than one case, junior staff suggested that certain senior curators 'just stepped in at the end to take the credit', suggesting that here authorship was merely assumed. In other cases, however, they talked of how difficult it was for anybody to change substantially the plans of the chief curator, though they sometimes succeeded in doing so. Designers and junior staff would talk of the 'lack of vision' and 'intransigence' of more senior staff, and would sometimes tell of subversive strategies which they had had to use to try to change the course of an exhibition. 'In the end we just cut it [the text] and didn't tell him, so by then it was too late unless he wanted it all redoing,' 'We had to put it in place and show him that it literally wouldn't work, so he had to agree in the end.' Moreover many, including the members of the Food Team, suggested that the passion of some senior curators for their own subject matter sometimes made them oblivious to how visitors might regard the exhibitions. 'A PhD thesis pasted onto panels, accessible only to the other three experts in the universe who are interested in the subject', 'Only woolly hats are going to be able to wade through that' were examples of comments made about such exhibitions – 'woolly hats' being a term used for 'buffs', lay individuals with a well-developed interest in, or even obsession with, particular kinds of objects ('the sort who will spend every weekend dissecting an engine' as it was once explained to me).[9] To be sure, this was to select particularly 'bad' examples, but it was this kind of single-author model that the new team model was meant to supersede. Altering the managerial structure was intended to alter the product.

Although Jane was the Team leader, and although she was on a higher grade than other Team members, she was not the sole author. Instead, the Team worked relatively collectively, with each Team member being assigned a particular part of the exhibition to work on (researching and writing its story-line, selecting its objects and conducting the organisation necessary to turn this into a finished exhibition). They referred to this as each 'owning' a particular area of the gallery, and used personal names or possessive pronouns to refer to these in everyday talk ('I'm worried about my bits of the gallery', 'Is that bit there Ann's?'), possession in this case being partly bound up with giving all members of the Team a sense of authorship. Clearly, *much* had to be done to make sure that the different parts of the exhibition 'fitted together' but this was a joint task, carried out in regular Team meetings and in meetings with the outside specialist exhibition design team. Sometimes, especially in the most fraught and pressured periods of exhibition-making, tensions arose which were expressed as hierarchical differences between the 'two offices' (the small office with Jane and Jan, Project Leader and Project Manager, and the large office with the rest of the Team – that is those on lower grades. Those in the larger office sometimes felt that they were being insufficiently consulted, but this was rare and mostly Team members proudly (and accurately) boasted that they worked very well together and even by the end had not 'fallen out being bitchy to each other' or 'ended up scratching each others' eyes out' as some other staff had predicted an all woman team surely would. The collective sense which the Team managed to create and maintain was also a function of their self-positioning *contra* the rest of the Museum (fed by their sense of doing something different, which might well be criticised by other curators). Of course, it was only to certain dimensions and members of 'the rest of the Museum' that the Team thought of themselves in opposition, but the drawing of this contrast helped to foster their own group coherence.

They were not alone, however, in doing this. The Information Age project did so in some respects even more strongly – insisting on being physically based in a building in a car-park outside the museum. The Project Leader described what going on in much of the rest of the Museum as 'the dough' or 'the syrup' (food metaphors seemed rather widespread at the time!). ('Get it past the plonkers' was one of the unofficial mottoes of this project.) The Food Team too, though still inside the Museum building, were spatially located at some distance from most other curators, and they too drew frequent contrasts between themselves and what was going on elsewhere (including in The Information Age project). In the case of Food, the gender of the members of the Team also became part of this self-marking of difference, as evident, for example, in their reference to some other Museum staff as 'boys'. There is no doubt that the gender and group solidarity of the Food Team could be disconcerting to some male members of staff. As

Sue put it: 'We have been referred to as the female mafia and those powerful women. I think that some men in the Museum do feel threatened by us.' This sense of threat could be seen on occasion. For example, one afternoon the Team was having a small party – eating cake and drinking coffee – in the large office when a male Museum worker came in. Faced by this group of relaxed women, leaning on radiators and sitting on desks, he was clearly taken-aback and blushingly asked where one group member (who was then absent) was, then hurriedly left. As he did so, we all burst spontaneously into laughter and Jan then said, with mock gravitas, 'They just can't cope with the fact that we're such strong women!'.

Designers and Interpretation

The use of an outside design service was not unprecedented in the Museum but it was unusual at the time for a major 'permanent' gallery such as Food. Hall-Redman Associates – with offices in Yorkshire and Cheshire, and known for previous work at the Bradford Colour Museum, Lancaster Maritime Museum and Manchester United Museum – had won the contract after a competitive tender. Again, this insertion of competition and the external was part of the conscious attempt to 'break with the past' that characterised this exhibition and the particular time of which it was part in the Science Museum. Like many other such changes, it was received somewhat ambivalently. For those involved, it was a chance to 'get something fresh, a bit different – you can get stuck in a bit of a rut if you always have the same designers on everything' or an opportunity to 'counter a strain of in-breeding in our exhibition development' (internal memo). But for those such as the Museum's own team of designers it was part of a more widespread demotion of expertise in the Museum ('Outside designers aren't going to understand the nature of the Science Museum and our visitors. They're probably going to think of it just like any heritage presentation') and of moves towards contracting out rather than maintaining expertise 'in-house'. ('There seems to be an idea that outside designers are somehow better,' said one of Science Museum designers ruefully.) As such, it was also part of a 'downsizing' of Museum staff: the number of staff in the design office had been shrunk by so-called 'natural wastage' (staff not being replaced when they left) from seventeen to 'only five and a half and one of those is on indefinite sick leave and most of the rest are thinking about leaving' (Science Museum designer). While overall staff numbers in the Science Museum had not shrunk significantly –

there were still some 440 employees in 1988 – this overall figure masked a decline in the number of jobs requiring traditional expertise and employed on semi-permanent contracts and an increase in lower grade (in civil service terms) and fixed-term contract jobs, especially in the new marketing functions of the museum. In this respect, the Science Museum was part of a more general reconfiguration of patterns of work prevailing in the UK (and many other countries) at the time.

Another unusual feature of the organisation of Food was that it was not based on, or concerned with exhibiting, a single existing collection as were the majority of the Museum's exhibitions. This had caused some concern in the Museum when the subject-matter was first announced, with one senior member of the Museum staff rhetorically asking at a seminar: 'What will it show then? A few ovens and a load of old cookery books?' The exhibition could, and did, draw on existing Museum collections, including Domestic Appliances (from where some 'old ovens' were indeed culled), the Wellcome collection of medical-related objects, and from Transport, Agriculture, Food technology, and Photography. However, the selection of a topic – food – which did not neatly map onto a specific collection, was part of a managerial strategy to try to sever what had come to be thought of as a 'natural' link between collections and exhibitions. Again, this was an attempt to alter the product by changing the structures of its production, an attempt which could be regarded as the according of at least some authorial agency to institutional structures themselves.

Linked to this was the fact that members of the Food Team were not appointed to work on this project because of their specialist curatorial expertise. Indeed, in another departure, one in keeping with changes discussed in chapter two, they were given the title 'interpreters' while they worked on the exhibition, the term 'interpretation' being used to highlight the orientation to visitors rather than the 'care' ('curation') of objects. Nevertheless, they virtually always referred to themselves as curators rather than interpreters or 'curator-interpreters'. In fact, before they began work on the project, all members of the Team had worked as curators and all had particular subject expertise. Some of this was relevant, though not strongly so (Ann's work on the Domestic Appliances collections, for example). Neither, with the exception of Jane (who had a degree in Microbiology) did members of the Team have any other special expertise in food-related subjects. All were happy to state that while they found food an interesting subject, and enjoyed eating it, they were definitely not experts in it. However, far from being perceived as a disadvantage, this was positively construed; for, in the process of 'visitor-substitution', lack of expertise was equated with a greater capacity for being able to identify and communicate with lay people. Members of the Food Team saw themselves as lacking the barriers which would cause them to be 'out of touch with ordinary people' – barriers created by too much specialist expertise. That they vaunted a lack of expertise at a time when, as various cultural commentators have observed, there was a widespread proliferation of expert systems and professionalisation, is not to be explained simply as an exception.[10] It was precisely in relation to a perception of science as highly and increasingly inaccessible to those who lacked the necessary specialised expertise that the Team members emphasised their shared sense of exclusion with 'ordinary visitors'. Moreover, lack of traditional kinds of specialisation and expertise was also equated with flexibility and adaptiveness. Nevertheless, as the 'flexible specialisation' couplet highlights, flexibility could, and indeed was, bound up with new forms of specialisation as increasingly specialist niches – and distinctive corporate identities – were sought out and promoted by organisations. In the Science Museum, this can be seen in the way that the task of understanding visitors, and more widely the business of the public understanding of science, became increasingly expert matters, with their own fast professionalising techniques, during the time-frame of this ethnography, as witnessed in a number of other 'departures' by the Team, such as carrying out visitor surveys and trialling prospective exhibits on visitors.

Also part of the attempt to reorient this exhibition towards visitors, rather than the expert and even esoteric worlds of science or of collections and objects, was the managerial location of the Team within the new Division of Public Services, of which Mr Suthers was Head, and, as such, the 'line manager' of the Team. Again, this was not uncontroversial in the Museum. While some staff found it a welcome disruption of the power of senior curators and a sensible bringing together of the Museum's 'public face' tasks, others remained suspicious. One curator involved in creating another exhibition was particularly critical, lamenting the 'dumbing-down' that he perceived in the move which now 'puts exhibiting in the same division as managing the toilet cleaning'. To him, this was evidence that the Museum was becoming what he called 'Bozoland', 'Lululand, Cuckooland, Nincompoopland', 'Wallysville', a crazy irrational place in which values had become topsy-turvy.

These, then, were the main differences in the way in which the exhibition which came to be called 'Food for Thought' was organised, relative to previous exhibitions. They were not the only ones, though; others related more to the way in which the process was carried out and the content and aims of the exhibition. No doubt in the making of any exhibition there is something of a rhetoric of newness and difference; after all, it is primarily through such claims that creativity and even worth is assigned in modernity.[11] This certainly was a feature, to some extent, of the other exhibitions which I observed or discussed with their creators, though in most cases 'newness' was restricted to matters of content and approach rather than ramified throughout the whole managerial process. The rhetoric of change and 'restructuring' – of 'sweeping away the old' – was about more than Food alone: it was also part of the more widespread changes outlined in the previous chapters – in and beyond the Museum – which came to bear particularly acutely upon this exhibition.

Why Food?

That the flagship exhibition of the new regime in the Science Museum should have been on the subject of food, that this subject should have been presented largely from the perspective of consumption, and that it should have received the bulk of its funding from supermarket sponsorship seemed like a perfect expression of the wider emphasis on consumers and consumption of the time. As I noted, many museums (and other public institutions) were embracing a vision of the public as consumers, and conceptualising citizenship as a matter of making informed choices. In museums of science the popularity of the concept 'public understanding of science' was partly an expression of this (though also of the waning of museums' former relationship to scientific knowledge). The theme of health and nutrition was as exemplary an extension of this idea – use-value and information to support individual responsibility in the domain of one's own body – as could have been dreamed up. It was, however, in many ways an odd or surprising choice for the Science Museum as comments by museum staff and some internal memos noted ('Surely this is a subject for the NHM, not us'), and as was confirmed in a questionnaire commissioned by Mr Suthers during the Food project, many visitors (50 per cent) would not have expected such an exhibition in the Science Museum.[12] So how did it come about?

An idea to mount an exhibition on a food-related topic had been around for some time in the Science Museum, the Royal Agricultural Society of England having proposed in 1979 that a new agriculture gallery be planned for 1988, the 150th anniversary of the Society and the 'Year of British Agriculture'. Letters and meetings followed, but did not 'progress. . . as smoothly as might be hoped', as an internal memo from the then Director, Margaret Weston, noted. A sticking point was that the Society, which proposed to support the exhibition financially, did not quite see eye-to-eye with the Museum about the nature of it, not an unusual problem when an idea was being instigated by an external organisation which was to foot much of the bill. In particular, the promotion of 'agriculture', which was a central aspect of the Society's remit ('to show agriculture as a developing professional exercise as well as a social necessity', as one rather dull 'scenario' produced by the Society put it), did not entirely tally with the Museum's idea of what might make an interesting exhibition. Matters continued to potter along but were partly put on ice in the mid-1980s by the fact that Dame Margaret was due to retire and it was easier to leave matters to her successor.

Jane was one of those involved in some of the earlier 'food and farming' ideas and she took the opportunity to suggest the idea of an exhibition on a food-related topic to the new Director. In doing so, however, she also reshaped the ideas, arguing that the agricultural dimensions should not be included in the Science Museum but displayed instead in a proposed new national museum of agriculture. As she explained it to me:

> I was keen on the social bits and the new Director was the sort who would go for that. The old one would have preferred ninety-one tractors in a line – she liked the technology, not the social. The new Director. . . wanted a radical change of approach to exhibitions, so the time was right to stick in more of a social impact. There's no point presenting something if the Director is not sympathetic.

Jane, who herself had an interest in nutrition as well as a commitment to the idea of communicating with a lay public, also emphasised the suitability of food as a topic to the public understanding of science.

A number of other things also conspired to make the topic of food one which would be given the go-ahead. First, it was something which lent itself to some of the 'departures' which we have already mentioned, especially that of not being based on a single collection. Second, food was a subject that was a matter of considerable public and media interest at the time – a real 'hot potato'. This was a period of mounting concern about factory production methods in particular, and health scares such as salmonella in eggs. During the making of the project, every week brought new articles – new findings (often seeming to overturn those of the previous week) and new risks – about food which caused some difficulty for the Team as we shall see later. Third, as a memo from a member of the Education department put it:

> The Museum is often castigated (particularly by teachers) for producing exhibitions which appear to ignore developments such as the rise of a multi-racial society, and the changing role of women in society. It is hard to see how most of our galleries could show an awareness of these issues, but F&N [Food and Nutrition] is different. It provides us with the opportunity to show that we are aware of them without, I think, being accused of tokenism or hypocrisy. Topic areas on "herbs and spices" or "staple foods" would take care of the "ethnic" issue.

Fourth, the topic seemed to be one with good sponsorship potential, with supermarkets and food companies being among the most profitable industries in Britain in the 1980s. (A list in the Food files lists food companies together with their 'profit after tax' and the response given to approaches from the Museum.) It was, in other words, a topic which undoubtedly 'resonated with the times', though individual initiative and much gathering of statistics and mobilising of arguments (including ones to overcome objections that the topic was inappropriate to the Science Museum) were required to translate this resonance into the local context of the Museum.

The Feasibility of Food: the Feasibility Study

In February 1988, after Jane had sent her proposals to the Museum's Economic Management Committee (made up of the Director and Assistant Directors), she was asked to prepare a feasibility study on the topic. She did so with Jan and Sue, whom she personally requested to work with her on this. The document which they produced in March was entitled 'Food and Nutrition: a Proposal for a Permanent Exhibition in the Science Museum. Food Project Feasibility Study'. To highlight their professionalism and difference from other exhibitions, this document was 'a glossy', with a 'Food and Nutrition' logo (a stylised shopping trolley containing this name alongside the NMSI coat-of-arms). It was based on extensive 'brainstorming' – the rather wonderful large sheets produced during this stage, full of many more joky ideas than are represented in the Feasibility Study, were still available for me to consult – and secondary research into matters such as costing and the possible audience. It drew too on the work that Jane had already done in her own earlier proposals. The study should, of course, be understood not simply as a statement of intention but also as a strategic and rhetorical document, designed to persuade the Director and the Trustees to give it the go-ahead (which they did soon after the Feasibility Study was submitted). I describe some of its content below.

Introduction and Audience

The Introduction to the study is as follows:

> People are interested in food. Recent surveys have shown that, increasingly, their interest focuses on health-related aspects. There is rising public concern about 'unhealthy' foods but little understanding about what is healthy or unhealthy, or how daily diet may be improved. At present there is no major exhibition in Britain which explains nutrition and food.
>
> The Science Museum proposes to mount a lively, entertaining and interesting permanent exhibition on food. The Science Museum's national collections illustrate the history and current state of agriculture and food technology, and hence it is uniquely placed to help people understand today's diet and answer some of their questions.
>
> 1989 sees the celebrations for British Food and Farming Year. This exhibition will be timed to open in September of that year providing a long term focus for the understanding of food and nutrition in the UK.

The claim of potential visitor interest in the first line is both a tactic to highlight the fact that this is a subject which might well attract a wide audience and also part of the placing of people, or visitors, to the forefront as is evident in other aspects of the document and in ideas developed later. The 'health' dimension is justified by its claimed widespread and growing public and topical interest (as witnessed by 'surveys', frequently invoked in the report). The mention of relevant collections is partly to counterbalance the opinion that a health and nutrition angle would not be entirely appropriate to the Science Museum as well as to contributing to the more general task of showing why the Museum should be the venue for such an exhibition ('it is uniquely placed. . . .'). We should note here too that the proposal is credited not to the authors of the report but to The Science Museum ('The Science Museum proposes. . .'). This is, perhaps, a somewhat premature, though no doubt rhetorically effective, subsumption of persons to the institution that we have already noted and that we shall see later in the making and reception of this exhibition. Timing is also justified: the British Food and Farming Year (Museums Year was later to be added too).

The adjectives first chosen to describe the exhibition are worth noting: 'lively, entertaining and interesting'. In everyday discussion these were oppositional adjectives, contrasting this exhibition with others in the Museum, described as 'boring', 'dull', 'book-on-the-wall'. Yet in the document as a whole a more earnest educational dimension predominates – the exhibition will 'explain' and 'help people understand'. As the Education staff member noted, this was to some extent a departure for the Museum too (he was contrasting it with the Natural History Museum next door) and one on which 'we have. . . a poor track record'.

One other theme should also be noted here: that of nation. 'Britain', 'British', 'national' and 'UK' are included in these few paragraphs in a rather low-key and taken-for-granted manner: the Museum is 'national' and the Food and Farming year is 'British'. National boundaries are taken as rather natural parameters, the incontestable fact of the Museum's national status. How this and its auto-production of categories such as 'the British diet' were negotiated in relation to what the Education officer referred to as 'the "ethnic" issue' is a theme to which we shall return in the chapter six.

Although the Museum receives many international visitors, a British audience is implicitly invoked in the proposal documents. As was a new imperative of the late 1980s, a 'target audience' was also explicitly defined: 'The exhibition will be aimed primarily at family parties, including parents who manage the family diet'. This is in some ways surprisingly specific given that in verbal accounts the Team tended to emphasise that the exhibition was for 'everybody' or 'ordinary people'. The statement, however, should not, I think, be interpreted to mean that they considered all 'ordinary people' to be members of families. Still more surprising is the fact that the Feasibility Study also identifies 'higher socio-economic groups' as its target. It notes that it is adults with children, especially in 'higher socio-economic groups', who exhibit most concern over matters of diet, that 47 per cent of Science Museum visitors attend with children, and 97 per cent are from 'higher socio-economic groups'.[13] These figures, we should note, derive from before the introduction of charging. At the time of the Feasibility Study admission charges had been mooted, though not yet confirmed, and this may explain the strategic mention of the fact that those likely to have 'disposable income' have a particular interest in this topic.

Exhibition Content

The discussion of the possible content of the exhibition begins with a list of 'basic principles'. While this is a somewhat heterogeneous list, it is worth quoting in full because it contains both the guiding principles which were to shape the exhibition and what I call the exhibition's political legibility – the politically significant readings which the exhibition seemed to invite or inhibit. As some of these principles were later lost (sometimes with significant consequences for political legibility), the list provides a useful starting point for the stories to follow. Here I provide a very brief note after each principle (or two) on the significance of each; I have numbered the list for ease of discussion though the emphases are original.

> (1) Successful exhibitions start with the familiar and move on to new areas. Most Science Museum visitors are from south-east England and few have direct experience of farming. Their experience of the food they eat begins, as children, at the dinner table and extends, as adults, to the supermarket shelves. Few know how their food reached there, or how it is packaged, processed, or stored.

This idea of starting with the familiar was a central dimension of the exhibition design and shaped various key features of it which would, in turn lead to its being read in certain ways. In particular, it privileged consumption and everyday knowledge in the exhibition.

> (2) Modern agriculture would be difficult to present adequately in an entertaining and interesting way in a gallery in the middle of London, with no room for livestock or arable land. In addition there are plans for a National Museum of Food and Farming on a greenfield site where these could be better displayed.
>
> (3) The exhibition will concentrate on food itself, and its 'processing' both in the home and in the factory. Basic production of food, i.e. at the farm, need not be covered *in detail,* although it must be mentioned. Accordingly the proportion of the exhibition devoted to agriculture itself will be reduced.

The loss of virtually all mention of agriculture and primary food production was to be a consequence of later so-called 'pragmatic' decisions. It was, however, also to have an important impact on the political legibility of the finished exhibition as these areas had been defined out of the exhibition's remit.

> (4) The Science Museum is the ideal place to show the large 3D objects used in parts of the food processing industry. Visitors expect to find such objects here, and expect to see them working.

Large 3D objects were indeed included, though they sometimes behaved rather obstreperously. Given the changes in the exhibition as it progressed into reality, they also came to shape the exhibitionary politics, partly because of their refusal to be thrown off their original physical and semantic trajectory.

> (5) The exhibition will be fun. Finding out about food should be as pleasurable as eating it. Current beliefs about the benefits of a mixed balanced diet will be explored.

'Fun' was a much used word in verbal accounts of the exhibition; and we will return later to a discussion of the politics of fun. The rather different point here about diet shows a clear awareness in the use of the term 'belief', that nutritional ideas are not static. How the Team attempted to deal with this is another theme that will be explored later, where we shall see it in interaction both with scientists (nutritionists) and visitors to the exhibition.

> (6) We will start by explaining what we need to eat and, on a simple level, why. Nutrition will act as the linking theme throughout the gallery, setting each area of the gallery into an overall context. Nutritional theories are constantly changing, so the gallery should be designed to allow for easy updating. However, this gallery need not deal with digestion (in the Natural History Museum) or the molecular details of nutrients (in future biochemistry exhibitions).

Here we see the principle of presenting easy ideas first, as well as the changing nature of (at least nutritional) science. The editing process of siphoning off certain areas to other museums or exhibitions as a justifying tactic is also used here.

> (7) Somewhere in the exhibition we should consider the foods people actually eat and drink, including coffee, even if these have no intrinsic nutritional value.

Later, this was to be cast as part of the broader principle of familiarity – a principle which, as we shall see, had exhibitionary (and political) disadvantages as well as advantages. It is also part of the popular and consumption emphasis of the exhibition.

> (8) The gallery should not be afraid to tackle controversial matters of public concern such as world food problems – shortages, food mountains (witness Band Aid), and additives. Indeed, MAFF's [the Ministry of Agriculture, Fisheries and Food] survey found that ingredients in food ranked third (after smoking and environmental pollution) in people's minds as damaging to health. They reported that public awareness of additives was 'media led' with a general belief that additives had adverse affects. Few people had any specific knowledge of their use.

Intentions to include controversial issues are clear here. All of these topics came to be included in the exhibition, though this was not always noted by visitors or critics for reasons that, as I suggest later, are rather interesting. A recognition of the Museum's possibly distinctive role as part of, or in contradistinction to, the media is made here.

> (9) The subject of food is very large. The exhibition should be designed to allow visitors to choose what they wish to see and provide more detailed information in the resource area.

The theme of choice in the exhibition was to become a central one and it came to ramify through many more matters than the provision of further information (which was done through computer programmes, themselves allowing 'choice' about 'routes' to take). This too was a crucial dimension of the exhibition's political legibility.

Figure 4.10 shows the topics which the study suggested should be covered in the exhibition. At the top we see the two main consumption-focused topics which were to orient part of the exhibition: Shopping and Eating Habits. Leading down from the latter is what was described in the document as a 'nutritonal spine'. Here, nutritional ideas were to be presented, oriented in relation to specific foods. Those listed were each supposed to represent particular nutritional contributions to the diet: Meat and fish (protein, fats, minerals, fish); Tea and coffee (dietary water). In addition, each of the foods exemplified certain production processes: Meat and fish (salting, drying); Vegetables (canning, freezing . . .) (here was where the big 3D machines were to fit in) there were various other (mainly historical) items of information such as 'the 1960s growth of coffee bars'. To this end, the Feasibility Study contains a number of case studies outlining the possible content of each area.

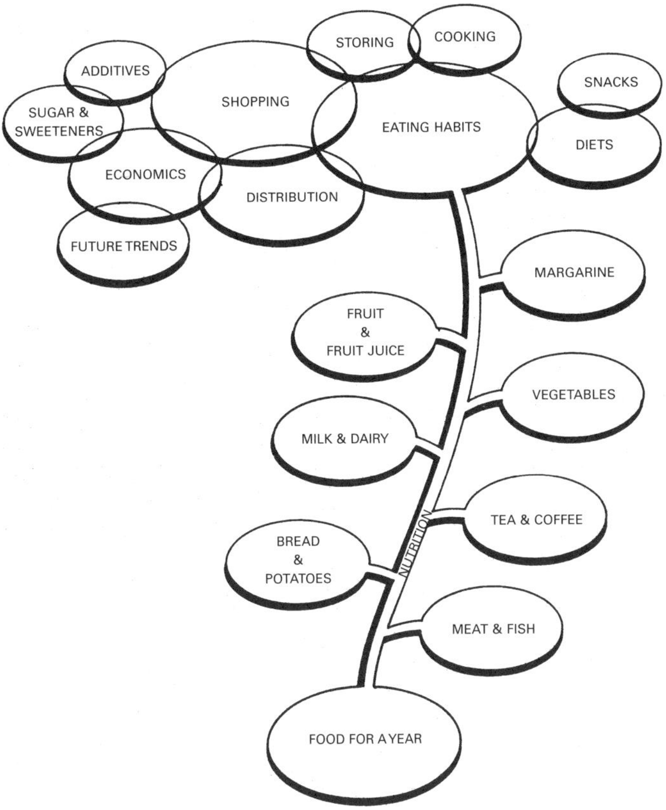

Figure 4.10 Possible exhibit topics from the Feasibility Study.

'Industrial Collaboration' and Budget

The study also covers the potential for what is called 'collaboration with the food industry', specified as the following possibilities:

- Expert advice on the range and content of topics covered in the exhibition.
- Access to technical expertise on the key processes of food manufacture.
- Financial support for the exhibition, either as a sole or joint sponsor.
- Support for the planned programme of educational literature and materials.
- Financial support for the continuing update of the exhibition over its lifetime.
- Access to archive and film material.

- Assistance with identifying and supplying three-dimensional material for the exhibition and for the national collections.

The report notes that 'to date, approaches have been made to a number of large companies and organisations within the food industry'. Looking for industrial sponsorship for both financial assistance as well as for what was often called 'assistance in kind' (such as provision of artefacts) was necessary for most exhibitions and in this Food was far from unusual, though the identification of particular aspects – the accompanying educational literature and its updating – as separate sponsorship 'opportunities' was relatively innovative.

As the next section of the study – the budget – made clear, such 'investment' (the word used) by the food industry was going to be essential to help to fund the set-up costs, which were estimated at nearly £1.5 million, and maintenance costs of £79,000 over the projected ten year lifetime of the gallery. The Science Museum (as author again) 'expects to fund most of the staff costs' (not included in the £1.5 million figure), the study states, and in an appendix calculates these as nearly £300,000. At the time, this was the most expensive exhibition that the Science Museum had undertaken.

Go-ahead and Sponsorship

As the Director and the Trustees had now approved the idea of the project, the following months were dedicated to trying to acquire some substantial sponsorship – 'patrons' as the main sponsors were to be called – for the exhibition to cover the large costs of the new gallery. As the study itself had noted, a number of potential 'industrial collaborators' had been tentatively approached. These meetings might have been over 'technical matters' – as when Jane visited Nestlé's headquarters and 'Alimentarium' exhibition in Switzerland – with sponsorship being 'slipped into' the discussions. Personal contacts, such as that of the Director with David Sainsbury (a member of the Sainsbury family which owned a large UK supermarket chain), were also mobilised, with representatives of possible sponsors invited to dinner at 'the Director's club' (London's Athenaeum). The decision was to approach two possible main sponsors ('patrons') in the first instance (Sainsbury's and Nestlé) and a number of other 'smaller' ones to fund specific aspects (such as the education pack).

By the end of April, the Gatsby Charitable Foundation – one of the Sainsbury Family trusts, and one which then was particularly interested in funding interactive exhibitions – had confirmed that it would contribute £500,000 and it was looking likely that Nestlé would contribute £250,000. So appointing further members of the Food Team went ahead in May: Jan was transferred to the project, and Sue and Heather were appointed to the two E posts after interviews. All began to work on developing the ideas – 'reading frenetically, we were starting from scratch, remember' – and making contacts for potential objects, all towards creating what were called 'outline scripts'. Ann and Cathy, also after interviews, took up the F posts in the summer, by which time, the designers had also been appointed. Hall-Redman Associates (HRA) had won the contract, not only because the interview committee (the Director, Mr Suthers, Jane and Jan, with Sue in attendance) liked their proposals but also that they were seen as 'people we could get on with'. Jan noted at the time:

> I liked their northern bluntness. I am keen that this project is 'curator led' and think that we are more likely to get this with HRA. This is not to say that they do not have their own ideas to contribute – from what I have seen of their work I think they do – but I have confidence in their listening abilities.

Here she expresses a fear common to curators that designers might 'try to take over'. 'Want to lead on CONTENT!' was the hand-written note by one of the unsuccessful competing companies.

Although Nestlé confirmed in May that they would contribute £250,000, they made this 'subject to achievement of a satisfactory form of contract between us which defines the commercial opportunities and range of activities in which our brands may feature'. The Museum was, however, reluctant to agree this, particularly as Sainsbury's had not made such demands. However, what had been agreed with Sainsbury's (by the Director in personal conversation with David Sainsbury) was that the name Sainsbury should feature in the name of the gallery. This was unprecedented in the history of the Museum and the subject of a mostly negative comment by curators. In June, the Sainsbury family offered an additional £250,000 sponsorship, but making it quite clear that 'the family name should be permanently and exclusively associated with the exhibition so that it is known as the Sainsbury gallery or exhibition'. They also specified that no other food retailer be involved as sponsor (or in terms of foods represented) but that food manufacturers could be. A suggestion by the Museum that Nestlé's name should also appear on the gallery was rejected by Sainsbury's, and although negotiations continued for many months, no agreement could be found satisfactory to all parties and eventually, after additional arguments over some dimensions of the content of the exhibition, Nestlé pulled out. Such negotiations, while here specific to this gallery, highlight some of the problems about sponsorship for museums of science in particular. Sponsors are clearly expecting something for their money, and the problem for museums of science is that sponsors are likely to support only exhibitions in which they have a subject-based interest. In some ways, naming a gallery after a sponsor (as was the practice at many other museums, in the case of the Sainsbury wing at the National Gallery), rather than allowing a direct influence in the content or more specific 'commercial opportunities', might seem a more suitable option. However, because of the subject link, the semantics are different from, say, art museums affecting the way the exhibition is read as we shall see in chapter eight.

All of those who eventually contributed financially to the Food gallery had an interest in the subject matter: the National Dairy Council – £50,000, Tate and Lyle and British Sugar – £10,000 each a year for updating the gallery for the next five years. The Meat and Livestock Commission, Mars, and Good Housekeeping donated smaller amounts. Given the widespread media coverage of dietary matters at the time which was mostly critical of dairy produce, sugar and meat, these organisations were likely to want to influence the representation of their products. The Team members generally emphasised that they themselves held what they termed 'curatorial control', that they alone were ultimately responsible for the content of the exhibition. However, they also conceded that it was sometimes difficult to be sure what had been informally agreed, given the 'gentleman's agreement' nature of the way in which sponsorship tended to be established. Furthermore, even if those individuals in a company with whom the deals had originally been done had not requested any input into the content of the exhibition, this had not necessarily been conveyed to those lower down with whom the Team dealt directly, and such staff (who were often PR staff because these were responsible for company trade exhibitions) might well take it for granted that their aim should be to ensure that their company interest be represented as favourably as possible.

The Feasibility Study had already set out a timetable (Figure 4.11) and this lists the activities which were to be undertaken and when. Despite the constant sense of over-running and being extremely pressed for

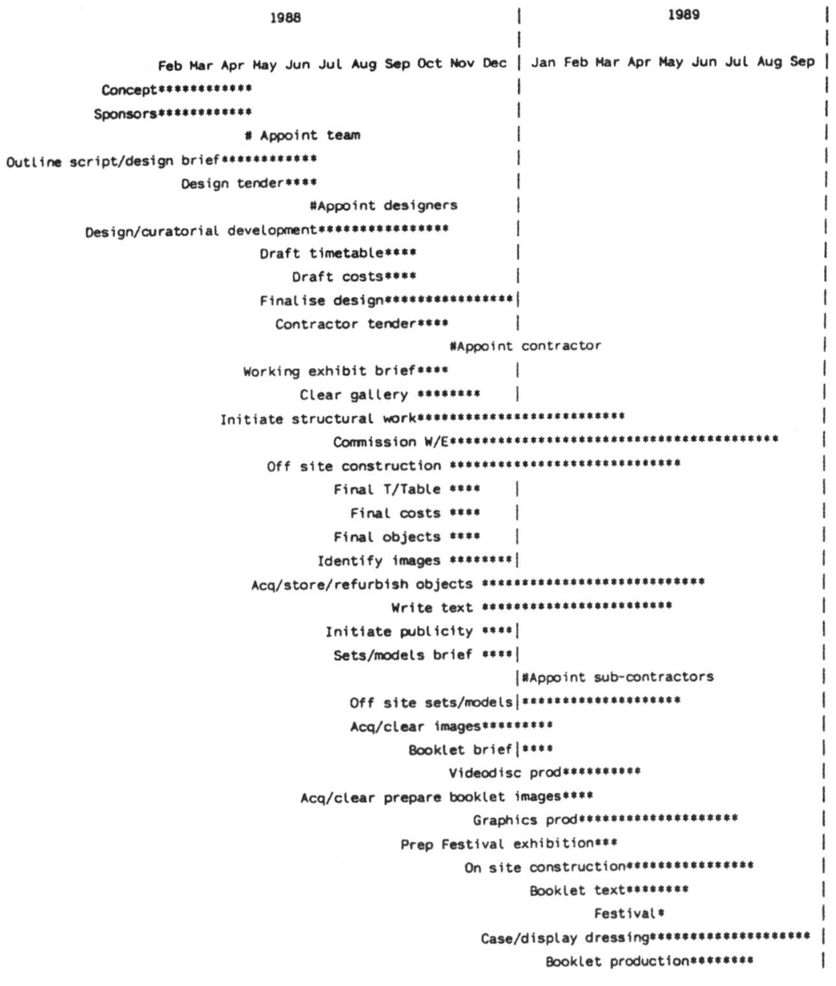

Figure 4.11 Timetable.

time during the exhibition's making, this timetable proved reasonably accurate with very little of what in the Museum was euphemistically called 'irrecoverable slippage' occurring. By the end of the summer of 1988, then, Food was steaming ahead. Not only had the main ideas been mapped out, the Team and designers appointed, the name partly decided and substantial sponsorship assured, it was also agreed that the exhibition should be on the Using floor in the former Astronomy gallery. This last decision was also a matter of some controversy for, although Astronomy was generally agreed to be in need of refurbishing, it was a particularly 'object-rich' gallery, both in terms of the quantity and importance of its displayed collection (which was to be put in storage). The list of objects (prepared for their removal) in the Astronomy gallery reads like a poem:

> Oxford Heliometer, Dondi clock, Wright Orrery, Original Orrery, Nasmyths Telescope, Groombridge Transit Circle, Kew Photo-Heliograph, Sissons Mural Quadrant, Bird's Mural Quadrant, Shuckburgh Equatorial, Rosse Mirror, Smyth Equatorial, Newtonian Reflecting Telescope, Short Reflecting Telescope, Butterfield Quadrant, Statue of Galileo, Jarvis Clock, Coronelli Globe, Jaipur Zodiac, Festival Orrery. . .

'They are ripping out Astronomy to put in a hamburger joint. . . Is the public expected to pay £2 for that? People come to see historic objects' said one curator caustically. As what was destined to be the first permanent gallery to open after the introduction of charging, the Food exhibition was in part going to be a test-case of what visitors did want. First, however, under what often felt like the rather hostile gaze of many Museum staff, the Team faced the task of turning their ideas into physical reality: the exhibition itself.

Notes

1. See Hall 1980; and chapters one, eight and nine for further comment.
2. For further discussion of authorship in relation to cultural production see, for example, Becker 1982; Born 1995; Burke 1995; Foucault 1995.
3. See Foucault 1995.
4. Derrida 1995.
5. The cost of the exhibition (and indeed any exhibition), which I so unreflectively repeated, is itself an interesting cultural construct, as Hilary Rose pointed out to me at that meeting. Why were staff costs excluded, for example? Museum staff explained to me that as they were already employed, this was not an 'extra' cost to the Museum. Nevertheless, the obligatory adding of 'excluding staff costs' was to alert hearers, especially imagined sponsors, to the fact that the Museum was in fact making a further contribution. Part of the background to this was that in negotiations with sponsors the Museum often suggested that it would contribute a certain proportion – for example that it would 'match' external sponsorship – but with the caveat that its contribution would be made at least partially 'in kind', particularly through the provision of staff expertise and time. As the latter were computational

matters in which the Museum could exercise considerable discretion, this produced a useful flexibility into negotiations. Even within the computed costs – amounting to £1.6 million in this case – there was room for discretion, though this could rarely be exercised by the Team themselves. Thus 'the budget' and 'expenditure' felt extremely intransigent, especially when the former was being exceeded by the latter.

6. See Feist and Hutchinson 1989a.

7. Other members of staff might be invited in special circumstances. So in December 1988, all members of the Food team were invited as they were working on 'the flagship project' as one wryly put it. Some staff expressed their resentment at the way that the Science Museum/Trustees party was paid for out of Museum funds, whereas other parties – such as Departmental ones (to which all staff would be invited) – were not. One member of staff who had never been invited told me that those below D were not allowed 'because they think we don't know how to behave ourselves. They're scared we might moan in front of the Trustees'.

8. Van Maanen 2001. In management studies, this kind of work structure is sometimes known as 'business process re-engineering' or just 're-engineering'. Keith Grint explains that this is characterised by the use of process teams, multi-dimensional work (perhaps requiring 'multi-skilling') and a shift of 'employee focus' – 'from concern for the boss to concern for the customer' (1995: 94) – in theory at least.

9. I never heard curatorial object love compared to or contrasted with woolly-hat obsession though they clearly share similarities in their relationships with objects. Perhaps 'woolly hats' – as the derogatory names for and comments about them suggest – were a disturbing category for museum staff precisely because of this similarity and extension of object love. There are interesting discussions of collecting and its classification as either legitimate or perverse in Elsner and Cardinal (eds) 1994, Pearce 1995, and Pearce (ed.) 1997.

10. On the proliferation of 'expertise' and 'expert systems' see, for example, Giddens 1990.

11. The 'cult of the new' is part of a broader cultural focus on 'originality' which is deeply intertwined with notions of 'individuality' (see Taylor 1985), and is also part of the 'imaginative hedonism' which Campbell (1987) has argued is a distinctive and crucial feature of modern consumerism.

12. See McManus 1989: 4.

13. The source given for this is an English Tourist Board survey of 1982 which the report says provides the 'most recent figures available'. 'Higher socio-economic groups' is used to refer here to all groups except Ds and Es. Twenty nine per cent are As and Bs according to the report, indicating that the Feasibility Study could have interpreted the results differently if its authors had wished.

'Reality Sets In': Managing and Materialising Dreams (and Negotiating Nightmares)

When I talked with the Team after the exhibition had opened, all of them described the process of making it as one of moving, as Sue put it, 'from very creative to hard slog.' 'Well, you start off with all of these wonderful ideas', explained Jan, 'and, then, well, reality sets in. Each one of the areas we'd defined could have been a whole gallery really, so in the end we just had to be brutal.' Their accounts told of cuts, of loss, of the unexpected intervention of 'practicalities', of constraints of time and of money. In this chapter, I look at some of that process of 'reality setting in' as the exhibition materialised into exhibits and gallery space. I do so not simply to tell an allegory of thwarted dreams but to try to highlight some of the particularly important players, processes and assumptions which shaped the outcome (sometimes in unexpected ways) of the exhibition.

This chapter continues to work through the authorial puzzle set out in the previous chapter, and the more general concern with the production of culture and science in the making that threads through the book as a whole. During what often felt like a roller-coaster ride of exhibition production the daily issues which crowded in were ones of what to put in and where, how to deal with lack of space or a wrongly shaped location, where to get hold of the right item to exhibit a particular idea, how to express a concept simply, how to find enough money and keep to budget, how to get all of those involved working to a time-table and simply how to manage the whole enormous multiplicitous business of creating the exhibition. Although it did not always feel like it, all of these, one way or another, had implications for the ways in which visitors were imagined, for the ways in which science was represented and for the later political legibility of the exhibition.

While numerous events and decisions throughout the exhibition-making process shaped the final outcome, there were three moments which seemed particularly consequential: (1) a relatively early intervention by the scientific advisory panel of the exhibition which was critical of one of the organising principles of the gallery and led to this being changed – an intervention that I call 'the Reorganisation'; (2) a first major editing phase, referred to as 'the Retreat', as the Team's ideas were mapped into the physical space of the exhibition and much had to be jettisoned; and (3) a later, and to the Team unexpected and at the time frustrating, editing of the exhibition, which they called 'the Rethink', initiated by criticisms from the Museum Director. I deal with each in turn and try to trace some examples of what came to be politically consequential inflections, showing how they became progressively solidified into the exhibition space. In each case I also use the particular intervention and moment in the exhibition's development as the basis for a discussion of broader issues in relation to: (1) the role of scientists in the making of science exhibitions; (2) the role of physical space, objects, media and designers; and (3) the role of some of the underlying ideas about knowledge, exhibition and 'the public'. In each section I am also concerned to highlight presuppositions and sometimes apparently trivial decisions or events which – like bugs in a computer programme – only make themselves fully evident as reality sets in.

Science and 'the Reorganisation'

In the making of most Science Museum exhibitions there is a good deal of contact with those working in relevant industries and it is not unusual to have somebody from a company joining planning meetings to give what is usually termed 'technical assistance'. So, for example, in the making of the Chemical Industry gallery, a [retired] member of ICI participated in regular meetings;[1] the Information Age project also intended to include somebody from a computer company on their Team to help to give them detailed technical information. In the case of Food this was deemed inappropriate: firstly, because the exhibition covered a wide range of topics and there was not a clear specific industry to go to, and secondly, because, as Jane explained to me, 'It was very difficult to get them to say anything against anything, even if it was not their company's product, because they worry about the impact it might have on the food industry as a whole.' Because the exhibition was to deal with potentially controversial matters such as food poisoning, additives and health, this was also problematic. Although Jane had originally assumed they probably would liaise closely with those whom she termed 'commercial scientists', she chose in the end not to do so.

Sponsoring companies were a particularly difficult category, as the Team learned early on when a representative of a sponsoring sugar company seemed very keen that sugar be presented in terms of 'energy' – deemed a more positive category than either one of 'carbohydrates' or 'calories'. This was resisted by the Team, who emphasised the importance of their 'objectivity' on the matter and Sue decided to include a representation of a slave ship in the section on sugar partly to make the point, to herself as much as anybody else, that the exhibition was not shaped by its sponsors. This example was taken by the Team as a warning of the 'wrangles' which could have ensued had sponsor scientists (Sainsbury's chief scientist, for example) been allowed much input into the formation of the project. This is not to say that sponsors were allowed no input at all: Sainsbury's were given regular presentations of how the project was going, and all sponsors were sent the draft text of sections of the exhibition which related to their products. This, however, was only after these had been discussed with the main official scientific input to the exhibition, a five-strong advisory panel consisting of those who held the title of Professor of Nutrition or Food Science and Technology. This panel met twice to review the early plans of the exhibition and its members were then available to discuss particular points and to check over the text produced. In addition to their explicit function of providing information and checking 'the factual accuracy' (a favourite phrase in this regard) of the exhibition, the professors also had an informal task (of which they may not have been aware) of helping to ward off 'commercial scientist' input by allowing the Team to say that their advisory panel had approved of particular things. These university professors were, then, a means by which the Team harnessed what was, especially in dealings with sponsors, termed 'objectivity'.

Although the professors provided the Foodies with a good alibi for employing terms like 'factual accuracy' and 'objectivity' in warding off attempts to change their own ideas and text, in many ways they highlighted the slipperiness of these terms. The professors also disagreed among themselves on various matters, such as the nutritional worth of particular nutrients and foods – a reflection of wider dissent, often noted in the mass media, within 'scientific opinion' where food and health were concerned. (For example, one of the professors argued strongly for a massive decrease in the amount of fat consumed whereas another attacked this as creating 'muesli-belt malnutrition'.) This led Jane to decide to highlight this lack of agreement within the exhibition. However, in another unexpected twist, when the professors were asked to come up with quotes illustrating their positions, they all chose rather uncontroversial ones, perhaps because they were aware that these were likely to be on public display for ten years or so. Thus Jane's intention was frustrated and the exhibition panel entitled 'Controversy or Consensus?'; showing the mug shots of the five professors and choice snippets of their wisdom, illustrates the latter far more than the intended former.

One aspect on which the advisory panel agreed was that the original idea of the Team to present ideas about nutrients via particular foods – bread to illustrate carbohydrates (as we saw in the feasibility document) for example – was inappropriate and 'old-fashioned'. They preferred that people should think of all foods as a combination of nutrients. This was the early editorial intervention which I call the 'Reorganisation' because it led to the Team making what felt at the time as annoying but relatively innocuous changes to the organisation of the proposed exhibition. In response to this criticism they decided to separate 'nutrition' (later to be renamed 'Food and the Body') to an area of its own (rather than use it as a 'linking spine') thus severing its connection with the food areas which dealt with food production. Nutrition and, more broadly, the health dimensions of food, thus became physically separated in the exhibition from the representation of food production. This separation later revealed itself as problematic in the light of the major issues of food poisoning and food contamination which began to hit the headlines with increasing frequency in late 1988 and which have continued intermittently ever since. In the next chapter we shall return to consider how the exhibition tried to deal with these within its fast 'concretizing' (as the stage of turning ideas into physical exhibits was called) framework.

It is clear from the Food experience that the representation of science to the public is not simply about taking ideas from 'science' and repackaging them for public consumption. Firstly, 'science' itself is far from homogeneous: there are different kinds of scientists, not only with different specialisms but also with different agendas, and those involved in exhibition-making do not simply 'pick up' scientific ideas and re-present them, they also negotiate between different kinds of scientific input. Secondly, the process is far from being a neat linear one. Interventions from the scientists come at various points during exhibition-making and some are only really evident as they interact with other decisions and in the finished exhibition itself. Moreover, in making their interventions the scientists are not doing so simply from the point of view of 'science'. They are also concerned with the reception of their contributions, how these will be understood by visitors within the context of the Science Museum, and with the possible public consequences of what they say. This is evident in the commercial scientists' reluctance to be critical of any aspects of food production as well as the professors' reluctance to have their more controversial ideas on public display for the next decade.

The Pleasure before the Pain – Proliferation

The advisory panel's intervention came relatively early on in the exhibition's production, after the Feasibility Study had been produced and initial ideas set out but before these had begun to be translated into the physical space of the exhibition. This interim stage was one in which Team members dived into researching the areas of the exhibition to which they had been allocated. They began reading 'basically whatever we could lay our hands on', beginning with library searches and recommendations from the advisory panel and others that they met, including children's books and newspaper articles as well as more scholarly books and journal articles. As Heather said, a little ruefully: 'What comes out may be like a Ladybird book but you've still got to do all the research to get to that point.' They also began to make visits to relevant factories and archives, investigating simultaneously the possibility of pictures and objects which might be included, especially large scale machines which might be able to be demonstrated in action in the gallery. In addition, they visited other exhibitions on the subject of food in Ontario, Chicago and Switzerland in order to refine their own ideas through comparison.[2]

While these trips helped to show some things that the Team did not want to do ('some of the interactives which had sounded a good idea did not really work that well') they also provided positive inspiration. Overall, this was a proliferation stage in which much got added, especially things that individual Team members liked. These were sometimes additional themes or ideas (like having something on 'why the British don't like ring-pull cans' or 'squirty cream and the ozone layer') though more often they were particular objects that Team members came across in their travels [Figure 5.1]. Heather, for example,

Figure 5.1 Object-feel (and smell): Cathy and Heather examine possible objects for the gallery.

found a 'rather gorgeous' Greek wine jug with a picture of fish on it in the Museum's own collections and reckoned that she could 'squeeze it in' to her section on fish. When Sue saw a tiny plastic gherkin in the Heinz archive, she was desperate to include it ('Isn't it wonderful? I've just got to have it!'). Less was abandoned than added, however, in these heady and expansive months.

At the same time, some of the 'basic principles' of the exhibition came to be reiterated and reshaped, both in the regular Team meetings and also in the daily interactions in the offices. One dimension of this was reacting against some of the criticisms of the exhibition that had been voiced in the Museum, including the Education officer's memo. The suggestion that the exhibition might be 'didactic' irked the Team and in response to this they re-emphasised their 'fun' approach, that they did not intend to 'be preachy', that the exhibition would not be 'boring'. One way in which they hoped to avoid 'the yawn factor' was by not using panels of text in the exhibition. Quite what to use instead had not been resolved, members often referring to panels, as did Jane on one occasion before correcting herself, 'or whatever we are going to have instead of panels, because we're not going to have panels, because panels are boring'. (In the end, however, there were 160 panels in the exhibition.) They were also keen to emphasise the experiential aspects of the exhibition – another key aspect of 'fun' – and that it would cater not just to sight but also to senses of smell (a cabinet of various spices and a food aroma unit), sound (an exhibit reproducing different sounds associated with food, such as a popping champagne cork, sizzling chips or crisps being crunched) and taste (at that point, there was to be a tasting exhibit as well as an eating area included in the exhibition). Joky and fun exhibits were to be included; the giant chocolate mousse pot and some fairground-style mirrors which showed visitors a little fatter or a little thinner were some of these, and there were plans to use cartoons. The Foodies were keen to include as many 'social bits' as possible, several Team members saying that they personally found these most interesting. This included what they listed as 'superstitions and fads in each area'. These sections were supposed to look at matters such as 'carrots and seeing in the dark, garlic and Dracula, salt and the Devil, Shrove Tuesday, gingerbread men', plus individual snippets of interesting historical and cultural information.[3] All in all, at this stage, the proposed content of the exhibition was undoubtedly 'busy', to use an adjective which the Team frequently and approvingly used to describe it.

Another characteristic of this phase, which we need to understand to see why later editing felt 'very, very painful' to the Foodies, was reacting against some of the criticisms of the proposed exhibition circulating in the Museum. The idea that the exhibition would not contain historic objects (as in the Astronomy versus hamburger joint comment) particularly rankled. Whereas the criticism of being 'didactic' irked by casting the Foodies as chalk-waving schoolmistresses, the 'object-thin' criticism seemed to impugn their identity as curators. In response to the Education officer's observation that this exhibition would be unlikely to contain many objects, they angrily listed inventoried artefacts that were to be included, such as 'the oldest can in the world', the original Birds-Eye pea-freezer, and a tea-packaging machine. On several occasions Team members would report on conversations they had had with other curators in which they had 'had to point out, that we *do* have objects actually'. Heather later described herself as having been 'paranoid about not having any objects' at this stage of exhibition-making and that this was why she had been 'desperate to get some in'. All, especially Jane (who was a member of the Gallery Planning Group), were aware of the concern among curators that displaying fewer objects could play into the hands of those arguing that curators should not be involved in creating exhibitions, and more generally for a 'downsizing' of curatorial numbers. Jane constantly argued vehemently against this. For example, she resisted a suggestion that an outside script-writer should be brought in on Food: 'as curators it is our job to interpret objects for visitors'. As curators too, all members of the Team often exhibited object-love and, despite the fact that this exhibition was to be 'message-led rather than object-led' (as the Director described it), they often felt themselves compelled ('gotta have it!') to incorporate objects on aesthetic ('I thought they were so freaky'), affective ('I really love it'), historical ('it's one of the first produced') or other grounds ('nobody will have seen anything like it', for example). This passion for objects, the desire to counter within-museum criticism and awareness of the political consequences of a dearth of objects contributed to their proliferation. This was expansive in terms of space for, while some of the artefacts were relatively small, such as 'the oldest can', others, like the tea-packer and the freezer, were space-greedy.

Other things multiplied too. There had from the beginning been an intention to use a mixture of media, including working demonstrations, audio-visuals and computers, with a particular emphasis on interactive exhibits. While many post-1960 Science Museum exhibitions also contained a combination of some of these, Food was regarded as unusual in the high proportion of interactives it intended to have. It was more a 'science centre approach with added objects' rather than 'object-based with added demos' to use some of the language in which these matters were talked about in the museum world. Moreover, as the Team liked to emphasise, the interactive exhibits were not to be 'just push-buttons' but 'properly interactive', which was defined to me as 'not just push-button, not so passive. . . we want something which involves the visitor more'. Thus, some of the exhibits were to be not just 'hands-on' but 'body-in'. Among other things they included at that time, was a tunnel which the visitor would be able to enter in order to 'experience what it is like to be a frozen pea', a 'smellerama' (in which visitors try to identify different food smells), a 'fun egg and spoon' exhibit, large 'egg-timers' for trying to shake oil and water together, a sugar centrifuge, exercise bicycles with panels showing how much energy was being used, and a supermarket checkout through which visitors could scan basket loads of fake food. Many of these exhibits, especially the 'body-in', were ones which would occupy a good deal of space. But the space in the gallery was finite – too finite to accommodate all these dreams.

Design and 'Retreat'

The first major curbs on the Team's proliferation phase came in October 1988 when they rented two adjoining cottages in Lancashire and spent two days with the designers trying to work out how the outline scripts – the basic ideas and artefacts the Foodies wanted to include – could be mapped onto the actual gallery space. This was not the first meeting with the designers; they had had meetings earlier, but the Lancashire Retreat was regarded by all concerned as a major 'moment of truth', of 'brutal cuts' and of 'reality setting in'. Unironically referred to as 'the Retreat' because the meeting was held at such a distance from the Museum (in order to prevent interruptions and enable a really concentrated effort on the task), the meeting could also be seen as a 'retreat' both in that it involved a re-treating of ideas, and in the sense that the Foodies had to step back from some of the many ideas that had already blossomed.

A general idea of which parts of the proposed exhibition would go where had been established at the earlier meeting. What the Retreat was about was a more detailed and specific designation of space – working out which particular artefacts and exhibits would go where and just how much space each section of the exhibition would be accorded. Given that the organisation of each part of the exhibition had been the task of a different individual, the Retreat also involved managing relations between different Team members over whether space should be taken from, say, X to give to Y ('trading' as one of the Johns called it).

The designers had been sent the outline scripts in advance and had brought their drawings of the possible layout of the exhibition with them. These were on large tissue sheets which could be laid over the a base drawing of the gallery and its structures (which showed various crucial structural matters including at which points it would be possible to place heavier objects). In some cases they had prepared alternatives and they had rubbers, pencils and rulers at the ready for redrawing as plans changed. The days proceeded with each Team member, in the presence of Jane and usually of Jan, going through the plans for their particular areas with one or other of the Johns. Far from being a matter of the designers just 'packaging' the Team's plans, this process was a much more constructive one in which some of the planned material was cut, condensed or reconceptualised. The designers also held opinions on what was likely to be 'interesting' or 'boring' as well as what would look good.

The designers were particularly concerned that the space would be 'confusing' and 'bitty', with too many small distinct areas, a consequence of the Team's desire for something 'busy' with lots going on but also of the fact that different individuals had worked on different sections of the exhibition. To try to reduce this potential 'bittyness' the designers suggested trying to group some of the areas together so that visually and spatially they could be linked. Everybody was rather pleased when they collectively managed to come up with a classification of sections of the exhibition into 'Where?' (the distribution and economics of food), 'Why?' (covering diet and eating habits), 'What?' ('what do you need from your food?' – an area which was now defined to include not only nutrients but also 'pleasure' and 'food safety'), and 'How?' ('how do you prepare it?' – covering processing, both domestic and industrial). This, however, was a further step towards solidifying the incision, initiated by the professors, between food production and food and health. Moreover, it gave each of them a particular, consequential, inflection. Under the label of 'How do you prepare it?', food production becomes a purely technical matter, illustrating the ways in which machines and technologies work. The 'What do you need from your food?', by contrast, becomes very individual-focused – an inflection which is written deeper into the story here by including individualised matters of taste alongside those of nutrition. This helps the intended presentation of diet as 'as individual as a person's clothes – what suits one person does not necessarily suit another'. The incision was made deeper too by the designers' call to make each of these areas physically or visually distinct. At the Retreat a lot of discussion was devoted to how to do this effectively, though none of us even considered the possible implications that this division itself might have. This was not just a matter of pragmatic and aesthetic interests predominating – though they often did – but was also a consequence of the modes in which the exhibition was projected forward and the visitor imagined. 'Busyness' and 'boringness', 'the yawn factor' and considerations of the visitor's physicality – whether they would be tired by this point, 'overloaded' – were the conceptual frameworks through which the exhibition, and indirectly the visitor, was planned into being.

One subject of particular attention was what was called 'visitor circulation' and 'visitor flow', the ways in which it was envisaged that visitors would move through the exhibition. In this imagining of an embodied visitor into the still virtual space of the exhibition there was a particular fear of what were called 'bottle-necks' (areas where too many visitors might congregate and block the way for others), 'dead-ends' (where visitors would have to retrace their steps instead of 'flowing' into a new area), 'throw-away space' (space which had to be left relatively empty merely to help visitor flow) and, perhaps most particularly, of 'confusing space'. This was in many respects a consequence of the 'busy-ness' that the Team wanted and their own resistance to the exhibition having any one specified direction. In turn, it was linked to their desire to create an exhibition which would not be too didactic, which they associated with unidirectional exhibitions. Important to them was that the visitor should not be compelled to take a particular route but that they would have choice in the way they moved through the exhibition. As we shall see in the following chapters, this idea of consumer choice was written deeply into many aspects of this exhibition. In this it was not alone as we have already seen in relation to the multi-museum idea discussed in chapter three. However, the desire for choice and variety on the one hand, created problems for visitor circulation and the creation of a 'non-confusing space' on the other. The resultant mapping created during the Retreat was to some extent a fragile compromise – an exhibition containing many small diverse sections and alternative directions which visitors could take, but nevertheless with routes of flow and certain broader 'theming' (which the designers intended to mark stylistically through what they called 'visual punctuation') to 'tie it together'.

Although there were moments, especially in the kitchen, when some of the Foodies grumbled that the designers were 'trying to have too much curatorial input', on the whole the 'brutal cuts' were managed in a relatively consensual and good-natured way. This was, perhaps, partly due to the manner in which the Johns, often supported by Jane, explained their suggestions (as well as the fact that they were careful to present them as suggestions even if they were more than that). It was, perhaps, also due to the informal surroundings (all were in jeans and we had to take turns making tea and stoking the fire) and most of all to the fact that it became quite self-evident that there was simply too much to fit into the available space. Now and then one of the Johns would whip out a large wooden tape-measure to show just how big a likely space (comparing it to the size of the room that we occupied) or exhibit would be. By physically demonstrating the 'spatial constraints', the necessity for cuts was made incontrovertible.

Making Cuts

The cuts were many and various. They included a large part of the section on 'sugar' (including a proposed computer game about factory production and a working demonstration of sugar packing) and on 'snacks', some of the area devoted to staple foods, and specific exhibits in many areas (the 'mediaeval market' shrunk to 'a mediaeval hag sitting with a basket on her knee'). Despite the variety of items cut, certain legitimations for doing so tended to predominate. One of these was whether an area was 'really' about food or 'really' relevant to a particular part of the exhibition. Thus, for example, Jane said that showing something on squirty cream and the ozone layer was 'getting too far off the topic'. Another justification was whether something would become 'dated' or a 'dead issue' by the time the gallery opened and into its lifetime, as was said of the emerging salmonella in eggs scandal. Whether an exhibit would have interesting interactives was often crucial, as was, to a lesser extent, whether there were inventoried objects or other three dimensional exhibits which would be included. Interactives demanded a particularly large amount of space – five square metres was reckoned by the designers to be the necessary area for these – and this sometimes meant that for already commissioned interactives to be included other things had to be excluded. Thus to include the interactive sugar centrifuge, other aspects of sugar processing and history were cut.

Sue's proposed section on the psychology of shopping, to take one notable example, fell victim to a combination of these. Sue had wanted 'to show, basically, how supermarkets try to con us into buying things' by explaining how, in the usual layout of supermarkets, shoppers are first confronted by fresh fruit and vegetables which are both colourful and appealing but also relatively expensive items that we might be more likely to miss out on when we have spent too much; how staple items, such as bread and milk, are usually located well into the store, meaning that one has to pass lots of other goodies before reaching them; or how more expensive items are often placed at eye-level. Most of these were ideas that she planned to show through text and pictures, though she did have some ideas for three-dimensional exhibits, such as one demonstrating how lighting is used to make meat look more appetising. This relative lack of interactives or objects, however, was one of the features of this area leading to the decision to cut it, particularly when Sue was faced with a choice of cutting other parts of her section on shopping which were to include interactives and original items, the creation and acquisition of which had already begun. In contrast with these, she herself came to the conclusion that the psychology of shopping was 'nebulous and difficult to do in a gallery'. The material world of the Museum could not afford it space. She was also persuaded by arguments that this section would rapidly become out of date as supermarkets would draw on new research and current wisdoms would become obsolete. She also acknowledged, with some reluctance, that it would probably prove 'very contentious, very awkward' with the sponsors. Generally the latter would not be something to deter her, though in combination with the other factors it could be seen as an element of self-censorship. Thus through these multiple 'pragmatic arguments', as Sue described them, the psychology of shopping was eliminated. Later, she was to regret this when the finished exhibition was criticised for being what food companies and supermarkets would surely have wanted.

One outcome of the Retreat was a realisation that for the exhibition to be ready on time, the Team would need to finalise 'scripts' much sooner than had been envisaged. That is, they needed to decide in even more detail just what objects and exhibits would finally be included (many were still in the stage of negotiation), just how large they would be, and how much text and graphic material would accompany them. On their return to the Museum, the Foodies went into overdrive to try to get all of this ready. However, something else was to shortly disrupt their timetable. This was a call by the Director for them to thoroughly 'rethink' the whole exhibition – only ten months before it was due to open.

The Rethink: Messages, Messages, Messages

What felt at the time like 'a major bombshell' (Jan) began as what was intended to be a carefully orchestrated presentation to the Director. The Foodies were concerned that he might 'try to throw a spanner in the works'; he was often regarded as wanting to intervene in how things were being done (though he insisted to me, partly perhaps in awareness of this reputation, that he was being 'extremely hands-off with this exhibition'). They planned to 'deflect his attention' by all going in and talking about their own areas, showing him some detailed layout plans and attractive objects, and making him wait until the end to ask questions so that he could not easily 'get on one of his bloody hobby-horses about history or whatever'. Sue has also picked up the phrase 'visual shorthand' on one of her industry visits and they planned to make use of this: 'It's not a museum word but the Director will love it.' Unfortunately for the Foodies, the strategy to 'deflect his attention' with lots of detail and historical snippets turned out to be a bad idea.

On the appointed day in November, all dressed rather smartly, we file into the Director's spacious office, quarter of an hour before the meeting is due to begin and arrange some choice objects – mainly food packaging – on the sideboard and coffee table, and place the plans of the gallery on the large board table. Dr Cossons enters, 'his usual boyish, enthusiastic self' (Ann), and says how much he is looking forward to hearing how things are getting on and how, as 'everybody knows what the project's about. . . you don't need to explain it all'. Jane takes this up to say that they will just give a quick account without stopping for questions at this point. She passes around a six-page paper, entitled 'Outline Story' which lists some of the main themes of the exhibition and their content. The document states that the exhibition is 'about food and how it has changed' and sets out the new 'What?', 'How?', 'Why?' and 'Where?' classification as well as the previously established headings (such as 'Tea and Coffee' or 'Shopping'), saying something about each of its areas.

In her introduction to the meeting, Jane emphasises the fact that the gallery is to be 'determinedly populist in approach. It's not a gallery for specialists, it's a gallery for the general public'. She also says that the Team has identified 'about five hundred possible objects for the gallery' (a consequence of the object love and attempt to counter in-Museum criticism), though they do not propose to include all of them. The rest of the presentation proceeds as though walking through the gallery, though entering from three different directions, with each Team member giving an account of the areas for which she is responsible. This all takes much longer than the allocated twenty minutes but Dr Cossons restrains himself from asking questions, though I notice that he is becoming increasingly fidgety. Jane winds up by concluding: 'But it's not a normal sort of Science Museum exhibition. . . in any way!' with which Dr Cossons laughingly agrees and begins, with a charmingly disarming modesty, what is to feel to the Team like a rather devastating response:

> That's as good a starting point as any, isn't it, because it seems to me that the gallery is not setting out to present a great collection. It starts off from a series of themes and there are materials in the Museum's collections which can underline or illustrate some of those themes and

in other areas you haven't got objects and you're going out to find them. In other areas objects aren't appropriate anyway so you're using other types of medium. And my initial reaction was that I've lost contact with your initial aims and objectives in what seems to be a wealth of statements and themes. And I'm just wondering whether it might be useful to step right back and say what the gallery is to say. Or what you want to say through the gallery. And how each of these contributes to the building up of that statement or series of things. I'm not suggesting that it doesn't, I'm just a bit lost or confused in my mind. The other one is, I think you're saying a fantastic amount in the gallery [Jane: Yes we are] And I'm just wondering whether the clarity of your central message might be lost in the wealth of individual elements within the gallery – and this is only a question at this stage, for debating – any one of which may in its own right be fascinating. But how does it actually contribute to that central message? [Jane: We are slightly concerned about the quantity of information] It looks, and I'm not suggesting that I've paced it out on the ground, chalked the floor and so on, tremendously densely packed with ideas and messages. And just taking for example the 'Tea and Coffee' one. . . what is the essential message of the 'Tea and Coffee' section?

Jane says that it is 'that tea and coffee are your main source of dietary water' to which the Director says:

> That seems a super, absolutely clear message which I missed in all this business about teapots and so on. I don't know what teapots contribute towards that message. We are familiar with teapots because that's what we get tea out of. But is anything to do with the history of tea. . . . anything to do with the essential means, basic means, of getting that message across?

The Director continues to press the Team to tell him what different parts of the exhibition are trying to 'get across' and what the 'central messages' are:

> So what is at the root of the gallery, then? I'm just trying to get down to one-liners if you like. Because I think that you will see much more clearly – I'm deliberately playing Devil's Advocate you understand – how each of these messages reinforces that central message. It's a sort of pyramid really, isn't it? There's a central message, and there might be a series of sub-messages which guide the geography of the gallery in each of your areas. And then there might be separate little messages and so on. My

> anxiety is just how much there is in it and how many messages you might have got and I'm just wondering whether we can trace each of these little messages right back up a hierarchy to some central one-liner which says the Food Gallery is to do this.

After some discussion of whether the message is that 'food has changed' (Director: 'Food has changed – yawn, yawn – so what?') Jane changes tack and says that it is 'to help people understand food'. The Director takes this up as referring to the nutritional content of food and challenges the relevance of various sections which have been presented to him. He is also concerned with how the 'messages' that the Team suggest are there are translated to visitors in the exhibition ('How do they know 'Tea and Coffee' is 'dietary water'?') and with whether visitors are likely to be interested in these messages anyhow. Several hours later, when many parts of the proposals have been explored and when I have at last had the pleasure of hearing one of the Director's infamous 'when I was a lad in Nottingham' anecdotes, the Foodies are sent away to come up with the 'pyramid' of messages – formulated as questions and answers – for which the Director has been searching. As they leave he tells them:

> The key thing is messages. The gallery will stand or fall by that. It is important for you to go through the process of wooing the unbeliever. The ultimate unbeliever is the visitor.

Back in the offices, although feeling rather deflated, the Team concede that they have ended up with far too much going on in the exhibition and that the Director's comments have been useful in helping them acknowledge this. However, Jane is concerned about the possible slippage of time that the kind of going back to basics that the Director has suggested will entail. They had expected that the Director would have liked the historical emphasis that they gave in the presentation – 'he's usually into this' – and concerned that if they follow his advice 'it will be all nutrients, all modern', 'it will be the historical bits that will go. . . these are the interesting bits'. Looking back at the transcripts of the meeting, however, it seems that what was involved was not the Director contrarily being 'not as keen on history as usual' – had there been some interesting core historical message he might well have been satisfied – but, because of an implicit tendency to contrast 'the history' with 'the science', his comments were prone to be read in an 'if not one, then the other' kind of way: today he wanted science not history.

More generally, the case was typical of a tendency that I witnessed in other contexts in the Museum for staff to calculate their actions in terms of what they perceived that the Director would or would not like, a consequence of the perception that only he could 'grant life or death'. In some contexts this could be a constraint on creativity and autonomy for, instead of sticking to thinking up their own ideas and trying to persuade the Director of their worth, staff would, as in this example, expend energy on trying to orchestrate a favourable outcome by giving him what they perceived he wanted. Yet this did not always work, because he was not necessarily looking to have what he had liked last time played back to him. Another consequence of this was that the Director was often depicted as contrary by staff, as 'changing with the wind' or 'going for the flavour of the month' because he did not always like what staff had prophesied that he ought to like.

In the following days, the Foodies grapple with what they call 'the Rethink', the two objectives of which, according to Jane, are 'to clarify our understanding and to get it past the Director'. It is decided that a 'rigorous conceptual framework' is needed and 'rigorous' becomes the word on all our lips (we sometimes even drink 'rigorous' coffee). At Mr Suthers's insistence, although the Team are initially not very keen on this, a consultant is employed to help them with their rigorous task. Over hours and hours of meetings the exhibition proposals are thoroughly dissected, titles change ('Tea and coffee' to 'Drinks') and a pyramid of questions and answers, as the Dr ordered, is produced. Some of this rethinking means that some of the physical layout of the exhibition needs to be changed (swapping around 'Sugar' and 'Snacks', for example), though this is kept to a minimum in order to make as little disruption to the ongoing design work as possible. The newly-defined aim for the gallery is 'to help people understand the impact of science and technology on our food', with an accompanying question: 'How does science and technology affect what you eat?' The foregrounding of 'science and technology' here is a product both of the contrast with 'history' mentioned above and of a turn to what is seen as fundamental to the Science Museum during this difficult time. In trying to formulate an aim which will satisfy the two objectives identified by Jane, and allow as much as possible of what was already going on to be included (so as not to disrupt the timetable too much), 'science and technology' is seen as a good bet because, as is said (sometimes a little wearily) on more than one occasion 'we are the Science Museum after all'. 'Science and technology' is also seen as relatively 'safe' and 'value-free', an easier route to display and one which, in providing for the inclusion of all of the large industrial machinery and interactive exhibits whose momentum is already thrusting towards the finished gallery, is fully and easily legitimate. What we see, then, is a kind of 'institutional regression' – a going back to what is seen as established and uncontroversial about an institution – at a moment of crisis.

Figure 5.2 shows the first line of the pyramid – the aims and questions for each of the exhibition's main areas. The 'How?', 'What?', 'Where?' and 'Why?' framework – which has now been deemed too difficult to 'translate' to the public – has been forgotten and instead each section has a title including the word 'food' which it is hoped will make sense to visitors. History has not been eliminated, however, but has become subsumed to the overall 'science and technology' message. In being pressed to be clear about the content of the exhibition, the Team defines part of its remit as being about the increase in food choice in Britain over the past century. Coupled with the 'impact of science and technology' main message, the story becomes one of how science and technology have brought us greater choice. At the same time, under the new explicit aim, explaining technical matters becomes central to the exhibition. This leads Heather, who fights hard to retain what she calls her 'more social' and 'more interesting bits', to worry that 'this exhibition is becoming a hymn to the food-processing industry'. Her concern, however, is not explored: the Team already feel themselves to be under too much pressure and too far behind schedule.

Managing 'Muscling-in'

The process of making the exhibition is one in which the Foodies must constantly manage relations with others; it is a process which in many ways is one of struggling to maintain a semblance of authorship in the face of other kinds of players 'muscling-in'. This is a process also of managing professional identities. The Foodies perceive their professional identities as entailing an authorial role and frequently talk of having 'editorial control', which they vest with a higher 'Science Museum' authority in referring to it as 'Science Museum editorial control'. This leads, them, for example, to insist that the role of the outside consultant brought in for the rethink is only as 'a wall to bounce our ideas off' and vehemently resist the suggestion that she writes the exhibition text. As part of their perception of their professional identity, they accept that they have to address the issues raised by the Museum Director, their 'line-manager', but nevertheless seek to do so in ways which limit the impact on what they are already doing.

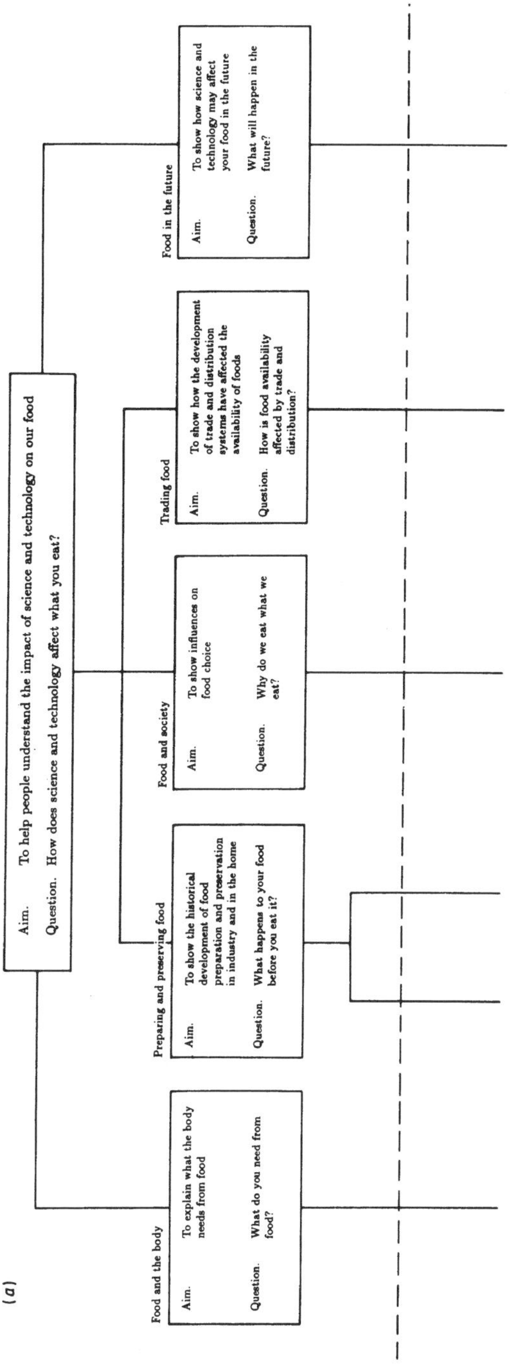

Figure 5.2 Part of the 'rigorous conceptual framework' after the Rethink.

In relations with scientists, and especially sponsors, 'Science Museum editorial control' is of particular importance to the Foodies. They manage relationships between different groups of scientists to keep at bay what they sometimes depict as the rather predatory 'commercial scientists' (who are perceived as wanting to use the exhibition to make a case for their own products). Notions of 'objectivity' and 'factual accuracy' – terms with which, it is assumed, no scientist can possibly quibble – are considered by the Team as crucial in this protection of their own professional boundaries. Yet in practice, it is infrequently on these grounds that disputes emerge and this rhetorical armoury is only occasionally appropriate and even more rarely successful.

In the days when Nestlé was still being courted as a sponsor, the company had objected to aspects of the way in which the Foodies intended to depict the history of the invention of instant coffee; more generally, Nestlé was said by the Team to want an inordinate amount of space devoted to this topic ('they would have us forget about everything else in the exhibition if they had their way'). In particular the company was said to want an account which would emphasise their own place in this history and ignore that of General Foods. While the Team countered that this would 'not be entirely factually accurate', it did not constitute as strong and incontrovertible an argument as the 'factual accuracy' gambit was always imagined to. Firstly, 'the facts' were disputed: both Nestlé and General Foods had produced their own historical accounts and there was no absolute higher authority. Secondly, it would be quite possible to tell a 'factually accurate' story of Nestlé's own invention of instant coffee – 'factual accuracy' is not in itself a protection against bias or artful silence. Thirdly, the rhetoric of 'factual accuracy' was of little use in relation to the question of the amount of space to be devoted to the topic. Rather than 'factual accuracy', then, most of the difficult cases concern more nebulous and perceivedly 'subjective' matters such as the best or 'most appropriate' way to say something to the public.[4] Another example of this is when a Department of Health scientist tells Jane that she has 'the story a St John's ambulance man [a non-professional paramedic] would know'; her account, in this case of food-poisoning, is 'useful but not strictly accurate'. This, however, he judges appropriate for a public exhibition as the more scientifically correct picture is too uncertain and too complex to be 'helpful' (and less likely to make people alter their habits to avoid food-poisoning).

In addition to the designers, also crucial for translating the Foodies' dreams into reality were numerous technicians and other workers, inside and outside the Museum. These included, for example, the outside companies whose facilities were used to edit film (mainly of factory production) for the exhibition, those which came to make the graphic and text panels, and those which supplied the fake food. These relationships were not always harmonious, especially when it came to issues of deadlines, and in some cases there were misunderstandings of the kind of product that was being produced. On the whole, however, they were relatively straightforward for the Team to manage because they were sporadic and for specified and clearly limited tasks. More difficult was the much longer term and absolutely crucial relationship with the company responsible for the physical construction of the exhibition and its 'shop-fitting'. Jan ended up spending almost all of her time in the last six months or so just making sure that all of this went to plan, which meant that she spent an increasing amount of her time in a room set up as the 'site office' directly adjacent to the gallery. She described what went on here as 'a different culture altogether' – one which involved her in a characteristic 'straight talking', different from the way that she dealt with others in the Museum. She seemed rather good at it; her northern accent would become more marked and she would adeptly shift from joking to being very firm and direct. It entailed mastery of a specialist language and knowledge; 'otherwise they'll try to fob you off'. There was a set of specific interests connected with the thickness of battening for the stud-walls (the partitions which divide sections of the exhibition), of the functioning and malfunctioning of the 'cherry-picker'(a kind of small crane) and dealing with the fire officer's regulations. This work had its own particular smells – the smoky office and the warm dusty gallery with its pungent top-notes of strong glue.

The building work was also conducted in conjunction with the Museum's own building department – Construction and Building Services (CABS) – which was responsible with the Team and the designers for drawing up the tender for the exhibition and for the provision of information and overseeing. Also smoke- and straight-talk-filled, meetings with CABS would often seem to me, I have to confess, direly boring with what seemed like interminable discussions of the weight limits of particular bits of floor. CABS had their base outside the Museum itself in one of the prefabs in the car-park – an indication, perhaps, of a role which was perceived as somewhat tangential to the main business of Museum work. Indeed, CABS tended to be talked about by curatorial staff as something of an irritant, a group which they depicted as almost out to scupper any creativity by its discovery of 'problems', slow head-shaking and even slower movement towards solutions. The use of an outside company to carry out the work on the gallery ('otherwise there would have been simply no chance of opening in 1989') was intended partly to 'break the hold of CABS'. Even so, negotiations with them were vital for the construction of the gallery.

Others groups within the Museum were also involved in the exhibition's making. Of these, some of the most important were the Education section (which created a pack for teachers and schools to accompany the exhibition), the Interactives unit ('Launch Pad') which created the interactive exhibits, 'Audio-visuals' which was responsible for technical assistance with the videos and handsets, and the workshops (which created any replicas or sets and which restored items for display). Of these, the relationships with the first two were considered the most problematic and the reason was, again, a question of 'creative involvement', 'interference' and the amount of professional autonomy which different groups were perceived to seek. In relation to workshops and Audio-visuals the boundaries of expertise were generally clear, the Team deferring to the technical competence of these groups which they saw as not infringing their own domain of 'content'. This content versus technique division was not so clear in relation to Education and Interactives, however. As part of the new Public Services Division arrangement, the Education section was supposed to have a greater involvement in exhibition-making and, to some extent, it did. The Feasibility Study of the exhibition was commented on by the Education section and later a presentation of the proposed exhibition was made to teachers in conjunction with a member of the Education staff. Nevertheless, despite Mr Suthers's hopes of forging closer collaboration, this did not really happen, due partly to the fact that the Team perceived the involvement of the educationalists as a potential threat to their own authorial autonomy (as 'muscling-in') and because they resented some of the remarks made about the exhibition by the member of the Education staff who had commented on the Feasibility Study. This, they suggested, showed that the educationalists did not properly understand what they were trying to do and looked at it too much through the narrow lens of education. One outcome of this relatively distant relationship was that the education pack produced for teachers depicted the exhibition in a way that was rather different from that envisaged by the Foodies, even giving sections different names and grouping them in ways not anticipated by the Team. The Foodies were very annoyed about this and claimed that this was one reason why teachers sometimes said that they found the gallery 'confusing'. The Education staff, in response, said that they had had to re-label the gallery for teachers in this way because it had failed to respond adequately to the demands of the new national curriculum (a common syllabus for schools in England and Wales which was being introduced at the time) and that the organisation of the gallery was difficult to grasp.

Similar disputes, which also revolved around professional identity and autonomy, occurred in relation to the Interactives group which was referred to by the name of the main Science Museum interactive area – Launch Pad. Many interactive science centres or exhibitions were being set up across the country, and as one of the relatively early groups working on these matters the Science Museum Interactives group were in some demand to advise others elsewhere and even under commission to create exhibits for other locations. As an earlier offshoot of the workshops, they had moved from their previous location in the basement of the Museum to acquire their own offices, and became increasingly unwilling to accept a relationship with curatorial or interpretive staff on the lines of the workshops-model. One dimension of this was that they asserted the needs of their creativity: theirs was not a task, they maintained, in which an exhibit could simply be built to order. Instead, it involved thinking carefully about the best way to achieve the idea that was wanted and a degree of experimentation. This made it difficult, Launch Pad claimed, to ascertain quite how long the making of any item would necessarily take. To the Team, this was frustrating because they were working to tight deadlines and needed to know exactly what would go where. They talked about Launch Pad as having become 'semi-detached' and 'too big for their boots'; and they interpreted some of Launch Pad's demands as more concerned with 'making their own political point' than with the task itself. Nevertheless, the Interactives team did also have to deal with some very difficult practical matters in which they struggled to find ways of overcoming physical dilemmas as they tried to create interactive exhibits that would realise the hopes invested by the Team.

More generally, materials – objects and the physical space of the gallery – also made their demands. They did so on quantitative (how much space?) and qualitative (what kinds of space and qualities?) grounds, and also in concert with curators' own rather particular affective relationships with them. Not only as the designers struggled to find spaces on their tissue-paper plans, but also later in the actual physical encounter with gallery space, objects and exhibits sometimes refused to go where it had originally been hoped that they might (they proved too heavy for the 'floor loadings' in certain positions, or they obscured access to important power points, or they demanded more space around them than had been envisaged). Sometimes they were altogether elusive. The body-in pea freezer that Sue had set her heart on including – the headline exhibit announced at a press launch held eight months before the opening of the gallery – was never completed, partly because Launch Pad never succeeded in solving what they regarded as problems with the design. Heather devoted enormous amounts of energy to including a sausage-making machine in the exhibition. When she finally found one that seemed suitable it proved awkward in terms of its weight and operating demands. Eventually it had to be surrounded by protective glass (to protect the visitors from it rather than, as in many cases, the exhibits from the visitors) and only shown in action at specified times with human assistance [Figure 5.3]. Even so, it insisted on producing repulsively pasty-looking sausages, causing the Meat and Livestock Commission to complain about its bad behaviour. (The Commission, of course, chose to blame the Food team.)

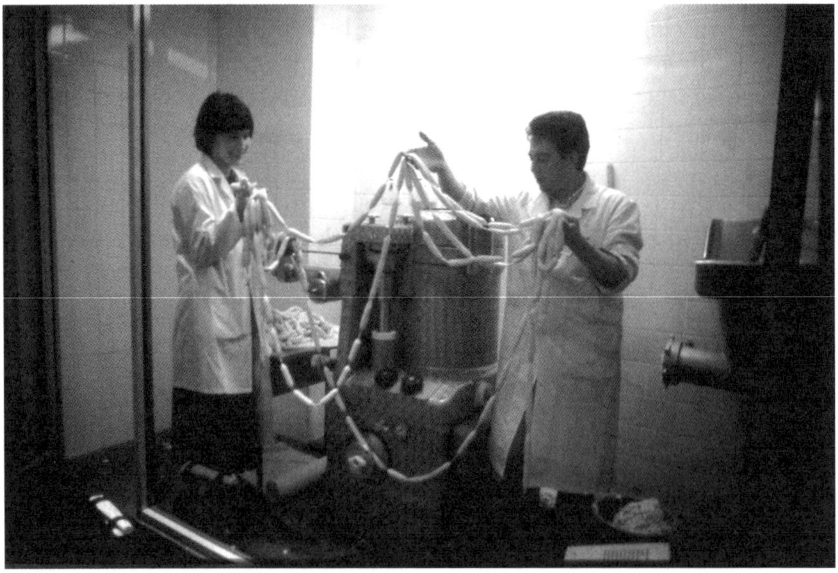

Figure 5.3 The naughty sausage machine performing at last with human assistance.

Money, or 'the budget', also made its intervention. Despite what seemed like a large amount of money to work with, the costs of many items turned out to be considerably more than had been envisaged. Jane struggled to 'keep to budget' and the search for extra sponsorship for particular items continued during the making of the exhibition. Some items which might have been included could not be for reasons of 'the budget'. The most notable of these was the accompanying eating area which right from the earliest days had been seen as an important accompaniment to the exhibition. The search for sponsorship for this was not successful – partly because potential sponsors did not want to be subsumed to 'the Sainsbury gallery' – and in the end this was not constructed as had been hoped.

Time was another crucial factor which often seemed in much too limited supply. Moreover, as the days ticked by, not only was there less time remaining before the opening date, but also there was reduced opportunity to unpick what had already been put into place. This gave the whole experience of exhibition-making a relentless hurtling forward character and any calls or suggestions to rethink or rework what had already been done were experienced as deeply disruptive. One consequence of this was a 'salvage tendency': much of what had already been done had to be kept, otherwise it would be as time lost. This salvaging was also understandably accompanied by a reluctance to 'dig too deep' or 'go too far' in any revisions – these were all perceived as running counter to what felt like the primary aim, to open on time, or at least not to 'slip' too far beyond the planned date.

What we have seen in this chapter is a journey from 'very creative to hard slog', from proliferation to constraint. It was not, however, a straightforward linear process: it involved far more than merely 'packaging' and 'transporting' ideas taken from one world (that of science) to another (that of the public). Imagined visitors, and sometimes real ones too, constantly intruded (as we shall see in the following chapter) even in the kinds of science that scientists themselves chose to present to the curator-interpreters.

My account here has, of course, been of the making of one particular exhibition in one particular institution. Other places, and other times, will, to varying extents, do things differently. My aim has been to highlight some of the assumptions and legitimations – some of which will have broader currency – that were mobilised during the making of this exhibition. In particular, by focusing on three 'key moments' – the Reorganisation, the Retreat and the Rethink – in the planning of

Food, I have sought to highlight some decisions – often thought relatively minor or innocuous at the time – which came to have greater significance in the finished gallery and visitors' interpretations of it. In the next chapter I will look more specifically at the ways in which visitors were imagined in the construction of the exhibition and at the related matter of how science, and more specifically the politically-sensitive subject of food, was represented.

Notes

1. See Bud 1988.

2. This is regarded as a significant aspect of museological training even though it is often not formalised. The Science Museum did, however, sometimes arrange group visits for its staff to other significant museums, visits which some staff referred to as 'jollies'. Sue, for example, had recently visited the recently opened science centre in Paris, the *Cité des Sciences et de l'Industrie* at La Villette, on one such trip.

3. I have told the story of the fate of these sections in Macdonald 2001.

4. See Handler and Gable 1997 for a discussion of the way that 'the rhetoric of fact at Colonial Williamsburg [makes it] often difficult to raise the question of what the facts are being made to add up to – of what, that is, particular histories mean' (p. 97).

Virtual Consumers and Supermarket Science

During the exhibition's making, it was peopled with a 'phantom public' – spectral or virtual visitors.[1] In this chapter I look at the ways in which visitors were imagined into the Food exhibition and more generally at the process of 'configuring the user' in the museum context. As Steve Woolgar puts it, configuring 'includes defining the identity of future users, and setting constraints upon their likely future actions'.[2] This process is also intimately bound together with the 'product' that is more explicitly being 'configured' – in this case, the exhibition and science itself. Just how visitors are perceived, and just how the practices of exhibition-making implicate virtual – and sometimes actual – visitors, inevitably has consequences for the finished exhibition and, to varying extents, the ways in which actual visitors will relate to it. This, however, is not a simple writing-in process in which the visitor will behave as the exhibition-makers explicitly envisage: on the contrary, as we will see in chapter eight, visitors refuse in various ways to conform to the visitor-model that the exhibition-makers construct. Neither is 'writing-in' solely concerned with the explicit matters of trying to define 'target-audiences' and draw up 'visitor profiles'. Numerous other, sometimes overlooked, matters also shape the way in which the finished exhibition will invite visitors to relate to it, and one aim of this chapter is to highlight the most significant of these matters which, to varying extents and with different inflections, are likely to be of significance in the making of many exhibitions.

The Food exhibition, as part of the new emphasis on consumer sovereignty within public services in the UK in general and of the public understanding of science approach in the Science Museum in particular, attempted to prioritise the visitor as never before. For the Food Team, this new approach was one which they saw primarily as positive and democratising: as a chance to create an exhibition which would be for 'ordinary people, for everybody' rather than one which would 'go over all normal people's heads'. It was an exhibition which they hoped would appeal to groups which they thought were under-represented by the Museum's current exhibitions, in particular, women and ethnic minorities. This vision was not simply a managerially-calculated approach designed in order to increase 'visitor numbers'. The Team was undoubtedly personally committed and enthused by it (especially at the beginning of the exhibition-making process before reality began to take its toll). It was a vision to which, as I noted in chapter four, they articulated their own gender and structural position in the Museum. At the same time, as we saw in the previous chapter, they also tried hard to maintain their 'editorial control', particularly in relation to 'commercial scientists'.

When the exhibition opened, as well as the Team's disappointment that it seemed 'a bit flat', they were also annoyed at some early criticisms: that 'it [did] not do much for women' (a female member of the Science Museum staff), that it had 'a supermarket logic' and was very much what Sainsbury's would have wanted' (Derek Cooper, *The Food Programme* Radio 4). How could the exhibition be read in this way given the intentions of the Foodies? What was going on between 'encoding' and 'decoding'? This chapter takes an ethnographic look further into these matters of authorship and authority, of the production of culture and science in the making, by focusing mainly, and first, upon the configuration of 'virtual visitors'. Then, later in the chapter, it looks at some aspects of the finished exhibition with particular reference to the ways in which science – and more specifically contentious and politically significant matters to do with food – was represented.

Imagining the Public

Food was one of the first exhibitions in the Science Museum to carry out what was called 'formative evaluation' – trialling some of its ideas and exhibits on visitors prior to exhibition completion and using new computer 'readability' programs to try to ensure that its text would hit the right visitor 'reading level'. All exhibitions inevitably construct a 'virtual visitor' not only through explicit statements about 'target audiences' and 'expected audience' but also, often more tellingly, through decisions about text (what knowledge and levels of ability should it presume?), about content (what will already be familiar?), about media (will it engage or distract?), and about aesthetics (will they be entranced or repulsed?). Exhibition-makers try to imagine visitor responses. Will they understand? Will they become fatigued (or 'exhibitioned-out')? Will they be able to find their way around – and out of – the exhibition? The questions that they ask, and the relative weight with which these questions are accorded, are all part of envisioning the exhibition visitor, and they all play into the shaping of the exhibition. Certain other questions are not asked, and certain exercises of imagination not made. These 'silences' or 'non-thinkings' are also crucial to the legibility of the ensuing exhibition.

Much of the time, exhibition-makers evoke a standardised visitor.[3] This is their 'ideal visitor', not in the sense that this is the best possible visitor that they can hope for but in the sense of an abstract vision of a fairly coherently behaving visitor. However, this ideal visitor will not necessarily be imagined free from contradiction. Just as anthropologists have found in other contexts, such as interpretations of ritual symbols, different meanings are only rarely brought together and made explicit.[4] Contradictions are not, therefore, brought out into the open. In addition, sub-categories of imagined visitors – or 'special visitors' – are also conjectured in some contexts. Thus, the 'woolly hats' or 'buffs' mentioned previously are one particular visitor sub-category for which some curators might try to cater (though the Foodies were adamantly against doing so). So too are specialists and scientists. Even in the case of Food, which was explicitly intended to be 'populist' rather than 'specialist' it was, as we have seen, regarded as essential to strive for 'factual accuracy' and to 'get our facts right'. One reason given for the importance of doing so (in additional to the reasons discussed in the previous chapter) was that to have a visitor (a scientist perhaps) point out an error in the finished exhibition would very embarrassing. Being 'shown up' in this way would cause professional ignominy by publicly revealing that a topic had not been properly researched.

This was a matter of concern even to curator-interpreters in the case of Food who simultaneously vaunted their lack of specialist expertise. Imagined critics here were sometimes reviewers in the public media, who at the same time were being increasingly sought out as another aspect of the Museum's 'cultural revolution'. (The press launch held so long before the opening date was an example of this new emphasis in the case of Food.) Most often, however, imagined critics were other Museum staff, especially other curators. As we have already seen, the Foodies were often preoccupied with how they imagined other Museum staff would react, and while they sometimes enjoyed the idea of making something which other – especially 'old guard' or 'boring fart' – curators would not like, they also sought to counter potential criticisms (by including objects, for example). In this they were certainly not alone and indeed it was often said in the Museum that 'exhibitions are made by curators mainly for other curators.' (It was to try to prevent this that the making of exhibitions had been transferred away from curators and to a Public Services Division.) Nevertheless, even in an exhibition organised within this new framework, the way in which an exhibition would be received by fellow professionals, who would after all visit the exhibition, remained a significant concern to the exhibition-makers.

In everyday talk in the Museum it was fairly common for visitors to be referred to as problems, as 'in the way', as disruptive and as 'stupid'.[5] As Woolgar observes in his ethnography of computers, one function of such talk is to reinforce divisions between 'insiders' and 'outsiders', in our case, museum professionals and visitors. While from the financial point of view there seemed to be too few paying visitors in the Museum, for staff who had to walk anywhere near the Museum's interactive displays, there were usually too many of them. Visitors were described as 'stupid' or 'sheep-like' for clustering in certain galleries rather than dispersing to emptier parts of the Museum. For many curators that visitors might not understand certain Museum-imparted information was evidence of visitor ignorance. Stories would circulate about visitors who had completely misunderstood exhibits in amusing ways – perhaps trying to look into the wrong part of an interactive or confusing an effect with a cause.

Visitors were also sometimes depicted as deviants, especially as vandals. In the making of Food a lot of energy was put into making the exhibition 'vandal-proof'. This was seen as a particular problem because of the exhibition's philosophy of trying to remove psychological and physical barriers between visitors and the Museum, between the public and science. Avoiding physical boundaries around exhibits, and allowing visitors as far as possible to get their hands on them, was seen as the logical materialisation of the aim to present science in as unintimidating a fashion as possible. Yet this often raised problems for the conservation and protection of objects and exhibits. In response, the designers endeavoured to provide barriers which would be as 'unobtrusive' as possible, often using clear perspex and a case design with few visible supports. The exhibition was also built to try to avoid certain other kinds of 'deviant' behaviour. Dark enclosed spaces were regarded by Museum staff as potential haunts for child molesters (this was said to be one of the 'real reasons' why the Science Museum's mining exhibit had been closed down). Sue, for example, had to be careful to provide as much lighting as possible in the lorry container that she was using as part of her section on the transport of foodstuffs. But it was not just child molesters and intentional vandals who were perceived as annoyingly deviant in their use of the Museum. One day when I walked with Mr Suthers on one of his regular 'site visits' to see how the construction of Food was getting on we passed a family squatting on the edge of an exhibit in the Agriculture gallery eating sandwiches. 'That's our biggest problem', he said to me as we walked on, 'not so much the ones who are out to wreck things as those who are so busy trying to cut corners and save a bit of money. It's middle-class families who are probably our worst hooligans!'.

The 'hooliganism' of the middle-classes was in some respects a side-effect of the Museum's emphasis on consumer sovereignty, just as Food's 'vandalism' problem was partly a consequence of its pro-visitor philosophy. In contrast, it is impossible to imagine visitors to the British Museum in the nineteenth century deciding to stop and snack in a museum gallery. As Kenneth Hudson describes, prospective visitors to the British Museum had to send in a letter giving their credentials and assurance that their motives were curiosity and study; if accepted, they would then be allowed a half-hour accompanied tour, on a specified date at a precise time, with no information given about the objects and no opportunity to stop and gaze at any artefacts in detail, never mind to eat a sandwich.[6] In the 1980s, however, the introduction of more interactive areas, the raised noise levels which these and audio-visual exhibits produced, and the reduced visibility of the policing of exhibition space (in the more relaxed style of dress of 'museum attendants' and in the demise of 'Do not touch' signs) helped to make certain modes of visitor conduct less clearly unacceptable than previously. Curators in the Science Museum often grumbled that the presence of Launch Pad introduced a type of visitor behaviour which spread beyond its boundaries.

> The trouble with Launch Pad is that they [the visitors] don't know when to stop, so they go round wrecking the rest of the Museum. You see them trying to press and pull and swing on everywhere. But the older galleries, they're just not built for it. They weren't supposed to be. And we don't want everything to be turned into Launch Pad anyway!

Including interactive exhibits alongside historical objects in one gallery, as was intended in Food, was potentially a risky strategy. The

Team were keen to do this, however, because of their exhibition philosophy and the visitor configuration that this entailed, which, to some extent, sought to elide the 'insider'-'outsider' distinction.

'Pick and Mix': the Visitor as Active Consumer

The projected visitor of Food was imagined as one who would want to participate, who would appreciate the opportunity to be 'active' and 'busy' and relish (if sometimes perhaps too much) a relaxing of boundaries, who would want a choice of modes of presentation and content, and who would be in the Museum in search not just of 'understanding' but also of 'fun'. As well as being likely to find traditional Museum presentation ('rows of glass cases' or 'brass and glass' as well as panels) boring, visitors were generally considered by the Team as uninterested in, and relatively uneducated about, technology and science. A number of strategies was devised to try to cater specifically for this entertainment-seeking visitor who would choose to come to this exhibition, or the Museum, only if the kind of 'product' they liked was on offer.

One strategy was the incorporation of 'fun'. Although the use of interactive exhibits in science museums and science centres has been especially justified by arguments about their educative potential, the fact that they would be regarded as 'fun' by visitors was of equal importance to the Team in their own informal discussions. While some of the interactive exhibits were designed to illustrate a scientific principle (such as the role of emulsifiers in mixing oil and water) others, such as an exhibit in which the visitor would be buffeted by cold air like a frozen pea, were acknowledged as being much more about entertainment. More generally, as noted already, there was an attempt to go further with amusing exhibits such as an enormous model of a pot of chocolate mousse. 'Fun' was regarded as important because it made exhibits accessible: it disrupted what was sometimes characterised by the Team as a distancing authority in the traditional Museum. As such, fun and pleasure were equated with democracy in a conflation that has also been identified in other contemporary cultural technologies.[7]

Also conflated with democracy was an emphasis on building 'choice' into the exhibition. Incorporating a mixture of types of media – interactives, inventory objects, audio-visuals, replica sets – was one way in which visitors were seen to be being offered 'choice' (see Table 6.1). Choice would mean that visitors would have to be 'active' rather than 'passive' (to use a distinction used in the Museum as well as in cultural,

Table 6.1 Mixed Media: Exhibit Types in *Food for Thought*

	No.
Interactives	48
Working demonstrations	3
Videos and/or handsets	11
Computer information points	6
Inventory objects	87
Replica sets	11

sociological and media studies): rather than just receiving whatever the Museum presented them with, visitors were conceptualised as actively making choices between different types of display. These were visitors as shoppers, busily making their way through aisles of products, picking things out and handling them, choosing whatever caught their mood.

Not only would the different types of media present a variety of modes of imparting information, but they would also encourage different kinds of visitor activity ('hands-on', 'body-in', 'using a handset') and the use of a full range of the visitor's senses. The visitor would be invited not only to use sight, but also touch (as in 'hands-on'), smell (as in the 'smellerama' exhibit or a spice cabinet), sound (as in the 'identify foods by their sounds' exhibit) and, in the original plans but not in the final realisation (due to health and safety regulations), to experience taste. The Team's wish to include a very wide range of different topics (which had caused some of the difficulty leading to the Rethink) was also a consequence of the attempt to provide 'choice'. In addition, visitors were to be provided with different 'levels' of text – one relatively short and straightforward and the other more detailed (see below) – so that they could select how much information they wished to acquire. This was taken still further with the provision of computer information points. Even in relation to visitor movement through the exhibition, the Foodies were keen to provide 'choice' or the opportunity to 'pick and mix', and 'visitor flow' had to be negotiated in relation to this. Again, this provision of 'choice' was regarded as democratising in contrast to other, 'more traditional', 'unilinear' exhibitions. The latter were regarded as 'didactic' (one version of 'authoritative'), as the Museum foisting an already formed story upon the visitor. An exhibition with multiple possible alternative routes, by contrast, was seen to offer visitors agency over where to go and what to see. So important was this to the Team that they struggled to make this idea work within a space for which it was in some ways ill-suited: namely long thin galleries which opened onto the Museum's central atrium on one side [Figures 6.1 and 6.2].

The Foodies' understandings of the roles that the particular technologies of display and exhibition architecture play have resonance with analyses in critical museology.[8] The presentation of unilinear narratives, and their mapping onto exhibition space such that the visitor must follow physically the narrative set out, has been seen as particularly significant in the representation of ideas of evolution and progress. This form of spatial configuration, especially characteristic of the nineteenth-century public museums (though continuing well into the twentieth century), thus tries to 'close off' potentially deviant or 'wrong' readings by coercing the visitor to proceed in the 'right' direction. To the Foodies this form of presentation was regarded as disempowering of the visitor and, therefore, anathema to the democratising politics which they embraced. However, whether more 'open' and 'multiple' forms of display can be seen as unequivocally empowering the visitor is far from clear. Just as we cannot necessarily and unproblematically

Figure 6.1 Empty but shaped space: the gallery about six months before opening.

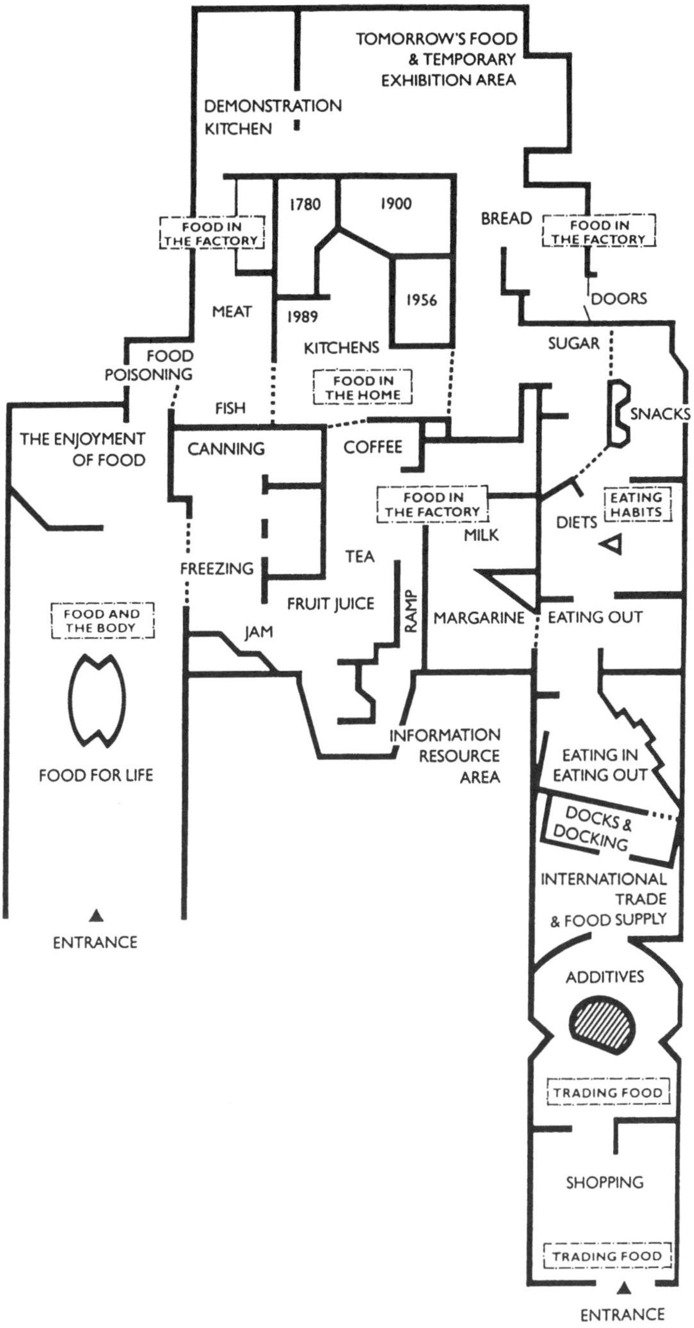

Figure 6.2 Plan of Food for Thought.

read an intended politics back from the finished cultural product, neither can 'culture makers' necessarily 'write in' their preferred politics by their choice of media and other display strategies. These are politically ambiguous. So too was the emphasis upon choice.

Choice was also a theme in the exhibition's messages. In the post-Rethink 'conceptual framework' the idea of 'choice' appears at several points: the aim of the section on food production is, for example, 'to show how the historical development of food preparation and preservation in industry and in the home have affected the choice of foods today'; the message of eating habits (now called 'Food and People') is 'to show what influences food choice'; and that of distribution (under a title of 'How has Science and Technology affected where you get your Food from?') is 'to show how the development of trade and distribution systems have affected choice of foods'. Although it is not explicitly stated, perhaps because it is viewed as self-evident, the assumption is that in all of these matters there is in Britain today greater choice than has ever been the case. Choice is, throughout exhibition-making, considered to be inherently a good thing. More choice is equated with more agency.

Consumer-friendly Science

Choice features as part of the exhibition's 'messages' in other respects too. As I have noted in the previous chapter, 'diet' was presented as a matter for one's individual lifestyle. It was also the intention of the Foodies that visitors should, as far as possible, be given information to choose between the views of different scientists (which, as we have seen, was to some extent sabotaged by the scientists themselves). This was again part of a conscious attempt to shift the balance of power between scientists and consumers by telling the latter that the former were not necessarily right: it was, therefore, up to consumers to 'make up their own minds' (a phrase frequently used by the Team). The Foodies attempted this in other ways too. One panel states: 'Not all scientists agree about a "healthy diet". Information and ideas about foods you should eat have changed and are still changing'. The exhibition also includes height and weight charts not only from the UK but also from the US, thus relativizing the scientific knowledge on display.

One of the biggest tasks of the Team, as they saw it, was to make science and technology 'accessible'. Presenting it as 'fun' was one strand of this. Interactivity also involved making science physically accessible, thus inviting visitors to interact with, rather than be passive observers of science. The aim was also to present all exhibits in a manner which would make them as physically and visually accessible as possible. Cases were thus to be avoided wherever feasible.[9] Another strategy was to present visitors first with familiar everyday experiences so that science would not seem difficult and esoteric. The exhibition's foregrounding of food consumption – shopping and eating – was integral to this strategy. This was one reason why shopping, in the form of a supermarket check-out with a scanner placed adjacent to a reconstruction of a 1920s Sainsbury's, was situated at the entrance to the exhibition through which most visitors were thought likely to enter. It was also the justification for organising the exhibition around 'familiar foods', such as baked beans and fishfingers.

Another indication of the importance accorded to making the exhibition accessible was the immense effort the Foodies put into making the text of the exhibition as easy to read as possible. After reviewing a number of recently completed galleries in the Science Museum, two members of the Food Team wrote a short report and the Team decided collectively upon the following conventions. Text would have two 'levels': a short 'story-line' with a maximum of fifty words in bold typeface, and a longer account of up to one hundred words. The Team decided to aim at a 'reading age' of twelve years old. At this stage, this was based not on formal criteria but selected because it was at the upper end of the classification of 'child' (before the teens) and so allowed for the ambition that the text would be accessible to 'children' without being unduly simplified and constraining.

Writing the text for the exhibition began in the February before the exhibition opened and took months to perfect. It was common in the offices as the Team wrote their text to ask each other about the clarity of their writing. For example:

Ann: Does this make sense? Do you really think it's clear enough?
Heather: Well, I understood it – and if I can understand it anybody can.

I was also enlisted in this, sometimes on behalf of my children: 'Sharon, what do you think would make most sense to your children – bacteria, bugs or germs?'. In such exchanges, visitors were imagined into the text of the exhibition as laypeople and as children. Women were considered to be particularly good at substituting such visitors. This informal visitor-substitution was also coupled with an extensive more formalised editing process. This entailed members of the Team first reading each other's text and commenting on it; then Jane and Jan read and commented on it; then another curator from elsewhere in the Museum (chosen because she was regarded as having 'good common sense', 'she's straightforward and sensible') did so; then a computer readability program was employed. After this process the text was submitted to Mr Suthers and Dr Cossons, to members of the advisory panel and also to all sponsors. Alongside, individual Team members sometimes chose to consult specialists over specific issues which they were finding it difficult to express (as with Jane's discussions with the Department of Health scientist over how to talk about food poisoning). Everybody found the whole writing process extremely exhausting and often somewhat agonising. As Sue recollected afterwards: 'The writing was a bit of a torture, just to get it right. And the cuts at first – well, squeals of pain. All those precious words! But then when you'd been through it a few times you didn't care any more. Yes, fine!'.

Each of the editorial layers, each of which constituted a visitor-substitution, inevitably made slightly different suggestions and the Team had to manage these, which they tended to do by according varying degrees of authenticity or objectivity to their visitor-substitutes. The curator from Collections Management tended to want more explanation. This meant that her suggestions were not always accepted and she was sometimes 'demoted' from her role as an 'ordinary visitor equivalent.' ('I think that's her wanting more technology but that's not necessarily what our visitors will want'.) The computer readability program's assumptions were more formally codified, though not into specific 'reading ages' as the Team had expected.[10] The Team selected 'children's story book' for the 'story-line' and 'simple newspaper or magazine article' for the fuller text. This latter was somewhat over the 'Ladybird-book' level that Heather had talked of, but, even so, the Team often found it difficult to convey what they wanted in terms which the program would not classify as 'pompous' or 'foggy'. The program highlighted complex syntax and vocabulary and offered synonyms but it neither corrected text nor 'knew' whether what was fed into it actually made sense or not. Nevertheless, its interventions and rather rude classifications were generally accepted without demur by the Team: a technological unlike a human commentary was perceived as 'objective', not bound up with personal positioning and as relatively discreet in that it would not gossip about the quality of the text with others in the Museum. This was the first time that such a program had been used in the Museum, and was another dimension of the fast expanding theory and technology for visitor management characteristic of the museum world more generally at that time.

Managing 'Real' Visitor Input

But what of 'real' visitors? Despite the rhetorical emphasis on visitors from the beginning of the project, research on what Museum visitors might have to say was done only after the project was well under way and largely on the prompting of Sue who had been inspired after having attended an international conference of Museum Evaluation (run by the World Heritage Association) in September 1988. There were mixed feelings about carrying out such research: one of the designers argued strongly that it was a waste of time because visitors wouldn't really know what they would want until they saw it (he also claimed that it was usually just done 'to be seen to have been done'); other members of the team thought it a good idea in principle but too late now that so much had been mapped out and that it would be potentially disruptive to the tight schedule. Jane told Sue that if this was what she wanted, she had to do it on top of her ordinary workload. In the end, Mr Suthers – who was trying to promote visitor research wherever possible – funded a consultant to carry out the research based on questions formulated by the Team, especially Sue.

It was not until February and March before the intended opening of the exhibition in September that the study was undertaken. By this time much of the three-dimensional design of the exhibition was complete, interactives had been commissioned, many objects selected, and the actual text had been begun. For this reason, the questions were all fairly specific and aimed at information which could, as the report put it, 'assess visitors' understandings and use of language with regard to certain topics in order that team members could gain insights of help when writing exhibit texts'. Questions asked were specifically intended to 'confirm and re-inforce decisions to include certain topics in the exhibition', though also 'if need be, [the Team would] modify planned presentations of them in light of visitor responses'. Questions like 'What is an organic food? What makes a food organic?' and 'How would you describe what a Calorie is?' helped to confirm the Foodies' suspicions that visitors were far from clear about these matters. Visitors were also asked (mostly in multiple-choice format) about whether and how often they ate canned and frozen foods as well as other foods which had been selected as 'familiar'. There was some difference over the interpretation of some of these results. The consultant, for example, noted that a high proportion of visitors (about a third) did not eat baked beans. Sue, however, who was responsible for the section of the exhibition on canning and who had chosen baked beans as an example of a commonly-eaten food, preferred to interpret this as a majority which did. Arguably, only a question inserted by Mr Suthers, held the potential to allow visitors a significant input into the exhibition content: 'Is there anything you would be especially interested in seeing or finding out about in our exhibition about Food and Nutrition?'. Slightly irritated by his 'muscling-in' ('He always wants to get involved. But what are we supposed to do with it at this stage?'), the Foodies breathed a sigh of relief when a third of respondents said 'no' or 'nothing in particular'; others mostly mentioned matters that were being covered, such as food-poisoning (a topic much in the news at the time) and nutrition (many comments being about healthy diets, good and bad foods), or those which could be defined as 'too specific to be representative' (a request to show something which would help to deal with a particular relative's illness, for example).

Later, in August, some prototype interactive exhibits and sample labels were taken into the Museum and to a Science Museum exhibition in Hyde Park to try them out [Figure 6.3]. This was only a tiny proportion of the overall number of exhibits to be included in the gallery but nevertheless it led to some minor adjustments. Like the other 'formative' (prior to exhibition completion) visitor evaluation, this was considered a relatively new attempt to involve visitors, albeit in a somewhat limited way, in the construction of the exhibition. It was also part of other forms of evaluation in the Museum, such as workshops being run for staff to help them 'assess the communicative effectiveness of exhibits' (as the information sheet of an evaluation workshop for Museum staff that I attended explained). The vision of the relationship between Museum and visitors implicit in much of this was of the Museum being in the business of conveying cognitive 'messages'. For example, question one of the list of questions at the workshop was 'Is the exhibit getting a clear message over to the public?', and others continued in similar fashion. Not only did this take as axiomatic that visitors were in search of such 'messages', but it also cast the conveying of messages as the task of the Museum. At the time, however, being 'message-based' and 'object-based' were more often seen as two different, and not easily compatible, enterprises.

The involvement of 'real' visitors in the exhibition's making was in many respects closely circumscribed. While given some agency to change the exhibition's content, this was strictly delimited by the

Figure 6.3 Formative evaluation: trialling food exhibits about two months before opening.

format in which visitors' participation was invited (especially the closed format of the pre-determined questionnaire), its timing (too late to change much) and the way in which it was interpreted (as far as possible not to disrupt too much). 'Real' visitors' involvement was circumscribed by the virtual visitors who were already imagined into the exhibition, whose desires, boredom thresholds, and 'reading levels' had already been decided upon.

The Nation's Diet

Another dimension of imagining the public into the exhibition was in the Team's invocations of 'Britishness'. As noted earlier, 'British' was regarded as a 'natural' category insofar as it simply continued the logic of the Museum's national status (as well as of 'British year of food and farming'). Moreover, 'the British diet' was often mentioned in the media at that time, as well as in certain official reports, as a generalised 'unhealthy' diet, based on mode- and median-based statistics. In the references to 'the British diet' in their study and general exhibition-planning, it was to this statistically-homogenised national construction that the Team oriented themselves, so reproducing and materialising this concept into the fabric of the exhibition. The exhibitionary principle of 'beginning with the familiar' and arranging the exhibition around 'familiar foods' was interpreted as referring to foods common to this 'British diet'. ('Natural and synthetic sweeteners have been chosen. . . as they are a familiar part of the British diet', to take an example from the Feasibility Study.) What was reproduced in the exhibition, then, was a 'British diet' – partly modelled on the Foodies' own (ethnically white) visitor-substitution – centred on the following foods: bread and potatoes, milk and dairy produce, fruit and fruit juice (with special focus on jam), margarine, vegetables (with baked beans and frozen peas as exemplars), tea and coffee, meat and fish (with sausages and fish-fingers as exemplars). Each of these was to be an area of the exhibition (an idea, which although it had been questioned, still largely remained). In this way, a rather stereotyped and homogenised vision of Britishness was deeply inscribed into the content and organisation of Food. Having a black woman next to a trolley-load of food for a month of 'an average British adult' (backing up against a white boy) at one of the gallery's entrances could be argued as incorporating potential 'difference' – of race, gender and age – into this homogenised national picture [Figures 6.4 and 6.5].

Figure 6.4 Representing gender, age and race: entrance feature.

Figure 6.5 Representing gender, age and race: entrance to the gallery, looking into Food and the Body.

At the same time, however, there was an awareness of both gender and age differences as well as what the Education officer had called 'the ethnic issue' – Britain as a 'multi-racial' society. The latter was tackled explicitly in the area of the exhibition called 'Eating Habits' which was to deal with changes in what was eaten in Britain over the past century and – for religious, cultural, ethical or medical reasons – among different groups. Like so many areas of the gallery, Eating Habits covered a very broad topic and there was an enormous amount of material which Heather was hoping to include: the development of eating-out and fast-foods, changing ideas about ideal body shapes, different people's diets, information about special medical diets such as low-salt diets for patients with kidney problems, different 'religious' diets, vegetarianism and so on. She brought some very nice ideas to this. For example, in the section on changing body ideals she included mirrors to show visitors slightly fatter and slightly thinner reflections of themselves, and she included silhouettes of some 'ideal' figures at different points in the century (including Twiggy and Daley Thompson – the choice of a black athlete as ideal showing the attempt to be racially aware). Moreover, her decision to use representations of particular individuals helped her to avoid the problem of looking as though she was implying that everybody held the same body ideals (the 'generalisation problem' inherent in concepts like 'the British diet').

Partly because of the large areas of material that she was trying to group together, and partly because of the generalised 'British diet' against which she was implicitly defining her material, Heather tended to classify all of the 'different' diets together in planning the gallery: medical (diabetic diets, for example), vegetarian, and 'religious'. The last were Buddhist, Jewish, Latter Day Saint and Moslem. As with the body ideals, Heather also individualised these sections, in this case with narratives from 'real people' who had agreed to contribute information. This was standardised into a common format: 'My name is [. . . .]. I am a [Buddhist, Jew, Latter Day Saint, Moslem, vegetarian]', followed by an explanation of what they do and do not eat, and in some cases an illustration of celebration meal (such as at Ramadan or Passover). A 'Christian diet' is not individualised in this way, however, but instead is associated with 'Britishness'. Thus a depiction of Christmas dinner has the caption: 'Christmas is the celebration of the birth of Christ. In Britain we traditionally eat turkey and plum pudding'.

Although in the final exhibition there is some spatial and stylistic differentiation between the medical and the religious diets, this is fairly slight and they use the same basic format. This is largely a consequence of their having been grouped together against the implicit norm: these were 'exceptions', or – in the language that Heather used as she created this section – 'restricted diets'. When I first heard Heather using this term in my early days at the project, I was horrified and dedicated a page and a half of my note-book to worrying over whether I should tell her just why I thought that defining all these diets together as 'restricted' was deeply questionable. I decided that I simply had to and the next day I said to her: 'You're not going to actually call it "restricted diets" are you?'. She looked at me as though I was slightly crazy and said, 'Of course not!'. It was, she explained, simply her own way of grouping these matters in order to fit them all in. At the time I felt relieved and, like Heather, did not really think about how it might look in the finished exhibition. However, as with other examples, groupings and terms used for convenience in the early stages of exhibition-making could leave an initially unnoticed imprint, rather like stains which seem to have been washed out but which reappear later.

The other area where ethnic difference was explicitly represented in Eating Habits was in a row of larders (one of which is a domestic deep-freezer). Again, this was a good idea for an eye-catching visual representation. (Heather had a special talent for this.) Again, Heather brought some more individualised life to the display by including taped commentaries about food by particular people (including Cathy's dad, Heather's gran and one of the manual attendants in the Museum) which would play as the larders were opened. During the making of the gallery, Heather found – as did all the Team to varying extents – that she had less space than she had hoped and she could not have as many larders as she had wanted. In the face of this, she decided to collapse together the themes of change over time and contemporary variation: thus the 1950s larder became Jamaican (the 1950s being a time when many Jamaicans came to Britain). This 'compression' was given added impetus too by the Rethink, during which one aim of the gallery became to show 'change in Britain over the last hundred years'. Although this had in many ways been implicit already, it was an explicit nationalisation of the main 'message' of the exhibition to which all sub-areas and themes had to be oriented. Variation over space – another main theme of the Eating Habits area – became subsumed to a narrative of increasing variation, or choice, over time. The Jamaican larder thus became part of a story about bringing more choice to Britain. At the same time, however, because of difficulties in getting many of the packages and foods to put into the 1950s Jamaican larder, and none at all in stocking the present-day deep-freezer, the larders could be read as a kind of evolutionary development, in which the Jamaican is back in the past, and a generalised fish-finger and frozen-pea-eating Briton is at the current apex.

In all of these examples, what we see is how the generalising force of orienting categories such as 'British', 'national', 'familiar' and 'increased choice over time', end up running against the grain of the Team's more explicit intention to be 'politically correct' (another concept in relatively new usage in Britain at the time). Just as ethnic difference is often argued to be marginalised within national constructions, so it is in the making of this exhibition, despite the best of intentions. The same problem could be said to be characteristic of the way in which 'political correctness' tends to be thought about, with emphasis on the evident visual or aural level – using the 'right' forms of language or images – and less attention on the underlying structures. What we also see in this example is how sometimes unexpected editorial decisions, interventions and events during the making of a gallery can lead to unanticipated connotations in the finished exhibition.

Pasteurised Production

The finished exhibition had other unexpected connotations too, though, again, ones whose archaeology can be unearthed from the ethnography of the making of the gallery. One was the way in which food production was presented in the exhibition. As I have noted, in the organisation of the exhibition, consumption was to be foregrounded and less familiar aspects of food – which included food processing – were to be introduced by way of consumption (and particular 'familiar' foods). Moreover, the 'familiarising strategy' was two-pronged in relation to factory production by also being conceptually linked with the preparation of food in the home. The processes involved in the former were seen as largely like those of the latter – just bigger and more automated.

At the same time, as we have seen, rather than being closely bound up with social and cultural information about particular foods, food production became a distinct area in the exhibition (a consequence of the various interventions and editing discussed in the previous chapter). Food in the Factory and Food in the Home were featured with an overarching aim: 'To show how historical development of food preparation and preservation in industry and in the home have affected the choice of foods today'. Another consequence of the editorial decisions discussed in the previous chapter was that matters of nutritional content and other qualities of foods were kept distinct from consideration of food production. In addition, a decision right at the beginning of the making of the exhibition had eliminated any attention being given to primary production – animal rearing and so forth – from the remit (chapter four above). While all of these individual decisions were based in sound localised reasons, together they produced a depiction of food production with a rather specific inflection.

Largely cut off from wider information, factory production is represented as a pure clean process of harnessing the capacity of 'science and technology' to do better and faster what is done in the home. The juxtaposition with Food in the Home acts to domesticate factory production, making it a safe and cosy process. Moreover, as with the larders, there is an evolutionary narrative here too. In Food in the Home a set of reconstructed kitchens is presented: 1780, 1900, 1956 and 1989. The oldest kitchen is relatively grimy, with a stuffed cat, and then each becomes progressively cleaner and more empty-looking. The newest kitchen is not behind perspex (one reason why it does not have the domestic clutter of the older kitchens) and it spills into the Food in the Factory section, creating a linkage between the two areas. As with the larders, this evokes an evolutionary reading, moving progressively from dirty old domestic practices to clean modern factory ones. Although, for practical reasons, the 1989 kitchen is next to that of 1780, it is noticeable that visitors often try to put the kitchens into a time order, looking from the turning information panels about the kitchens to each in turn, and swinging round to try to get them 'in line'. Such reconstructed scenes are, after all, typical of historical narratives in heritage exhibitions and, as such, the mode of display invites this kind of reading. At the same time, the large and clean processing machines themselves – mostly behind clear perspex in order to protect them from the public and *vice versa* – appear as traditional museum objects. They sit, inviting the visitor's admiring gaze, and tell little of the (perhaps) difficult lives in which they were entwined. Neither do they tell of the possible nutritional and health disadvantages of factory processed foods: nutrition and health are not the concern of this part of the exhibition. These objects – a milk pasteurisation plant, a sausage-making machine, a margarine homogenizer – have all this possible 'dirt' removed: they are themselves 'pasteurised objects', 'pasteurised against the threat of indigestibility'[11] [Figure 6.6]. So – partly as a consequence of fears of presenting the public with too heavy an exhibitionary diet – processing ends up as largely a matter of the domestic writ large and how to do it faster, on a larger scale, better.

'You should always wash your hands': Food Poisoning

Another area of the exhibition in which the consumer focus led to a representation of food production as relatively 'innocent' was that concerning food poisoning.[12] This was also an issue which became considerably more prominent in the media during the period of the exhibition's making. Concerns were raised in particular about salmonella in eggs. A major storm followed an infamous claim in November 1988 by Edwina Currie, a junior minister at the Department of Health, that most of the egg production in Britain was infected with salmonella. Mrs Currie's claim was highly controversial and she was sacked for making it, only to be vindicated later when, following a number of deaths from salmonella poisoning, the government had to issue guidelines warning 'vulnerable groups' against consuming eggs. During the course of 1989, as the Food team struggled to prepare their exhibition for opening, other 'food scares' (as they were often called) also appeared in the media: listeria, botulism and BSE (or 'mad cow disease').

Figure 6.6 Pasteurised production: clean machines on display.

Indeed, scarcely a day went by without there being some reporting of food concerns in the newspapers. As Jane remarked in a mixture of exasperation and pride: 'This subject is so bloody topical it's just not true!'.

Its topicality, and the uncertainty about 'just what are the facts?' (Jane), created problems over how to deal with it in the exhibition. One of the questions raised by some, especially in the farming lobby, was whether there was really an increase in the incidence of food poisoning or whether there was just more reporting and more 'scare mongering'. Were the cases of 'listeria' poisoning, for example, a reflection of a genuine increase in this type of infection or was it 'listeria hysteria' (a term used in many newspapers), a moral panic fanned by the media itself? If there was an increase in food poisoning, what was its cause? Were more intensive farming methods and contaminated animal feeds to blame? Or new types of food processing (perhaps using parts of animals not previously used)? Was storage during transport and in the shops a problem? Or were consumers at fault because they failed to follow sensible and sound food hygiene practices? Getting at 'the facts' was, as Jane observed, 'almost impossible!'.

So how to deal with these controversial matters of food safety in the exhibition was extremely difficult. Not only were 'the facts' elusive, but also there was a sense that information was changing rapidly and 'the facts' today might be proved wrong tomorrow. Jane was also concerned that the subject was surrounded by 'a lot of media hype' and might in retrospect look 'like a bit of a storm in a tea-cup'. Salmonella in eggs, in particular, would, Jane judged, 'be a dead issue by the time the gallery is open – all the infected flocks will have been disposed of or something.' Moreover, food poisoning became 'a major issue' in the press after the Food exhibition had not only been mapped out but had also gone through some difficult layers of editing. Although there had already been an intention to devote a small part of the section on Food and the Body to food safety, the question was whether this could be expanded when so much else was being cut. And how could this subject, which did not look very promising in terms of including either objects or interactives, be represented? In the end, an area of Food and the Body bordering onto that of Food Production was devoted to the topic (promisingly opening up the possibility that links might be drawn between the two). The name was changed from Food Safety to Food Poisoning (Jane – 'Quite frankly there doesn't seem to be any point in calling it anything else now'), and the 'message' from 'Most food we buy is safe. The way that we treat food at home can make it unsafe' to 'Our bodies need safe food. What is food poisoning?'.

Nevertheless, the fingerprints of the earlier idea that 'we' make food unsafe at home remain clearly visible. The food poisoning section contains five panels – all topped with a dramatic yellow warning sign showing a skull and crossbones – and an exhibit set into one wall which shows apparently clean cooking implements which glow purple when a button is pressed. This exposes, as the surrounding text puts it, the 'Hidden Menace', warning the viewer that 'even though your dishes or hands may look clean they still carry hundreds of germs'. A panel next to this, entitled 'How do Germs get onto Food' [*sic*], shows pictures of domestic kitchens and continues the message: 'Hands that look clean can often carry germs. They need to be washed frequently, especially before handling food and after going to the lavatory'. This panel also lists some of the foods that are most likely to cause food poisoning, and it explains that: 'The common food poisoning germs are often found in the gut and dung of animals we eat for food. When animals are killed such germs can be left on the carcass. . . If we prepare food carelessly at home or in a factory we spread germs from these sources onto cooked or clean food'. Although there is a brief mention (in small print) of the possibility that contamination may occur in a factory, the emphasis is on 'us', the consumers. We need to wash our hands and take care to follow proper hygiene rules. This is further emphasised in a panel entitled 'Golden Rules for Avoiding Food Poisoning'. All of these are what 'you', the consumer, or 'we' the consumers (the elision of viewers and the makers of the exhibition runs throughout) can do, such as 'Cook prepared food exactly as the packet says'. While this is, of course, potentially useful for consumers, it does not address the fact that one could follow all of these rules and still end up getting food poisoning because contamination can occur long before the food gets to 'you' or to 'us'.

A neighbouring panel, headed 'Why is Food Poisoning Increasing' (the graphic designer has an aversion to question marks), notes the increase in reported cases ('22,000 reported in 1987, over 44,000 in 1988') and states that: 'Scientists are convinced the increase is real but argue about the reason. Some say that new ways of raising animals, preparing or cooking food produce infected food. Others say that we ignore basic hygiene at home and do not treat our food properly'. (Jane had decided, somewhat reluctantly, that those arguing that the increase was just a matter of more reporting were too much of a minority 'to count'.) Given the fifteen consumer-directed 'golden rules' on the following panel, the viewer could easily conclude that the exhibition was saying that the 'others' were right.

Despite the fact that the Food exhibition, in some ways unusually for a Science Museum exhibition, covers a controversial topic and one which could potentially lead to major criticisms of the way that food is produced (and has certainly led to major public concern), it scarcely even touches upon the areas of how food can become dangerous before it reaches us. The reasons for the lack of attention to this were partly the earlier assumption that 'most food is safe' but also that primary production would not be covered at all in the exhibition, that the food processing sections of the exhibition should have a 'how it is done' message and that the exhibition would, overall, foreground consumption. The last of these was interpreted as the things that visitors could do at home to help to protect themselves.

Visitors, Politics and Supermarket Science

Earlier decisions – often conceived as purely organisational or pragmatic – joined with the vision of visitors to produce an exhibition which could in some respects be seen as having the 'supermarket logic' that the critic identified. Foregrounding consumption, presenting production as pure technology unimplicated in environmental or health risks, assuming a wholehearted narrative of progress, and celebrating choice all contributed towards a representation which could be read as 'very much what Mr Sainsbury would want' (as the critic put it) or 'a hymn to the food processing industry' as Heather had feared. David Harvey's comments on commodity fetishism, and the way in which looking beyond immediate appearances is closed off, are ones which can be readily applied to the Food exhibition:

> The conditions of labour and life, the sense of joy, anger, or frustration that lie behind the production of commodities, the states of mind of the producers, are all hidden to us as we exchange one object (money) for another (the commodity). We can take our daily breakfast without a thought for the myriad people who are engaged in its production. All traces of exploitation are obliterated in the object (there are no finger prints of exploitation in the daily bread). We cannot tell from the contemplation of any object in the supermarket what conditions of labour lay behind its production.[13]

Similarly, contemplation of any object in the Food exhibition does not lead to a revelation of the conditions of labour lying behind it. This was not, however, due to a calculated strategy to present the food industry in this way. On the contrary, the Team attempted to distance themselves from the food industry (as in their avoidance of 'commercial scientists'), and saw themselves as 'rather radical even' (Sue) in their championing of visitors and of a consumer-choice perspective, as well as in the making of references to women and ethnic minorities. So how did the exhibition come to be legible in this way?

In this chapter and the previous one I have shown how earlier decisions acquired unanticipated inflections. As in the 'Hidden Menace' exhibit, invisible 'germs' which had made their way in earlier could show up when put under the spotlight later. The conclusion that I wish to draw from this is not that exhibition-makers can never really know just how an exhibition will turn out (which may well be true at a banal level) but that we need to understand what kinds of practices and ways of thinking lead to particular results. We need to understand how inflections slip in; the consequentially implicit needs to be made explicit.

The virtual visitor of the Food exhibition was in many respects conceptualised as a child. In casual discussion as the exhibition was made, Team members often thought about whether children would understand something or not: they aimed for a text of Ladybird or children's book level, they enlisted me as a vicarious child-visitor substitute, and when they formatively tested their exhibits in the Museum they made sure that they paid attention to children's responses. This was not the studious adult imagined into so many exhibitions: the visitor to Food was anticipated as easily bored, possessing only a short attention span, lacking in knowledge and advanced cognitive skills, seeking fun and choice, and relatively uninterested in science. All of this was done to avoid creating an exhibition which would 'go over the heads of ordinary people', which would be inaccessible to those without the prior knowledge, skills or patience that so many other exhibitions demand. Imagining visitors in this way, however, also meant that certain other exhibitionary features were not given such emphasis. In particular, visitors were not conceptualised as likely to make a rigorous political critique of the exhibition. While the Team was well aware that some visitors (some curators and some pressure groups for example) might, they did not build a consistent interrogation of political inflections of the exhibition into its making. Instead, the overwhelming critique to which the exhibition was subjected during its making was to questions of its internal coherence and the clarity of its messages. These received considerable time and effort but there was no process in place to assess the potential side-effects.

This is not to say that the Team members never thought about the political legibility of the exhibition. On the contrary, they did, both in terms of what they sometimes referred to as their 'exhibition philosophy' and in relation to specific topics and perspectives (such as gender and ethnic minorities). Yet as I have shown in the examples above, in both cases these could become readable in ways not entirely anticipated by the Team. In order to identify more fully what was involved here and in more generalizable dilemmas, it is worth looking at them and at some further examples more closely. I begin with some of the specific politicised topics and in the following section consider further the Team's exhibition philosophy and the conception of the visitor and Museum role that this entailed.

Incorporating reference to different ethnic groups and to women was perceived as important by the Team in 'getting away from a Great White Male perspective' (Sue). As Sue explained to me, just including any reference to different ethnic groups or to women was 'pretty revolutionary in this place'. She was not alone in this perception, and indeed after the exhibition opened one female member of the Museum staff came up to her to say that she had found it 'so refreshing' that here was an exhibition that 'actually includes some images of women'.

Simply to include images of, and text mentioning, women or ethnic groups was a creditable achievement. At the same time, the very fact that it was seen as such was part of the problem: mere inclusion seemed to be enough. The language of some of the planning documents, which noted how certain topics would help to 'deal with' or 'tackle' 'the ethnic issue', and comments during the making of the exhibition about 'getting in' an image of, say, a women or black person, are illustrative of this way of thinking. There are two related dangers with this. The first of them is that of 'tokenism' (with which the Food exhibition was charged by a feminist curator from another museum), topics or perspectives being included without any significant challenge to the *status quo* (the feminist curator claimed that the exhibition did not 'do much for the representation of women'). That we might see an image of, say, a female cashier, would not be likely to change ideas about women and science. The other danger, highlighted by the example of 'ethnic' diets, is that in the effort to 'get something in', the alternative narratives through which it might be read (such as an evolutionary narrative) are not investigated.

Museum staff may undoubtedly find themselves in a difficult position here for they are often rather ambivalent about their role in relation to the *status quo*. Is their task to try to change things or to 'represent reality'? Including images of women and ethnic minorities was talked about by the Team as 'redressing the imbalance' of other exhibitions: theirs was an exercise in the 'remembrance' of the existence of these groups which other exhibitions tended to 'forget'. This, they saw as a legitimate and even necessary task. But whether they should go further and try to 'do something' about the way in which women or ethnic minorities were perceived more generally was reasonably seen as beyond their remit: they could seek only to 'represent reality' not to change it. In another exhibition whose planning meetings I attended – the Information Age project – this matter was rather more hotly debated. This group had been told by the Museum's management that the gallery might make an important contribution to government and industry initiatives to get women and girls more involved in computing. The planning team was therefore asked to see what they could do to show more women and girls involved and to encourage them to regard computers in a more positive light. Some on this team, however, saw this as contrary to the Science Museum's representational role: 'It's asking us to do social engineering and that's not what we should be in the business of doing. That might be the government's job but it's not the Science Museum's.' This response was part of a more widespread insistence that the Museum must stick to 'the facts' and 'factual accuracy' (an insistence which was also a means for exhibition teams to reject suggestions from others).

Facts and Social Responsibility

'The facts' and 'factual accuracy', while generally regarded as safe and unproblematic (provided you could 'get hold of them'), could themselves generate dilemmas. As discussed in the previous chapter, many areas of dispute could not be resolved by recourse to 'the facts', being more about matters of slant, exclusion or presentation. To give another example: at one point in the making of the gallery, Sainsbury's suggested that there ought to be the inclusion of a reference to alcohol somewhere in the exhibition as this was becoming a more common element in British people's diet. At one of their planning meetings the Team discussed whether or not it should be included. Jane agreed that it was 'a fact' that more alcohol was being consumed today but then, in a familiar move, argued that it was now too late in the exhibition's making 'to do anything major about it'. Nevertheless, the 'obvious place' to include 'something' on the subject, she thought, was in Food and the Body, an area predominantly about nutrition. But what 'facts' about alcohol would be included? The Team discussion went like this:

Sue: So, are you going to say that alcohol rots your liver?
Jane: No. And we don't in Sugar [one of Sue's areas] – don't say that sugar rots your teeth.
Sue: But that's because Sugar is about processing.
Jane: Hmm. . . We could say how many calories there are in alcohol?
Sue: But we shouldn't be encouraging drinking. We should say about the health risks
Jane: We are not talking about health risks anywhere in the whole gallery – not even in Fats.
Sue: But we shouldn't be encouraging drinking – especially in the present climate. Edwina Currie was on the front page of the *Guardian* today about drinking, you know, the Christmas campaign.

What we see in this exchange are many of the factors that come into play in negotiating the presence or absence of particular topics or angles on them: (1) 'the facts' (what can be said 'factually', such as the 'number' of calories); (2) the framework already mapped out (what different areas of the gallery are 'about' and what the gallery is and is not doing overall); (3) social responsibility (health consequences); (4) topicality (whether or not a topic or angle can be ignored given its external significance). This fourth factor also shows awareness of the political legibility of the exhibition – without warnings about alcohol the gallery would be likely, 'especially in the present climate', to be seen as socially irresponsible. The negotiation of all of the different elements eventually led to the inclusion of beer as one example in one of the interactive games in Food in the Body but with a note added about government recommended levels of alcohol consumption (a note which forgot the usual casting of the visitor as a child).

What we also see in this example, as in Nestlé's arguments about their role in the history of the invention of instant coffee (chapter four), is that sponsors were also capable of mobilising a rhetoric of 'the facts' in order to try to persuade the Team to accept a particular topic or angle. Another instance of this which caused considerably more difficulty than Jane's limited acceptance of the inclusion of alcohol in the exhibition concerned the reproduction 1920s grocery shop. This was in the Shopping section of the exhibition organised by Sue, one of the Team members who was most likely to voice concerns over the politics of subject-matter. In researching this section (and some others) of the exhibition, Sue had used the Sainsbury's archive amongst other sources, and the archivist had become quite interested and involved in the exhibition. She helped Sue to find good source material for the shop reproduction. Sue's idea had been to have a generalised reproduction rather than a specific shop but the archivist challenged this, arguing that it would be 'more accurate' to include a specific shop, and provided information for reproducing a 1920s Sainsbury's. Sue was reluctant to accept having a Sainsbury's grocery store in the exhibition, fearing that it would 'look too much like sponsor bias', and she tried to accept the basic model but without the actual shop name on the reproduction. This led to some heated exchanges in which the archivist argued that the reproduction would be 'inaccurate' if it did not include the name because this was part of the 'authentic original'. By mobilising the usual arguments used by Museum staff – arguments about accuracy, the facts and authenticity – the archivist won the case. Sue's concerns about political legibility, which were not so fully a part of institutionalised priorities, had to be put to one side (to her considerable annoyance). As we see later, this very visible presence of Sainsbury's at the exhibition entrance (where Shopping had already been placed because of the consumption-focus) was to have marked consequences for the visitors' reading of the exhibition.

In these examples, what we see, then, are specific decisions being taken – often legitimated by a rhetoric of 'factual accuracy' – without their possible consequences for the political legibility of the finished exhibition being fully extrapolated. What often matters is the specific physical arrangement of exhibits – where they are laid out relative to others, their positioning at certain 'key points' and so forth. Yet, these are often matters to which little attention is paid. 'Messages' are thought of as essentially explicit and verbal, and more subtle three-dimensional matters are given much less shrift in the exhibition-making process.

Democracy, Citizenship, Choice and Enterprise

The exhibition did, however, have a philosophy shaped by a politicised vision of the role of the Museum and the nature of the visitor. This was followed through into ideas about the mix of types of exhibits, the gallery layout and the mode of presentation. Key aspects of being 'democratising' in the exhibition were the emphases on choice, consumption and fun. All of these were implicitly associated with agency. Providing more choice, consumption and fun was providing more agency and, therefore, was more empowering of visitors. This was a concept of the visitor as an 'active citizen', which contrasted to the more passive visions of them elsewhere.

It was part of a broader shift in understandings of citizenship which has been identified as under way at the time. Nikolas Rose, contrasting this 'new' vision with an earlier one, explains: 'Citizenship is to be active and individualistic rather than passive and dependent. The political subject is henceforth to be an individual whose citizenship is manifested through the free exercise of personal choice among a variety of options', and he notes that the then Home Secretary argues that '"The idea of active citizenship is a necessary complement to that of enterprise culture"'.[14] As Rose argues further, this reconceptualisation of citizenship is not confined to the political Right of which the Home Secretary was part and it is not simply articulated through 'technologies' directed by 'the State'.

While there may be broad agreement that citizens should be encouraged to be active rather than passive, there have also been criticisms of the ways in which this is conceptualised within an enterprise culture perspective. In the casting of citizens, and, more fundamentally, 'properly constituted persons', as choice-makers, consumption comes to have iconic status as the realm *par excellence* in which citizenship and personhood are performed. The metaphor of the shopper becomes, perhaps, especially apt not only to characterise museum visitors but this new kind of citizen. But what kind of shopper? Not the careful constrained shopper desperately trying to make ends meet on a limited budget who might well find shopping a depressing chore, but like the imagined shopper of the Food exhibition, a shopper actively seeking pleasure and fun from their experience, relishing making choices, not particularly wishing for in-depth information but being happy to be 'busy', to act on impulse and desire. This casting of choice-making as central to citizenship is part of what Marilyn Strathern terms 'prescriptive consumerism': personhood becomes a matter of making choices, and individuality comes to be seen as a cumulation of the choices that we have made. Choice becomes 'the only source of difference'.[15] Moreover, 'prescriptive consumerism dictates that there is no choice but always to exercise choice'.[16] You cannot choose not to be an active, enterprising choice-maker. However, while the enterprise perspective celebrates difference in some respects, it simultaneously fails to recognise it in others. Not only is the option to be not entrepreneurial not countenanced, understanding consumers as 'sovereign' also fails to recognise differences which affect the choices open to them, for example, those of income, education, and upbringing. In the enterprise perspective, differences of life-outcomes all become a result of different lifestyle choices (just as diet becomes a matter of individual taste) uninfluenced by social, political and economic structural factors.

The celebration of choice *per se* also ignores the fact that choices must be made from the range of whatever is on offer. As Strathern, among others, observes, not only are the choices on offer ultimately determined by producers, they are often tightly bound up with perceptions of what 'customers want' in a self-perpetuating feedback loop.[17] Thus, not only are consumers cast as responsible for the choices that they make, they are also cast as responsible for the choices on offer. We are being given, we are told, what we want. If visitors seem to want something in a finished exhibition that is not there, then at least part of the blame lies with those visitors consulted during formative evaluation, matters of responsibility being shifted from producers to consumers. However, as in the Food exhibition, where the idea that visitors should 'make up their own minds' threaded throughout the making and much of the finished exhibition, this begs the question of what information we are given to make our choices.

One implication for knowledge provision of this emphasis on what consumers want, argue Heelas and Morris, is a 'lowest common denominator effect'.[18] Because not all possible consumer desires can be met in practice, there will be a tendency to go for majority wishes – which may be relatively uninformed – and those that can be relatively easily met. This easily panders, they suggest, to philistinism and perhaps rather superficial cultural products. Moreover, while requests for 'knowledge' tend to lead to 'what knowledge exactly?', those for pleasure, fun or entertainment are more likely to be perceived as 'in themselves', requiring no further elucidation. This also makes them the most likely candidates of 'what people want'. And if fun is 'what people want', fun, and the popular more generally, come to be seen as innocent of any socio-political influences ('fun is fun, and has nothing to do with power').[19] This positions fun and the popular beyond critique: they are seen straightforwardly as democratic expressions.

More generally, knowledge comes to be regarded not so much as a body of accumulated truths but as a matter of information from which consumers choose that which they want or need: it is turned into a matter of 'pick and mix'. This kind of 'knowledge', while undoubtedly worthwhile in many respects, is also limited by the fact that it is localised to matters of individual choice; as such, it is not capable of 'travelling', of being transferable to other persons and fields. For example, in Food for Thought there are many exhibits, such as the distorting mirrors and the exercise bikes, whose aim is not to provide a kind of generalisable knowledge that can be taken away and applied elsewhere, but which relates to individual experience and subjectivity. As has been argued for other aspects of consumer and enterprise culture, this privileging of the individual and experiential can also be a diversion from asking questions about politics and production. It could also, in other words, contribute to a 'supermarket logic'.

In highlighting these alternative possible ways in which the Food exhibition was legible, my intention is not to say that it 'really' meant one thing or the other. It was legible both ways (and more). One of the reasons for this, as Rose points out, is that the conception of citizens as active is much broader than the enterprise perspective alone, and many of the basic ideas involved are shared across the political spectrum.[20] David Marquand points out the overlap between the enterprise culture perspective and what he calls, after Samuel Beer (1982), 'romantic revolt': 'a new assertion of the "romantic" values of authenticity, spontaneity and individuality and a corresponding rejection of hierarchy, bureaucracy and externally imposed classifications and identities'.[21] For members of the Food team, as for many other museum staff at the Science Museum and elsewhere, this period felt like one in which 'romantic revolt' might just be possible and they liked to articulate what they were doing – to a degree – in such terms. They were against traditionalist, patronising, masculinist ways of doing things; they were for the public, the popular, ordinary people.

At the same time, however, much of the rhetoric was also shared with the New Right, many of whose views were not shared by the 'romantics'. Talking about 'active visitors', 'participation', 'access', 'accountability', 'choice', 'consumers', 'public understanding of science' – and seeking to champion visitors – was part of the same language but with rather different political inflections. As we have noted in other contexts, different inflections do not easily come to light precisely because of the fact that they share a common form.[22] Moreover, in the practice of exhibition-making they are often embedded non-verbally in three-dimensional exhibits and this also easily contributes to obscuring their different possible legibilities. Coupled with the lack of institutionalised means for exploring the potential readings of an exhibition, this leads to it being open to interpretations which might even be distasteful to its makers.

In the next chapter we see something of this as we follow the gallery through to its opening and reception by the media, other Museum staff and by those who have made it. Let us turn to the frenzied preparations for the big day – and beyond.

Notes

1. The term 'phantom public' I take from Bruce Robbins 1993 (who in turn borrows it from Walter Lippmann 1925) who uses it in a discussion of the difficulty, or even impossibility, of creating genuinely participatory forms of citizenship as well as to highlight the rhetorical or political place of 'the public' in debates about society and citizenship.

2. Woolgar 1991: 59. The notion of the 'implied reader' in literary studies is similar to, though not perhaps as extensive as, that of configuring the user. So too is the notion of 'preferred reading' used in Hall's encoding/decoding model (1980). The metaphor of a text, used also to some extent by Woolgar in his study of computers, is useful but fails to get at some of the interesting questions about materiality and objectness which are so relevant in the case of the museum. A similar point is made by Silverstone in his emphasis on television as technology (1994, 1999).

3. Or 'generalised user' as Woolgar 1991 terms it.

4. The classic example of this is Victor Turner's study of the Ndembu 'milk tree': Turner 1967. See also Cohen 1985. Ardener's concept of 'hollow categories' (1989) also captures the way in which different meanings can come to occupy a shared form. A similar phenomenon, in relation to a natural history museum, is discussed by Star and Griesemer 1989 in terms of the formation of 'boundary objects'.

5. Cf. Woolgar 1991 on 'atrocity stories' about computer users, and Forsythe 1992 on 'blaming the user'. Staff at Colonial Williamsburg also talk of 'clueless visitors' (Handler and Gable 1997: 28). A recent book about what goes on behind the scenes at the British Museum includes a list of amusingly ignorant questions asked by visitors (Burnett and Reeve 2001: 104). There are similarities here too with the ways in which students are sometimes talked about within universities. Consider, for example, the common practice of sending around email lists of 'exam howlers' – foolish things that have been written on exam scripts.

6. Hudson 1975. See also Wittlin 1949. These rules were officially changed only in 1963, though their enforcement had been relaxed (Hudson 1975: 190).

7. Berland 1992: 47; and see discussion below.

8. See, for example, Bal 1996; Bennett 1995; Duncan 1995; Jordanova 1989.

9. Cf. Harvey, Penelope (forthcoming). A similar aim for transparency and interactivity in as many domains as possible characterised the display of a historically important computer at the Manchester Museum of Science and Industry.

10. They used a program produced for IBM by Scandinavian pc systems, 1988. The way that this program, and other similar programs, works is by identifying matters such as the length of words and certain syntactical structures. Such systems cannot detect semantics and therefore whether something makes sense or not is beyond their remit. Long words are automatically considered 'difficult' – even though children may find certain long words easy to recognise. See Carter 1999 for a discussion of some of the readability tests used in museums.

11. Silverstone 1994: 174. He is writing here of objects of consumption more generally and arguing that commodities are not so much alienated objects as ones which have been specially prepared for our consumption.

12. This is discussed more extensively in Macdonald and Silverstone 1992.

13. Harvey, David 1989: 101.

14. Rose 1992: 159. He explains: 'Mentalities of government in the first half of this century operated in terms of an image of the citizen as a social being. They sought to open a kind of contract between government and citizens, articulated in the language of social responsibilities and social welfare. In these

forms of political thought, thc individual was a locus of needs that were to be socially met if malign consequences were to be avoided, but was reciprocally to be a being to whom political, civil and social obligations and duties were to be attached. This political rationality was translated into programmes such as social insurance, child welfare, social and mental hygiene. Pedagogic technologies from universal education to the BBC were construed as devices for forming responsible citizens. Planned and socially organized mechanisms were to weave a complex web that would bind the inhabitants of a territory into a single polity, a space of regulated freedom' (1992: 158). See also Roche 1992.

15. Strathern 1992: 172, 170. See also Strathern 1992a and 1992b.

16. Strathern 1992: 170. See also Giddens 1991: 8; and Marquand 1992.

17. Strathern 1992. See also Miller 1998.

18. Heelas and Morris 1992: 14. See also Susan Leigh Star's (1991) argument about standardization and the problem of dealing with minorities, a problem also noted in George Ritzer's account of McDonaldization (1996), and more extensively discussed within Bowker and Star 1999.

19. Berland 1992: 47.

20. Rose 1992. See also Cohen 1992.

21. Marquand 1992: 65.

22. See footnote 4 above.

Opening and Aftermath: Ritual, Reviews and Reflection

The months before the exhibition opened were extraordinarily hectic. There had been a sense of working at high pace against an impending deadline for much of the previous year but now things moved up another gear. Although the 'slog' of writing was finished and the panels were all in production, and much of the content was now decided upon, making sure that everything that was supposed to be in the finished exhibition actually arrived seemed to entail endless 'chasing up' and a myriad of miscellaneous tasks. The 'manatts' described the Team as 'running around like demented bed-bugs' – a description which they quickly adopted for themselves.

Here are just some of the things going on in the penultimate week. Heather is busy getting recordings done for her larders; Sue spends much of a weekend sticking lids on jars for her 1920s Sainsbury's and has to take a taxi to Paddington to buy a bag of builder's sand so that the workmen can construct a wall in her Sainsbury's shop; Cathy, Heather, Jan and I spend an afternoon making up frozen-pea boxes; Jane says that she has to keep a notebook by her bed so that when she wakes up worrying about something she must do she can at least write it down and hope to get back to sleep. The Team makes numerous trips to Wandsworth to the company making the panels to check that these are correct before they are finally completed (otherwise correcting them is considerably more costly); even so, some eventually turn up with the pictures missing or with the wrong text. The Team also goes to the Science Museum's warehouses and workshops to inspect objects and exhibits prior to installation in the gallery. Sometimes, together with the designers, they roam the gallery – now at the stage called 'shop-fitting' – checking that all is going to plan and trying to map the workmen-thronged tangle of stud-walling, wires, rolls of carpet, and cases onto their visions of how the gallery will, hopefully, finally look [Figures 7.1, 7.2 and 7.3].

There were, of course, 'last minute disasters', unexpected hassles, disappointments and frayed nerves. Only just over a week before the opening did it become clear that the frozen-pea blast tunnel interactive would not be finished (though it might be added to the gallery after its official opening). 'I could kill', fumed Sue. 'In fact, I think I will. . . . I don't think the bloody gallery will be open on time. I really don't. There'll still be contractors working.' The hydrogenation demo also looked likely not be completed, though an intervention by the Director meant that it was – late on the day before opening. Many of the working demos 'played up'. The milk-bottling plant, for instance, had a tendency to drip, to smash the milk bottles, and it proved surprisingly difficult to create a milk substitute which looked convincing but which could also be easily washed off (otherwise the bottles looked permanently grimy, which the National Dairy Council found 'very unsatisfactory').

Practical problems come in rapid succession. The tea-packing machine will not fit flush against a wall as intended and then turns out to be covering a duct. The 'unobtrusive' cases that have been selected for displaying many objects turn out to be rather dangerous – they jut out

Figure 7.1 Inspection time: Jan, Mr Suthers, Jane and John Redman in the gallery about five weeks before opening.

Figure 7.2 The exhibit that never was: Sue inspects what there is of the pea-freezer tunnel about three weeks before opening.

Figure 7.3 Taking shape: Giant chocolate mousse pot goes into the gallery six days before opening.

further from the wall than expected, have sharp corners and are not made of toughened glass; moreover, they have no base and so everything has to be wired to the back. The Foodies are annoyed with the designers about this. They have also to acquire new transparencies for the bakery as the frames these are to fit into turn out to be smaller than expected; the brackets to hold the video monitors are wrong (I drive to Oxford to exchange them – though even the new ones have to have ugly bits of wood attached to make the monitors fit); Ann desperately tries to 'age' the settle in her 1780s kitchen with turps, Oxo and coffee; Heinz keep sending Sue the 'wrong' cans for her canning exhibit; one of the famine medals she had wanted to include can't be found; and she has to get the Jamaican High Commission to fly her in a piece of sugar-cane as Safeway's are out of stock. Heather is distraught when she finds that her silhouette figures are not 'real-life' height (the graphic artist had reduced them in order to make them fit in the space available); she is still struggling to get the sausage-machine to function (it seems now to be demanding an extra attachment); and Lionel, who is being interviewed for the Jamaican larder, doesn't come up with quite the right answer when he says that he would buy foods for his special celebration meals from Sainsbury's.

There are also some last minute difficulties with sponsors: somebody from the National Dairy Council phones up a week before the opening of the gallery having 'noticed some changes' in the script (and is told that 'unfortunately it is too late to change it'). The Sainsbury's archivist comes to have a look at how the supermarket reconstruction is going and a row ensues about the light-fittings which Sue has, with great difficulty, found. The archivist says that they 'are much too ornate'. (Sue later transforms this into a hilarious story about the archivist having thought that the fittings were 'too phallic'.) Sometimes it seems that there are so many hassles that the only answer is to joke about them. Jan comments: 'I'm sure that the magnitude of seriousness of each problem is going down now – it's just that there seem to be lots more of them', and Cathy remarks: 'I think that we've got to the point where we don't care any more – we just want it to be finished. I suppose we'll start worrying about whether it is right after that.'

But it is an exciting time too. The first object, a coffee-roaster, goes into a case at 11.10 a.m. on Tuesday the 3rd of October, nine days before the official opening, after a 'hairy moment' when it looked as though it would not fit. (Cathy has to leave out three other objects which were also supposed to be in the case.) We all celebrate this as a significant marker in the move towards the completion of the gallery (and I am told to record it precisely). At last it seems to be possible to see that the exhibition really will be completed, that the dream will – somehow or other – actually become 'reality'.

Counting-down...

As well as finishing the gallery itself, there were also other matters to attend to in the last couple of weeks. One was dealing with reviewers from newspapers, radio and television. Jane generally handled this (though most reviewers also interviewed the Director) and she sometimes found it quite difficult to move between dealing with the hassles of completing the gallery and presenting an up-beat account of it. Coping with some of the reviewer comments was also hard, as I discuss further below. Also to be dealt with were the preparations for the opening ceremony. This was to be a grand affair, performed by the Duchess of York who was Patron of Museums Year. Invitation lists had to be drawn up, invitation cards specially designed and decisions made about what 'gift' to give the Duchess – the Director wants something 'loony and foody', not the usual plaque, and when an exquisite basket of flowers made from sugar is planned he excitedly asks, 'Is it in bad taste? Is it kitsch? Is it St Paul's cathedral in matchsticks?' Safety and anti-terrorist precautions have to be put in place, school parties selected, 'baby-sitters' found to look after special guests such as the sponsors, the protocol of where to put eminent guests figured out ('Where do we put the Duke of Kent?'), and the whole day and route carefully planned out and rehearsed, taking into account the Duchess's dislike of escalators and back-tracking ('Oh no, that means she'll have to go through the Agriculture and Gas galleries'!).

In the last couple of days before opening the Team work almost non-stop around the clock getting things into cases and cleaning the gallery. Audio-visuals only start being put in place two days before. Late into the last night panels are still going up, joiners are still sawing and hammering and many objects still need to go into cases. We all vacuum and polish madly, trying to get rid of the dust that seems to pother up constantly and cling to all surfaces. Everybody is comparing this gallery with others that they have worked on, nearly all of them saying that this one is running dangerously late, though stories abound about working until minutes before opening and having to stand in front of certain exhibits on the big day to hide the fact that they are incomplete.

Sometimes, populated with their objects at last, cases and sets look strangely empty, so we hasten to find things to provide background.

On the day before the gallery opens, for example, I am sent rushing off to buy a 1950s-looking drainer for Ann's kitchen and a small rucksack ('preferably khaki') for one of Sue's cases, as well as some 'gardenia-coloured' paper for Sue to make fake labels because the 'real labels' had turned out to be too big for the case. Looking at this list in retrospect, it looks like the Team might have been trying to get rid of me: to stop me taking photographs and making myself unpopular by announcing that 'these are my 24-hours-to-go photos' [Figure 7.4], or 'these are seventeen hours to go', perhaps! But we are all racing around dealing with what, now, in retrospect, seem like incredibly arcane and specific details, which, at the time, felt absolutely crucial.

On the last day before opening there is also another unexpected intervention from Sainsbury's. The archivist had noticed, on one of her visits to help with the reconstruction, that there were some foods from another supermarket in a couple of exhibits. The Director soon received a complaint from the Sainsbury's Press and Publicity manager saying that the company had stipulated in giving their sponsorship that no other retailer's products should be shown (though branded products were acceptable). Most Team members seem to be unaware of this stipulation or to have forgotten it and are very annoyed, not

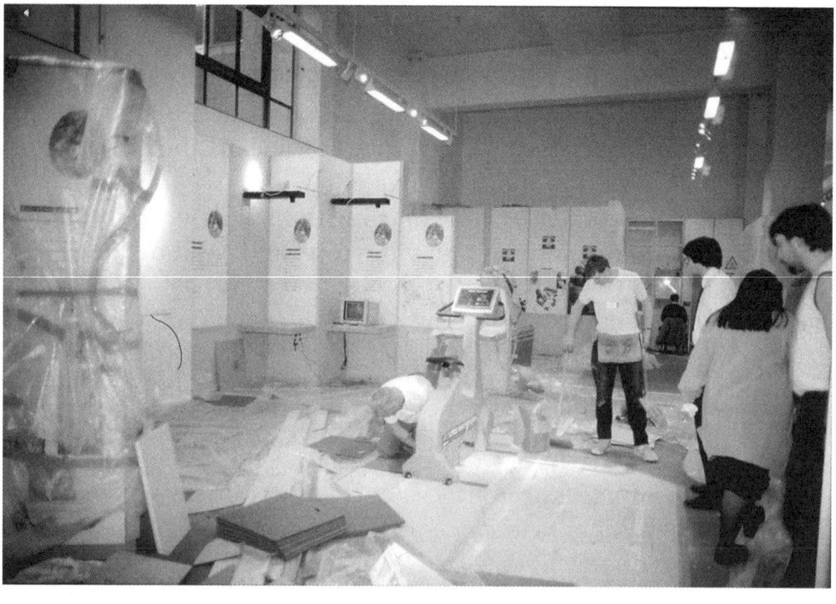

Figure 7.4 Counting down: the gallery at 24 hours before opening.

least because this is yet another matter to deal with at this late stage. Cathy exclaims: 'They're having their pound of flesh. I think they think they've bought the gallery and can do whatever they like. They're just screwing the Museum for all they can get, pardon the expression.' Other Team members think that this is nothing to do with 'the Sainsbury family' but is just about some of the 'minor employees throwing their weight about'. Later, up on the gallery, the Director says to me, in front of the Sainsbury's archivist, 'I'm looking forward to seeing what you write' – reminding her, I suspect, of my 'reporter' role. All the other supermarket foods are replaced, however, with Sainsbury's packages and tins that the archivist herself provides [Figure 7.5].

The Big Day

On the night before the opening of the gallery, work goes on into the early hours. Jane and Jan stay at a hotel nearby and are back at 7 a.m. and the rest of us are there soon after [Figure 7.6]. Things are still at 'panic stations'. During the press briefing at 9.30 there is hammering and sawing to be heard (joiners were still at work at 12 when some panels were still only just going up), making it hard for me to hear

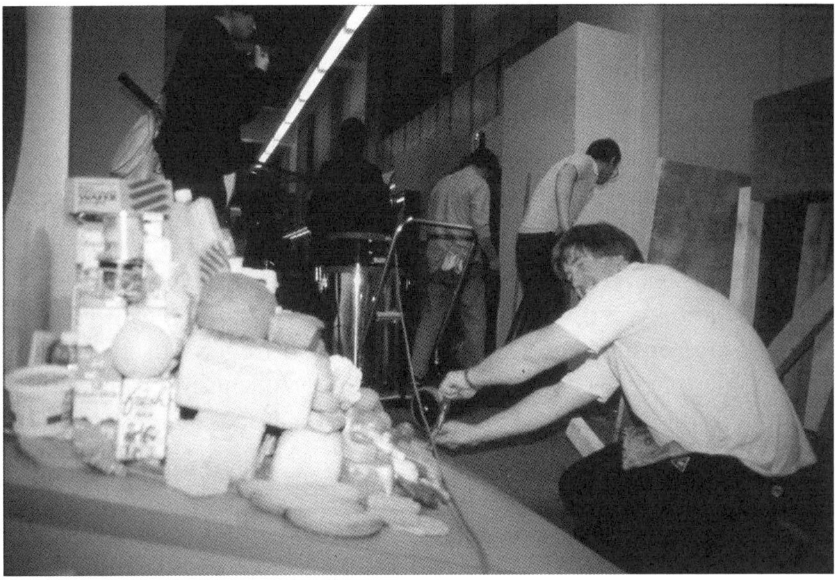

Figure 7.5 Changing names: removing non-Sainsbury supermarket products, fifteen hours before opening.

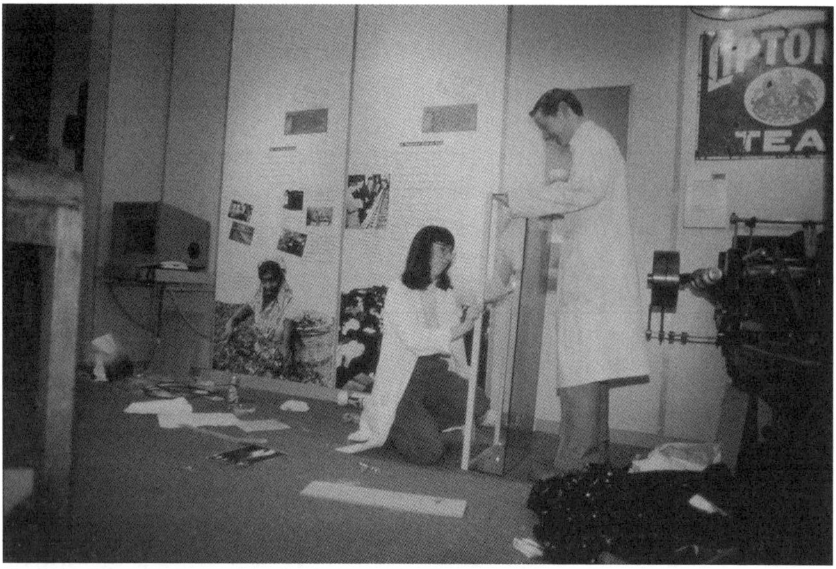

Figure 7.6 Will it be ready?: Fitting a case at 8 a.m. on opening day.

some of the questions, though it is clear from their answers that the Director and Jane are facing questions about sponsorship and the line that the gallery is taking on various aspects of consumer advice. I can't attend directly because, so thoroughly enlisted in action, I am busy making the bread rolls for one exhibit. When the press come round the gallery after the briefing session, some members assume that I am giving a demonstration specially for them (and even take my photograph). At lunch-time I go on yet another shopping errand – this time for a bin to place next to the sugar-packing machine (otherwise the litter scatters everywhere), some greaseproof paper to wrap Ann's fake cheese in, and a pair of tights for Cathy. We all race around with vacuum cleaners and dusters yet again and then dash to get ourselves ready. The Foodies have begun to refer to the gallery as 'this monster' and, as I comment in my notebook, 'there is a feeling of it as being something organic, with a life of its own'. Will it condescend to be ready on time?

Quite extraordinarily, it does – or at least, it puts on an appearance of being so, there still being hammering from behind the scenes as we wait for HRH. The Foodies, all looking amazingly smart and elegant after their frenetic days, are waiting at various points in the gallery to greet the Duchess and answer any questions that she may have about their areas. I sit in the audience, looking in on the gallery from outside now, the giant chocolate mousse pot just visible through the entrance between the white screens which bear the exhibition's logo and title, Food for Thought: The Sainsbury Gallery. The Duchess arrives, flanked by the Director and Lord Sainsbury, and all make speeches. The Director emphasises the way in which this gallery is a 'first' for the Museum – in its subject matter (which he observes was not so topical when exhibition-making began), in having the privilege of such extensive patronage and sponsorship, in being a new way of doing things in the Museum, and in having been created by an all-female Team. He does not say that it is the first exhibition to be created from start to finish under his directorship, one of the particular significances that this gallery has acquired within the Museum and the wider museum world; also he effectively cautions against reading into this *the* direction in which the Museum will be going in future. Lord Sainsbury says how honoured his family charitable trust is to be the Patron, notes the Sainsbury family's more general support of interactive exhibitions, and says how much the trust wanted to contribute to this enterprise because it saw the exhibition as 'part of our aim of letting our customers know as much as possible about the products that they are buying'. The Duchess makes some general comments about the importance of museums and endears herself to the audience (and the Team) by saying how delighted she is to open an exhibition on a topic in which she has such a keen personal interest. She is presented with her gift amidst a flurry of camera flashes, and then taken into the exhibition. The gallery is now officially open.

Later, after a lavish tea in the Fellow's room, we go back to the offices and just sit there, rather bedraggled. One of the Johns falls asleep; Ann and I, out of some strange urge for distraction from our exhaustion, do a crossword puzzle. Later we go back up to the gallery for an evening reception to which many more guests are invited than the more exclusive gathering earlier in the day. It is also an event intended to thank the many people who have helped in one way or another with the making of the exhibition. In my exhaustion, compounded now by too much wine, I drop and smash my camera. This feels strangely symbolic, as though my own observer role has come to an end.

The Ritual Process

In some respects the making of the exhibition seemed to follow the classical structure of a rite of passage as set out by Van Gennep: ritualised separation, followed by a transitional or liminal ('betwixt-and-between') period, and then, often the high point in ritual terms, a ceremonial reincorporation in which a new life-phase and status are marked.[1] Like a group of initiates for a coming of age ritual, the Foodies went through special ceremonies (interviews, preparing the Feasibility Study and joining the select group) which performed their symbolic separation from the rest of the Museum. This entailed a degree of physical separation too: they moved to their own offices set apart from those of other curators as well being separated from many of the humdrum tasks and events governing the everyday lives of other Museum staff. For the initiates, there followed months of battling to achieve tasks which had been set for them by their elders, a transitional phase during which they had to face and overcome numerous physical and psychological hurdles. It was a time of being tested – sometimes to the limit. It was also a liminal period in which the Foodies were neither 'normal' curators nor clearly 'non-curators' either. On the one hand set apart from the rest of the Museum, they were simultaneously central to it. The Museum's reputation would rest, at least in part, on how well they coped with the tasks they had been set.

The liminal period, Victor Turner suggests, is often characterised by a symbolic emphasis on 'anti-structure' – a highlighting of difference from normal or ordinary structures.[2] Rituals during this period may turn normal practices or relationships upside-down. In so doing, they also serve to highlight those normal structures or practices. In the case of the Team, and other exhibitions in the making that I observed, anti-structuring was evident in a pervasive rhetoric of difference from the 'usual' (or 'traditional') way of doing things. This rhetoric thus highlighted, especially by caricature, the normal. One effect of this was also to generate a sense of 'communitas' – of belonging – within the group. Alongside the anti-structural rhetoric, however, there was also an affirmation by the Team of certain key aspects of cultural 'normality', fundamental principles which, whatever else might be turned on its head, ultimately remained sacrosanct. Even if, at the beginning of the ritual process these were symbolically thrown into question, by the end their sacredness was affirmed. In the case of the Food exhibition, these sacred principles included 'objects', 'curatorial control', and notions of 'being the Science Museum' and all that this was seen to entail.

The ceremonial opening of the gallery was the ritual high point marking the end of the rite of passage. Preceded by rituals of cleansing, of purification, (our manic dusting and vacuuming, the changing into smart outfits) as is very common at this stage of initiation rituals, the ritual high-point is in some respects a denial or 'deletion' of the preceding months of work and difficulty.[3] Mess, dust, imperfections, sweat, under-eye shadow – all must be hidden in this performance of completion. It is a kind of epiphany, a moment of truth, though one which rests on a lie. One effect of this lie or denial is a performance of incontrovertibility: negotiation and struggle are erased and things are presented as inevitable. Like the clean machines, which do not tell of the lives entangled in their earlier history, the gallery presents a face cleansed of the struggles to achieve it. And the opening ritual – the moment when the gallery is officially declared ready to be visited by the public – is the marker of this newly pure state.

High point rituals also often contain within themselves a symbolism of journey, the crossing of thresholds and opening up. All of these can be seen in the opening ceremony: the Duchess's walk through the now presentable gallery can be seen as the transformative moment when all of those earlier work-oriented journeys through the gallery give way to a new kind of journey – that of the visitor. One reason why it is so important that everything is as perfect as possible for this first visit is that it regarded as an omen for the future of the gallery, for all of those journeys that are to come later. The opening ceremony is also a performative utterance of the importance of the gallery and, vicariously, of the Science Museum itself. The presence of a member of the Royal Family and a member of the House of Lords, a long and distinguished list of guests, and a stylish and opulent ceremony, tea, and evening drinks all serve to signal that the gallery's opening is a significant event: they bestow a kind of magic upon it.

For the gallery itself, the ceremonial opening was also its own opening onto a new life. It marked a new beginning, a new phase. For the Team, however, this was only partly the case. They had been initiates on the long and difficult journey; they had dealt with adversaries; they had pulled through. But what now? While they moved into a new phase – they would no longer be preoccupied with completing the gallery for October 12th – it was not quite clear whether the transformative process which they had undergone would result in a new status. Would they just return to their previous jobs and grades within the Museum? At this point it looked as though they might. Cathy and Ann both received rather abruptly worded letters just days after the opening telling them that they should attend a training course for the grade which they were on (G) before they worked at their temporary higher grade (F) on the exhibition. So rather than the rite of passage leading to a sense of renewal and effervescence as Van Gennep suggests is usually the case, it led more to a feeling of deflation – of 'coming down to earth' as Jan bluntly put it.

Entangled Identities and Authorship

In some respects the gallery's 'completion' is a fiction and the opening ceremony a ritual punctuation of a process that might otherwise have no clear end-point. Once the gallery is officially open the Team continues to work on it, mainly carrying out what they call 'snagging', (dealing with things which were not quite complete or with new 'hassles' that arise as the exhibition meets its audience). This includes getting some of the panels corrected, adjusting the colour on all of the videos, repairing the sugar centrifuge which is already breaking down and trying to find ways of protecting exhibits from the unexpectedly bad behaviour of visitors. The Team also has to write thank you letters to those involved and, in some cases, deal with sponsor complaints. (Heather refuses to answer her phone for days because she thinks that the Meat and Livestock Commission will be ringing to complain about the colour of the sausages, a problem she is still struggling with; and she receives a letter from the National Dairy Council saying that if the bottling machine cannot be improved the Museum 'should find a new way of representing bottling'.) They also have to prepare documentation for all of the exhibits, with lists of suppliers and other information, so that knowledge which is currently personally held by them can be transferred into more general knowledge, useable by others in the future. All of this is important work, and Jane manages to get a 'stay of execution' for the Team to remain together (on their current grades) until Christmas to complete it. The process is also, though, one of disentangling themselves from their own very intense and personalised involvement – a disentangling which is in many respects very difficult.

I am engaged in a similar process. After the exhibition has opened I continue to spend a good deal of time with the Team. Being there at this time is important for seeing how the gallery continues to be 'constructed', not only physically but also in the emerging discourse about it within and beyond the Museum. It is also important to see how the Foodies reflect back on their experience and the gallery, and it is an opportunity to check on paperwork as they tidy their desks. It is a time for chasing up various people for interviews, for hanging around the gallery itself and thinking about how to do research on visitors. But there is more to my continued presence in the Museum than this: I have become a bit addicted to the place, to the Team, and

I'm not sure that I'm ready for the degree of disentangling that I need in order to move to my own next stage of trying to make sense of it all. I feel almost 'lost' or 'bereft' now that the gallery is open at last and the heady hectic days are over.

Another reason why the disentangling process is difficult for the Foodies, however, is that, while formally their involvement with the gallery is coming to an end, talk about the exhibition within the Museum and beyond serves to entangle their professional identities with it still further. I have written earlier of how museum galleries (or collections) are often identified by reference to their curators and *vice-versa*. This identification, which has begun during the making of the exhibition, ramifies once the gallery is open to public view. No longer do other Museum staff need to rely upon rumours and leaks about the exhibition: now they can go and see for themselves what they think about it – and about Jane, Jan, Sue, Heather, Cathy and Ann. But, of course, their views are based not only upon their own observations but also on sources such as the comments of others and reviews of the gallery which appear in the media. These all circulate rapidly around the Museum, reviews being eagerly devoured and discussed, especially negative reviews. As Heather observes: 'People in the Museum love it when we have had a bad review.' One reason for this is the entanglement of professional identities with galleries. As Jane points out, these reactions are a consequence of the fact that Museum staff 'can't divorce what they think about the gallery from what they think about us.' And in the Foodies' case, Jane thinks, staff are predisposed to hope that the gallery will not do well because:

> As a team we did avoid a lot of the depression and flak that hit the rest of the Museum while we were working on the project. We were to an extent isolated from all the horrors that were going on in collections management. . . And we were definitely seen and to a certain extent are still seen as the Director's little buddies. . . . Some people were very jealous I suppose that we had a lot of access to the Director while we were doing the project and that he spent quite a lot of time with us. . . everybody got very uptight about that you know.

The others agree and explain how they think they were viewed by others in the Museum:

Heather: There was also a feeling that it was about time that we were slapped down actually.

Sue: Put us back in our places: 'Back in your box!'

Heather: There was definitely a feeling like that you know: 'They have had their moment of glory – now put them away.'

Sue: What would really actually enchant them even more is if we didn't get our promotions. That would actually be the epitome of joy for quite a lot of people. . . . Because they like people – there is this malicious thing – they like seeing people fail. It's quite extraordinary really. . . . People are very jealous by nature. . .

Cathy: . . .should see it as somebody succeeds for the whole system. They tend to see it individually: 'Oh, they've done very well, therefore it must look like I'm doing badly. . .'

Sue: . . .I mean, surely we are all here for the greater good of the institution not for our individual selves. Surely that is what the aim of this is all about.

Jane: Yes, but . . .this place is very anti-. Doesn't see things as a corporate venture at all. Sees it as perhaps theirs.

Team members point to a more general tension here: between the individualisation that goes on within the Museum and the fact that galleries are officially the product of the institution as a whole. (The names of the Team members do not appear on the list of credits at the gallery entrances.) Within the Museum, the opportunity to create an exhibition is a valued and scarce resource. This creates competition and jealousy among staff as they vie for this opportunity, the bestowing of which is largely in the hands of the Museum's Director. Consequently (in ways reminiscent of an analogy with the court of Elizabeth I that some Museum staff suggested to me), charges of favouritism abound, together with attempts to discredit those favourites so that the continued flow of scarce resources their way may be stemmed.

The tension here is also one of the politics of signatures and the local construction of authorship – of who is said to be the author of the exhibition. This is almost always an ambiguous matter. Here, the Team is saying on the one hand that the exhibition should be recognised as the product of the Museum as a whole – and we have seen earlier how Team members are sometimes willing to subsume their own work to the institution, to allow 'being the Science Museum' to override other ambitions they might have. On the other, they want individual recognition for their creativity (and the promotion that they think this should bring). Not only is the Science Museum positioned as an alternative author to the Team, but so too is the Museum's Director

– and, indeed, much that goes on in the Museum is perceived as entangled with his identity. Many reviews of Food for Thought discuss the gallery with reference only to the Director – as though it is his creation alone. This is a source of some annoyance to the Team. A review by cookery writer Prue Leith, for example, while mentioning Jane as 'the new gallery's curator', began:

> Neil Cossons, the 50-year-old director of the Science Museum is, in the museum world, something of a phenomenon. Anti-bureaucratic, pro-the-public, as keen (if not keener) on making museums exciting places to be as on improving the minds of the masses, he is the perfect man to produce the nation's first Gallery of Food and Nutrition.

The piece concluded: 'Dr Cossons doesn't think it can fail and, since he was the man behind Ironbridge, I don't think it will either.' Sue described to me the reception of this particular review:

> Four days after the gallery opened somebody came in – who shall remain nameless – and waved it and said 'have you seen this?' And of course we had. We had seen it two days ago. It was the sort of glee on that person's face as they came in the door – it really was quite visible. I just said 'Go away!'.

The fact that other Museum staff know that this is a review which the Team will not want to be reminded about – even though it is a very favourable account of the gallery itself – highlights the touchy nature of authorship and ownership. It also indicates the discomfort that the Team felt about the way in which the long labour of producing the gallery was sometimes talked about in terms of producing 'the Director's baby'. All of these constructions felt like an erasure of their own input and work, that also seemed to have a gendered dimension in the construction of their role as one of mere 'carrying'.[4] At the same time, the Director was not fully comfortable with the role that he had been allotted in this nativity story. When I interviewed him he seemed keen to try to disentangle himself from too much responsibility for the gallery, stressing, as I noted before, that he saw himself as having 'a very hands-off approach'. In some of his public statements too he seemed to be wanting to distance himself from the gallery, a stance also noted by some other Museum staff (who were always attuned to reading nuances and subtexts into the Director's utterances).

Also sometimes credited as author in reviews of the exhibition was Sainsbury's. This was, of course, the name which always appeared under the main title of the exhibition – Food for Thought: the Sainsbury Gallery – and it was probably unsurprising that it was read as an authorial signature (even its font looks signature-like) [Figure 7.7]. Moreover, there was a clear link between the subject-matter and the sponsor, making it seem likely that Sainsbury's would be the author in a way that would not be the case with, say, their sponsorship of a wing in the National Gallery. The fact that a member of the Sainsbury Gallery was present at press launches and made statements about the importance of helping people understand food served to cement this. A review in the *Daily Mail*, beginning and ending as follows, was typical in attributing the existence and aims of the gallery to Sainsbury's:

> No-one knows better than David Sainsbury of supermarket fame that we are sometimes baffled by the choice and variety of modern food. 'Forty years ago we could get fruit and vegetables only in their normal season. Packing and refrigeration was minimal', he says. 'The housewife was much more knowledgeable about the food she prepared. Now it is much more difficult because of the range of what we buy'. The answer to this problem was some lateral thinking. And yesterday the Science Museum unveiled their plans for a major new gallery dedicated to the impact of science and technology on food. . . . David Sainsbury said: 'The time couldn't be more right. The problem at the moment is a lack of information. People need the confidence to make up their own mind about what they should eat'.[5]

Figure 7.7 The politics of signatures: the gallery name.

This piece depicts Sainsbury's giving the Science Museum the task of creating a gallery which would help the supermarket aim of giving people confidence in their food choices. For this reviewer this seems to be wholly acceptable. For others, however, it was not. The accusation that the gallery was 'sponsor-led', and in the lap of the food industry, was also made in reviews of the gallery. The account by Derek Cooper on Radio Four's 'The Food Programme' (broadcast three days before the opening of the gallery) was one of the most damning of such reviews. Derek Cooper asks about the presence of Sainsbury's and McDonald's, each of which Jane justifies ('They're [Sainsbury's] a very good example of a grocer's shop in the 1920s. . .'), and whether essentially the gallery is 'saying that 1989 is better than 1889', to which Jane agrees, observing that it is because in 1989 there is more choice. The programme winds up saying that the gallery is a 'non-controversial approach to Britain's food. . . . it is ducking all the issues. It offers very little real food for thought at all'. The identity of the gallery, such reviewers were saying, had become much too entangled with the identity of the supermarket.

Responses and Reflections

What did the Foodies make of these criticisms? And how did they themselves see the exhibition now that it was completed? Why did they think that it had turned out as it had?

In response to negative reviews the Foodies were often defensive and bullish, particularly to other Museum staff, precisely because they knew that their own identities were also at stake. 'I'll defend my areas to the hilt' announced Sue the day after 'The Food Programme' review. Being up-beat about the exhibition and pointing out the positive as well as the negative reviews was part of a continued impression-management in which the Team also sought to influence the information circulating in the Museum.

But the Foodies were also rather surprised by the amount of negative coverage that the exhibition received. To some extent this was because more press coverage had been sought than for previous exhibitions. In addition, Food was covered by the national and popular media to a greater extent than most Science Museum exhibitions (which tended to be covered only by more specialist publications). This was because of the 'topical' subject matter: food. It was also because of the greater interest that museums were generating in the media generally, especially in the new context of charging for admission. And it was in these terms that most reviews were framed. Thus, some reviews looked for information relevant to the current food scares and controversies, seeking, it seemed, an authoritative answer from the Museum. This was evident at the press launch at the opening and the Director had to repeatedly emphasise that the exhibition 'had been overtaken by events', thus it could not cover all the most recent matters of concern (the 'inertia problem' of the exhibition medium discussed in the previous chapter). Also, Jane tried to point out that scientists were not always decided about these matters and the gallery represented this uncertainty too. Reviews framed in terms of museological concerns were likely to point to the existence of charging (as in the cartoon depicted in Figure 7.8) and of sponsorship, and to suggest not only possible 'sponsor-bias' but also an 'aggressive populism', dumbing down and a denigration of 'the power of objects'.[6]

The Foodies frequently complained that the reviews were 'unfair', that they had 'missed the point' of what the exhibition was trying to do, that the reviewers had failed to 'read it [the exhibition text] properly', and pointed to aspects of the exhibition or even areas where supposed omissions were mentioned. For example: in response to a

Figure 7.8 Charging at the check-out: cartoon of Food for Thought. Courtesy of Colin Wheeler.

critical review in *Hotel and Catering Management,* which stated that the exhibition did not say anything about cash-crops, Sue is annoyed that they do not acknowledge what she has included on famine; and Jane points out that of course they hadn't discussed cash crops because this was concerned with agriculture and thus beyond the scope of the gallery. Heather is surprised that her inclusion of McDonald's has caused so much criticism because as she saw it she was simply saying that 'this is what is actually happening in 1989' and she does not see inclusion as endorsement [Figure 7.9]. More generally, the Team also dismiss accusations such as those of 'dumbing down' by accusing the reviewers of elitism and failing to recognise what the exhibition was trying to do: 'to speak to ordinary people'. What the Team's responses also show, however, is that they want the exhibition to be read thoroughly, like a book, and as a text in itself, in terms of the messages and objectives which they had set out. Instead, for the most part, reviewers 'looked at' the gallery rather than read it; the 'messages' that they picked up were not drawn from what was written on panels but from the three-dimensional exhibits and the impressions they drew from them. Furthermore, their accounts were framed not by the internal pyramid

Figure 7.9 Representation as endorsement? McDonald's in the Sainsbury Gallery.

of interlinking aims but by external concerns about food or the way that museums were going more generally. It was these alternative framings that the Team had not fully bargained for.

As the Team acknowledge, however, the exhibition does not make its rationale very clear. Heather reflectively points out: 'We don't say anywhere that we are covering the most popular food in 1989. I think if we had said that explicitly somewhere. . . We have no explanation for why we lighted on the areas that we did light on.' Looking back after the gallery is open the Foodies are, amongst themselves, critical of other things about the gallery too. One of them is its overall feel. This they sometimes describe as 'not as lively as I'd expected', 'it's a bit flat', 'lifeless', 'I think we felt there ought to have been a bit more excitement there'. This is sometimes related to a 'loss of quirkiness' – the main outcome of the Rethink as the Team describe it. The demand for clear messages is regarded as having eliminated odd things which were included just because of the Team's attraction to them. But they equate this loss with one of individuality and 'life' (rather than questioning other aspects of the Rethink procedure).

Heather also explains that the opened gallery seems less original and different than she had expected:

> I think my greatest problem was that it doesn't look so very different from everywhere else. I think that we all thought that it was going to be – and whilst it is wildly different from other things in the Science Museum – it's very similar to things in other museums, local government museums, and all those. So I think my complaint would be that it isn't so very different.

Much of this, they suggest, is a visual matter. In particular, 'it's still panels and cases and things to do. I didn't originally want it to be like that' (Jane). Yet none of the Team members seems sure quite how it turned out like this and what they might have done instead. Jane suggests that the problem was money: 'Once we got the costings in for the overall building and things it became very clear that there wasn't enough money to do very adventurous things. I mean we had to go back to the panel.' More generally, the idea that money was the ultimate limiting factor in the exhibition's shortcomings runs like a mantra through the Foodies' reflections. It is understood as something incontestable and beyond the agency of those involved.

But there are other suggestions too. Some Team members think that the designers should have come up with some 'creative solutions'. ('I think it's probably something up to our designers to be honest because I don't know that there is any other way of getting all that information across': Jane). And, more generally, while they had specifically wanted designers who would not 'try to lead on content' and while they had bitterly opposed some of the cuts that they felt the designers had forced them to make, Heather suggests that in retrospect that 'we were very curator-led in the end and it's backfired a bit'. Other designers, she thinks, 'would have just said "you can't have a panel there whether you want one or not. There isn't room. You've got to change your ideas"'. The general sense of insufficient 'liveliness' of the gallery they think may be partly due to the designers' choice of a 'muted colour scheme' – fashionable grey carpeting and walls and cream panels with splashes of primary colours. Accusations that the gallery layout was 'confusing' should, they think, also be directed at the designers who had not made the organisation clear enough. The designers themselves disagree about the lack of 'liveliness' and the colour scheme, though they suggest that there should have been 'more visual punctuation' in the gallery. Presenting a layout is, however, always a difficult matter because, the designers think, nobody ever stops to look at an overall plan of a gallery. From their point of view, trying to deal with so many staff and such a large gallery was a difficult task and 'not the ideal way of creating something that really hangs together'. Although they agree that there are too many panels, their perception is that they pushed the Team to reduce this number as far as they felt they could within the difficult circumstances of the Rethink and the time slippage that this generated.

In response to some of the criticisms about the politics of the exhibition the Team acknowledge that there were some sections of the exhibition, notably Shopping, that 'took on a life of [their] own', an expression which again illustrates the extent to which the Team felt that their own agency in the matter was depleted. The way that the Shopping section, which lies at what is the most used entrance to the exhibition, 'has Sainsbury's written all over it', is seen as particularly unfortunate. Part of this was due to the archivist's insistence on authenticity (and thus the prominent display of the name) in the reproduction of the 1920s shop, and to the replacement of some foods by Sainsbury's labels. Additionally, however, the tins and packages supplied for the interactive supermarket checkout scanner are all Sainsbury's' – just because these were supplied free by the company. As Sue observes: 'It's cost basis – practicality of replacements. It's easier for us to do it through Sainsbury's. And OK you have, there's a compromise there, you lose perhaps, people might say, integrity for practicality.' Nevertheless, she feels that the purpose of the exhibit was to illustrate the use of bar-codes and in the terms in which she intended it, the exhibit is successful.

This kind of reasoning, in which presence can always be legitimated in relation to intended aims and objectives, is, as we have seen, common in the making of the exhibition. So too is legitimisation in terms of the nature and aims of the institution. In discussions about the way that the gallery has turned out the Team make comments such as: 'We are a museum of science and technology – it's not our job to tell people what to eat. We have to talk about processes'; 'The Corporate Plan is to raise the public understanding of science – how can we then rush off on a completely different tack?'; 'I don't think that we considered any other approach really to be quite honest. I don't see how you can in a museum of science and industry. . . We were keen to *add* the social history in.' As Sue explained, 'If we had to cut. . ., science and technology would have to remain in because objectively that had to be so in our gallery by definition of the nature of our Museum.' While Cathy expresses doubts about this 'science and industry' approach, she too thinks that there is an inevitability to the gallery's stance:

> What can you expect though with sponsorship? It's also being the museum. You can't expect ever to say anything that isn't biased. If we had wanted to do a green version of things the Director and Terry, never mind the sponsors, would never have let us get away with it.

Whether Cathy and the others are right or not about what might have been allowed (and it is difficult to know given that it wasn't put to the test), what their words highlight is their perception that only certain approaches were going to be possible in the Science Museum. This was their own 'secular theodicy'.[7] It defined the horizons of the thinkable from the very beginning. It also meant that other ways in which the gallery might be read, and in particular dwelling on the unsaid or unrepresented, were only rarely countenanced.

In this chapter we have moved from the final stages of preparing the exhibition, through the transformative moment of its ceremonial opening and on to some of the reflections on it by the Team themselves and reviewers. But as the Team sometimes pointed out (especially in response to reviews which they classified as elitist or specialist), what really mattered with an exhibition like this were the visitors. The proof of the pudding, so to speak, was in the eating. In the case of this exhibition, which had been explicitly populated with virtual visitors of an 'ordinary people' variety, what visitors would make of it would be crucial. It would be crucial within the Science Museum's public understanding of science approach and cultural revolution more generally. So what did visitors make of it? It is to this that we turn in the next chapter.

Notes

1. Van Gennep 1960. Originally published 1909.
2. Turner 1967.
3. See also La Fontaine 1985, and on the 'deletion of work' Bowker and Star 1999 (especially ch. 8).
4. See Delaney 1991 for an anthropological analysis of such gendered conceptions.
5. *Daily Mail* 23.3.1989
6. Deyan Sudjic 'Science Museum offers food for thought' in *Sunday Correspondent* 7.1.90
7. This term is from Herzfeld 1992.

The Active Audience and the Politics of Appropriation

Sometimes, especially when school parties 'descend' (to use the word often used by museum staff), the Food gallery throngs with noisy, 'busy' visitors. There is scrabbling and pushing as children snatch tins and packets from the shelves at the checkout and scan them; receipts – churned out by the till – scatter the floor; at the chocolate mousse pot visitors press buttons to turn a plate of chips blue, they pump air into flour, expanding its volume, and, at the other end of the gallery, they peddle frenetically on the exercise bikes and race around pressing buttons and piecing together puzzles which show the nutritional components of pizza and fish and chips [Figures 8.1 and 8.2]. But at other times the gallery receives just a slow trickle of visitors and it is rarely as busy as Launch Pad or even galleries such as Space on the ground floor, and some parts of the gallery, especially the displays of production processes, seldom teem. Some visitors stroll through, hands in pockets, casually surveying the exhibition, only occasionally tempted to stand a little closer to a panel or to peer into a reconstruction. Others flit from one thing that catches their eye to another – a visitor type which has been called a 'butterfly' in contrast to the 'strollers' who have been characterised as 'fish'.[1] Some visitors begin with studious attention (owls perhaps?) but then give up and metamorphose into either butterflies or fish. There are also 'ants' – visitors who move purposively as though looking for something in particular; there are those who back-track or beat a hasty retreat, others who seem bemused or lost, and some who are definitely more interested in their companions than anything on the gallery walls.

This chapter looks at what visitors make of the exhibition, the creation of which we have ethnographically followed in the earlier chapters, and asks whether these visitors, who variously scuttle or

Figure 8.1 Visitors getting their hands-on at the check-out.

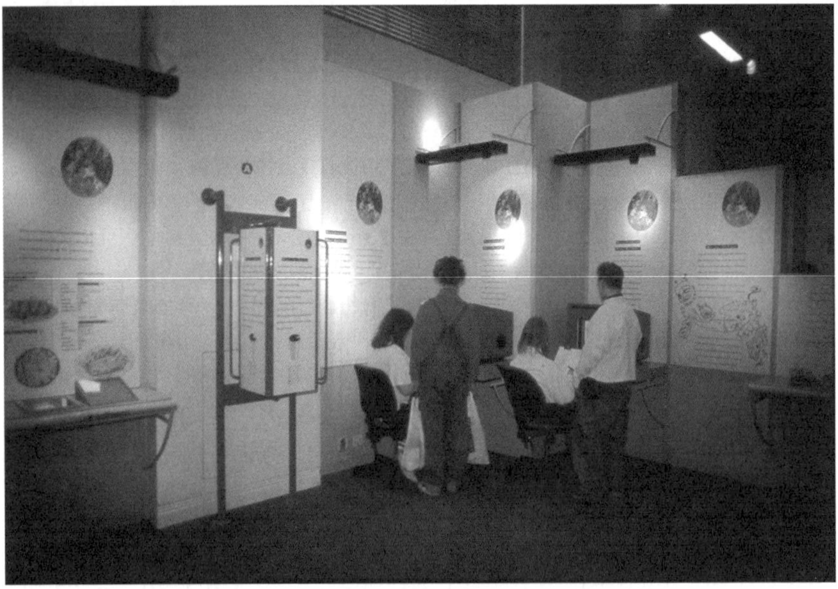

Figure 8.2 Getting the message? Visitors in Food and the Body.

saunter through the now opened gallery, bear any relationship to the phantoms who helped shape that display. More generally, this chapter is concerned with the question of how audiences engage with, or relate to, exhibitions; and how this can be researched.

In this chapter, I describe visitor research on Food for Thought which I carried out with my colleagues.[2] This research aimed to consider the reception of the exhibition in relation to some of the dreams and virtual visitors implicated in its making and also, more broadly, in terms which visitors themselves employed. That is, it sought to understand how visitors culturally framed their experience: how they recoded as well as decoded the exhibition. In so doing, the research sought to go beyond the often rather cognitive emphasis on 'what visitors have learned' or whether they have 'got' or 'not got' the 'messages' intended, which has been typical of a good deal of museum visitor research.[3] Such an approach characterises the audience as relatively 'passive'. It is based on a conveyor-belt model, like that of scientific literacy noted in chapter two, in which information does or does not succeed in being effectively 'transmitted' to the public, and in which the emphasis is often on discovering barriers (which might include, say, educational ability or pre-existing 'false' ideas) that might impede this process. This approach has been characteristic of some work in, and also received criticism within, various fields, including cultural and media studies and the sociology of science (with particular reference to the public understanding of science), as well (though generally more recently) as museology.[4]

In response to this criticism a new wave of research has emerged which has begun from a premise of the audience as 'active', as constructively appropriating cultural products in potentially myriad ways. Yet some of this new wave research has also been questioned for its tendency to celebrate uncritically anything that audiences or consumers do as 'active' and to regard these as manifestations of 'agency' or even 'resistance'.[5] As we have seen in the virtual construction of visitors discussed in chapter six, the conceptual conflations involved construe 'activity' as in itself a manifestation of 'democracy'. However, as I argued there, this may involve a framing of activity or participation – as well as 'choice' more generally – in such a way that rather than opening up possibilities for critical engagement these are actually restricted. Thus, rather than just reading off 'democracy' or 'empowerment' from 'activity' or 'choice-making', it is important to try, as in earlier chapters, to understand just how activities are conceptualised and performed by those involved, what kinds of questions are asked and, equally crucially, what are not.

Another feature of some of the new wave research – sometimes called 'the new audience studies', 'the new revisionism' or 'the popular culture project'[6] – is an emphasis on the diversity of individual interpretations amongst audiences, which, as Roger Silverstone has pointed out, is itself again conflated with activity.[7] While it has surely been important to highlight the fact that there is rarely a single uniform response to any particular cultural product, the specificity of cultural products is sometimes ignored.[8] The other problem with this approach is that the notion of audience variability is sometimes extended to suggest that the range of potential readings is so infinite that analysis is almost redundant. This was a perspective sometimes voiced in the Museum and at other museum events in which I participated, some museum staff suggesting that as the possible range of visitor interpretations was infinite, it was hardly worth trying to take them into account.

As will be described in more detail below, the visitor research in Food for Thought did show differences amongst visitors. However, amidst the variety were also certain patterns which, while not necessarily common to all those studied, could be seen as part of a repertoire of prevalent interpretations. These varying interpretations and modes of engaging with the exhibition did not seem from our study to map neatly onto any particular social variables – no distinct differences between, say, men and women emerged from the account – though our research methodology may have made us less able to map differences in this way (see below). Nevertheless, neither did the patterns identified seem to be groundless or the chance outcome of purely individualised constructions. On the contrary, they needed to be understood in relation to wider types of cultural framing (concerning, for example, the nature of a museum visit or of science) and also to more specific cultural accounts produced from the encounter with this exhibition, such as issues related to the subject matter, the exhibitionary media and specificities of content and display.[9]

Catching Cultural Accounts

The research on visitors to Food for Thought was rather different from the ethnographic research on the exhibition's making. Visitors' own experience of the exhibition was relatively fleeting: typically, they would come just once, for half an hour or so. Research with the visitors was likewise relatively fleeting: about twenty minutes discussion with them after their visit. This was coupled with a degree of general hanging around the gallery and observing, visiting ourselves and with friends and relatives, as well as discussions with the museum staff such as warders and explainers (whose task was to help visitors use the interactive exhibits in particular and to give help more generally). The Foodies carried out some of their own visitor research and also struggled to deal with some of the consequences of visitor misbehaviour in the exhibition. This also informed our understanding of visiting. Overall, however, the research on visitors was framed by the encounter with the exhibition itself rather than the lives of those visiting; though some of our questions were oriented towards the place of the visit within those lives.

Because an encounter with an exhibition is three-dimensional and physical rather than purely cognitive and verbal, part of our research involved direct observation of visitors in the gallery. This entailed some fairly unstructured general observation and also more structured 'tracking' – that is, following visitors through the gallery and charting their movements, recording which exhibits they spent time on, what they said about them (if this was loud enough to overhear), and their overall length of visit.[10] Partly because we thought that interaction among visitors would be of interest we decided to focus the research on small groups rather than single individuals. We further justified this to ourselves in terms of the fact that the gallery was specifically aimed at 'family groups'. Consequently, we chose to track groups which consisted minimally of one 'child' (somebody looking under about 16) and one 'adult' (somebody who looked over about 18), and we aimed for as broad a range of possible participants as possible.[11] In addition, we tracked groups entering the gallery from two different entrances ('Shopping' or 'Food and the Body') in proportion to the overall usage of these (which we monitored first): almost three-quarters entered through 'Shopping'.[12]

After groups had been tracked, the researcher (most often Gilly Heron, sometimes me) approached the group, explained that we were from Brunel University, that we were studying the exhibition and asked whether the visitors would be willing to be interviewed. Not all did so. In total forty-two groups (composed of 123 individuals) were both tracked and interviewed.[13] Group interviews took place in a room adjacent to the gallery and were tape-recorded. These interviews lasted on average nineteen and a half minutes, the shortest being ten minutes and the longest fifty-five.

We began with an open question which aimed to elicit visitors' own accounts of their experience in the exhibition: 'Could you please describe where you went and what you saw?' and followed this up with, 'What did you think of the exhibition? Please feel free to say whatever you want'. We used prompt questions where we felt that we needed clarification or further information, and tried to draw in all members of the group (as there was sometimes a tendency for just one member – generally one of the adults – to adopt a role of spokesperson). This was followed by a semi-structured interview with questions concerned with the following (the full interview schedule is in the Appendix):

(a) *The visit* – our interest here was in the way visitors framed their visit, their motives for coming, and their patterns of museum visiting and leisure activities in general;
(b) *The exhibition* – as well as the account of their experience we also asked about who they thought had created the exhibition, about its content, whether it was 'scientific', and how they saw it in relation to other exhibitions;
(c) *Science* – here we asked about interest in, and views of, science;[14]
(d) *Visitors* – socio-demographic information on age, occupation and levels of formal education.

In discussing some of the results from this visitor research below my intention is to focus on a number of matters which are of particular relevance to this exhibition in terms of issues raised earlier in the book but which also have wider implications. I begin with the ways in which visitors framed their visit, for this partly shapes the way in which they read the exhibition. I then explore some of the ways in which they talked about this particular exhibition and how they interpreted it. What is of particular interest here, and of broader relevance, is that visitors seemed predisposed to read the exhibition in ways which had not been anticipated by the creators but which took cues from the exhibition itself. These cues included the exhibition media, the nature of the institution and perceptions about the genre and topic, as we shall see in the following sections.

The Visit: 'on the List'

Why did visitors come to Food for Thought or to the Science Museum at all? How did they talk about this? In the responses to a question about why they had come I was struck that visitors often seemed to employ the idea of a list or programme. For example:

> It's just on the list isn't it? (Research manager from Brussels visiting with wife and son)[15]

> We had a list of things to do and one of them was the Science Museum [laughs] (Man from Sussex visiting with wife and with three children from Canada)

> We've planned a programme of various things. The Science Museum was on the programme always and it just so happened that this is the way we've fitted it into our programme, but it was always a definite slot, always (Male economic consultant from Ireland visiting with twelve-year-old daughter).

The idea of lists is analytically suggestive, as Jean Lave has suggested in her work on supermarket shopping. It allows us to try to identify wider socio-cultural patterns as well as to consider visitors' own strategies for compiling their more individualised lists.[16] So what sorts of lists feature 'the Science Museum' as a place to visit? From this research four could be identified: a day out, life-cycle, place and education.

A Day Out

The characterisation of the visit to the Science Museum as 'a day out' was predominant in the interview responses. As such, it was part of leisure activity set apart from ordinary daily practice – 'a kind of routinized non-routine' as John Urry puts it.[17] The Science Museum was on this metaphorical list of places set apart for demarcated 'special' time. Sometimes important to this idea of a 'day out' was the notion of 'family'. This was a 'family day out' – an opportunity for the family to be together. Some visitors talked of the difficulties of trying to find activities which would interest all members of the family: a male sales manager from Bedfordshire, visiting with his wife and two children (seven and four) explained, for example, that Food was a good exhibition because of its capacity to interest different family members – 'Anything that's of interest to the family as a whole... I mean, you know, it's gotta... when you go to something everybody's interested in it'. Some visitors explained their presence in the museum in terms of school holidays, perhaps saying that they liked to do something 'different' during them; and several were there to celebrate the birthday of a child, again showing that the Science Museum as a special site could help demarcate special time and special social relations. This also connects to one of the more specific framings of motivation to visit, that of life-cycle.

Life-cycle

Some visitors talked about visiting the Science Museum as something which should be done at a particular stage in the life-cycle (especially between about eight and twelve years old). There was often a sense of imperativeness about this – of the visit as a naturalised part of the life-cycle. For example, a female barrister said of bringing an eleven-year-old relative: 'I think we mainly wanted to bring A because we've been and it's part of his childhood'. In three-quarters of our interviews at least one adult had visited the Science Museum previously and a semi-nostalgic motive of providing the same experience for the children was evident in many interviews. For example, a male estate agent, visiting with his wife, their two sons (aged seven and two) as well as the mother's brother and an adult male friend, explained: 'We planned to bring the children to show them round the museums. It's something we did as children and we thought it would be good for them to do it'. As this example suggests, bringing children could also be something of an excuse for adults to have a reason to revisit the museum themselves.

Place

The Science Museum was often talked about as one of the 'things to do' in London (or sometimes, for overseas visitors, in England). For example, a twelve-year-old girl visiting with her mother and a friend told us: 'We haven't been to London for a long time and we're doing, like, different visits and this is just one of the places we wanted to come.' Again, the museum is one possible item on the longer list of possible places to visit. This is sometimes further specified by type of location, especially 'the museums' or 'the tourist sites'. Visitors were sometimes 'doing the museums' or going to other tourist sites (including Madame Tussauds, the London Dungeon, Buckingham Palace and the Docklands Railway). The language of 'doing' is perhaps of interest here, suggesting a list of things which can be ticked-off when they have been dealt with.

Education

While most of our visitors did not specifically give education as a motive for visiting the museum, there were some who did. A maths teacher, for example, told us: 'It's educational. That's what you come to a museum for really, isn't it? To learn.' Moreover, some visitors contrasted the museum with other kinds of leisure activities, especially theme parks (for example, one girl was visiting instead of going on a school trip to a theme park). A primary teacher from Twickenham visiting with two teenage relatives from Edinburgh explained: 'We do one educational visit and a few not so educational visits [laughs]!' There were also a few visitors who had a specific interest either in the subject matter of food, such as a mother and daughter who thought it would help with the school and college work that they were both doing. More often visitors had an interest in another subject in the Museum such as Space or Trains and had also visited Food because it was new. Visitors with a specific subject interest were more likely to be frequent visitors to the Museum (some were making their fourth visit in the course of a year) than were visitors on the life-cycle list who were often making their first return visit in twenty years or so.

For any visitor to the exhibition, therefore, their own motives for visiting might include a combination of these or perhaps other factors. There was, for example, one group which had intended to visit the Natural History Museum but had made a mistake and ended up in the Science Museum instead. This should, perhaps, be assigned the category of a particular type of visit (though not a specific list) for some staff claim that many Science Museum visitors do indeed really mean to end up at the museum next door!

Reading the Exhibition: Cues and Connections

Visitors undoubtedly bring much 'outside' information – drawn from their own lives and experiences – to bear as they visit the exhibition or talk about it. In some cases, exhibits become props for personalised, often nostalgic, accounts. The reconstructed kitchens and shop were particularly likely to produce these, with especially older visitors often standing in front of them and reminiscing about the kitchens and shops they had known. Exercise bikes and information about diet, as well as the thinning or fattening mirrors, often produced (mostly negative) comments by visitors about their own bodies; the food poisoning exhibit could produce memories of bouts endured by visitors themselves; and exhibits about the making of jam or bread, say, might lead to visitors talking about their own experiences of making these. Sometimes, however, the exhibition acted as a cue for much more 'exhibition distant' accounts, such as a child, on seeing the stuffed cat in one of the kitchens, talking about a pet cat that had been run over or the exclamation from one visitor about hating gherkins on seeing Henry Heinz's marketing gherkin. That exhibitions can provide a topic for group discussion – especially where it is pleasant and nostalgic rather than distressing – is undoubtedly part of their appeal.[18] Two female pensioners whom I met in the gallery one day were reminiscing about all kinds of subjects which the exhibition prompted and they explained their enjoyment of being provided with cues to do so: 'It's nice to be reminded, you see, taken back a bit. We enjoy being nostalgic.' She added, however, lest I think otherwise: 'Don't get me wrong. We don't spend all our time being nostalgic and looking back. We're interested in the new things too. But, yes, it's nice to have the opportunity now and again.'

Among the diverse personalised accounts, there were some themes which recurred, especially those of the body and the past. In addition, however, there was a related tendency to read the exhibition as being 'about' certain topics. The latter arose at various points in the interviews, particularly in visitors' general descriptions of the gallery and in response to a question about its theme. The former was especially interesting to me because what became evident in many accounts of the exhibition was that visitors gave an account in which they linked together disparate exhibits into a narrative which did not relate directly to the physical sequence which they had encountered. Moreover, in doing so, they also conceptually linked exhibits which had not been linked by the Food Team and which were not formally linked in the rigorous conceptual framework that the Team had struggled so hard to create. Two narratives, in particular, occurred many times in the interviews. These were a historical narrative – a story of transition from the old days to the present – and a health narrative, about which foods are good for you and which are not.

The History

In creating a historical narrative, visitors often talked of the historical reconstructions – especially the 1920s Sainsbury's, the delivery bicycle, the market woman, the chestnut seller, the larders, the tea-house, and the kitchens, often alongside 'newer' cases, such as the checkout scanner and the McDonald's. These would be talked about as though there was a theme mapped spatially into the gallery, moving from 'the old days' into the present. As a journalist and her visiting relative (niece?) from the US put it: *Journalist*: '[It] was well laid out, just sort of progressed from, you know, one logical thing to the next', *Relative*: We started out in the modern part and came through the history into the 1900s'. That there is no such neat historical development written directly into the layout of the gallery – and other visitors perceived it too – illustrates the power of this kind of reading. It is, perhaps, not surprising given that this is a typical mode of presenting exhibitions and one which is very common in relation to the kind of media which these visitors select.

While many visitors talked about the theme of the exhibition being 'food through the ages' or 'history of food in the shops and what it's like, or in the home', and while all saw the exhibition as emphasising the degree of change, there were different views over whether or not this was a good or bad thing and what the exhibition was saying about this. We did not specifically raise this issue ourselves but many visitors spontaneously talked about either things having been 'better in the old days' ('less of all that processing') or as having improved over time (the larders and the kitchens were both mentioned in this respect). What may have been happening here was that visitors were reading the account from already decided positions (they had pre-formed ideas about whether things had got better or worse on the food front) though the nature of the display, which was not altogether clear on the matter, may well have also allowed for some ambiguity. Interestingly, visitors tended to offer a clear-cut 'better' or 'worse' account rather than to suggest that it might be a mixture of the two (though in one interview participants argued about which it was). This may have been because they expected a museum exhibition to be giving a single perspective on the matter.

Good Foods, Bad Foods

The reading in of a categorical statement from the Museum was evident in the other prevalent narrative, that of 'good and bad foods'. Here, visitors again linked together exhibits from different parts of the exhibition, especially those concerned with additives (in the chocolate mousse pot), the section with the distorting mirrors, silhouettes and scales, and – at the opposite end of the exhibition – that on nutrition. Again, common display media seemed to prompt visitors to make these linkages, many of these being fairly interactive areas. Of interest here was not only that visitors made connections between exhibits that were neither spatially nor conceptually linked according to the Team's own plans, but that they specifically interpreted the exhibition contrary to a 'message' that the Team had hoped to convey. This message was, as one of the panels stated, that 'no one food in isolation is "good" or "bad"'. Several visitors said that the gallery was about saying 'what is good for you' or about 'healthy eating'. As a female accountant from Bishops Stortford put it: 'There's a lot of emphasis on healthy eating and what are the right foods to be eating.' A twelve-year-old girl from Surrey was specific that the exhibition was about 'good foods and bad foods', and a male lorry driver from Southend stated: 'What's good for you and what's bad for you, ain't it?'

Of course, in many respects there is a marked theme in the exhibition about a healthy diet and what a wood-turner from Huntingdonshire described as 'sensible eating'. What was interesting, though, was that visitors did not pick up the information about not regarding particular foods as good or bad, or, for the most part, about scientific uncertainty (on which, more below), but seemed more likely to read the exhibition as giving them fairly didactic information about what should and what should not be eaten. Again, this shows a tendency to read the exhibition in a way which is characteristic of other types of exhibitions – in this case health education exhibitions.

Vanishing Technology

The 'official' main theme of Food for Thought – the theme that crystallised out of the Rethink – was 'to show the impact of science and technology on our food'. A few visitors did suggest that the gallery was about this, the most clearest articulation being from a home economics teacher from Sussex who stated: 'I thought the theme was obviously going through the ages looking at the way [food]'s been processed and changed. . . how technology has changed food and made it more healthy.' Few visitors, however, mentioned science, technology or food processing in response to questions about what the exhibition was about, which we found in many respects surprising given that this was an exhibition in the Science Museum and that the exhibition contained many large processing machines. Part of the reason for not expressing the theme of the gallery in these terms may have been that the topic was not for the most part perceived in this way and that, as the two narratives discussed above suggest, alternative framings took precedence partly because of the topic and partly because of some of the display media. Indeed, when, later in the interviews, we specifically asked visitors whether they had expected such a topic to be covered in the Science Museum, the great majority said not.

Also contributing to the infrequency with which science, technology and processing were mentioned as themes of the exhibition was the fact that half of our visitor sample missed out the Food in the Factory section of the exhibition altogether and half of those who did enter it walked through it very quickly. Thus, although conceptually central to the main message of the exhibition, and physically central in the exhibition's layout, this section was marginalised in the way that it was appropriated by visitors. One likely reason for this was that, shorn of the social and cultural dimensions which were once to have been part of it, it seemed relatively 'lifeless' and so fewer visitors chose to take this route. Managerially pasteurised, factory processing was, it seems, less palatable to the consumers after all.

Choice, Transgression and Confusion

Food was regarded by its makers as challenging 'authoritarian' exhibitionary modes in its attempt to remove barriers between visitors and exhibits. Hands-on interactive exhibits were central to this but the principle was extended as far as possible to inventoried objects too. Another area perceived as challenging was the offer of choice to visitors – choice over route, over types of media, and over content. So how did visitors respond to these?

Visitors that we interviewed frequently stated how much they liked being able to 'do and touch', this being a point which children often made (in response to a general question about what they liked about the exhibition). For example, a ten-year-old girl said: 'It's fun. There's a lot of things to touch and do . . . hands-on and things. So it's very interesting', and a twelve-year-old boy told us: '[I] like this – where you can do things and touch things.' Some, such as a seventeen-year-old girl, specifically contrasted this with reading: 'It's nice. You could do things. It's not just like reading. Like take part, which is really good.' And others, such as a forty-three-year-old man, contrasted it favourably with 'more traditional' Science Museum exhibitions: 'It's so refreshing to see something where people can interact with the exhibits, take part and actually touch things. It's quite different to, for instance, the Science Museum of my childhood when everything was in glass cases and you had to read a lot of very small print to know anything.' For a few visitors, however, there was not enough to do and some specifically complained about the amount of what one, tellingly, described as 'written work'. A woman explained of her children aged ten and twelve, 'They have to stand and read and they don't want to. They want to get in and do it. And I think that's a big criticism of it really.'

Ironically, the popularity of the hands-on dimension of the exhibition was one of the main sources of consternation for the Team members who had, during its making, seen interactivity and allowing touch as vitally important. The problem was that some visitors were *too* active. Some of this seemed to be outright pilfering and vandalism in a relatively unprotected exhibition: items like knives and forks and fake food from exhibits 'walked', pieces were broken off one exhibit, and fake carrots were stuffed in the mouths of the figures in the Sainsbury's reconstruction. But the bigger problem seemed to be the mix of exhibits itself which all Team members decided 'just doesn't work'. What happens, Sue suggested, was that this 'hypes people up. . . so they have a go at an interactive and they start wrecking everything else'. She described some visitors climbing on the tea-packer and 'hanging off it like monkeys'. By the time that we carried out our visitor research the exhibition had already been altered to some extent to try to fend off over-enthusiastic visitors: rope barriers and perspex panels had been put up to protect some of the most frequently damaged exhibits and others had been repositioned. The Team had not, however, gone as far as putting 'Do not touch' or 'a big red cross' on some of these exhibits, although they had considered doing so at a particularly low point of despair.

The idea of choice was not something about which we specifically asked visitors but there was nevertheless material in the interviews which can be interestingly read in relation to this. In giving an account of the gallery, not only did many visitors reconstruct it into the narratives discussed above, but also many seemed perplexed about not being able to detect a clear route and narrative. Moreover, as well as those accounts which reconfigured the exhibition into a story of 'the history' or 'good foods and bad foods', there were many others which jumped from one thing to another with no order that we could discern and with no correlation with the gallery layout.[Figure 6.3] For example, a trainee teacher and her nine year-old son gave the following account of the exhibition:

> *Boy*: We went all around it and we saw, we saw the computer thing of how they make Stilton cheese. I thought that was good. We went all around to – I liked the McDonald's bit where they showed the McDonald's and all the other things
>
> *Woman*: That, it was interesting the way you perceive your own body and they all change shape from the fat one. Yes, it was interesting looking

> at the old kitchens and that but more so looking at the technological and that Tetrapak thing. And, you know, I go to Sainsbury's always to do my shopping and it was interesting to see some of the things that you see on the shelves, and some of the additives and things.

Some visitors themselves described their own movements through the exhibition as 'totally erratic', 'peripatetic', 'skated over' or 'just here and there', reflecting the apparent 'free-association' of the accounts. Our own observation notes too are full of words such 'drifting with occasional "dipping in"', 'a bit erratic' or 'wandered'. Some visitors assumed that they had somehow done the gallery in the wrong order. For example:

> I found it a bit confusing, perhaps because we came in at the output end of it. There's no clear direction indicating which end you should approach the gallery. And obviously it would be better to deal with the basic nutrition and things, and move around the gallery with the marketing and output of food as the final piece. That's a bit confusing. And perhaps a clearer direction indicating that you should come in via the clock exhibition would have been of some use (a local government officer).

Others also found the lack of a sense of direction disorienting:

> I had difficulty following the theme through it. So it wasn't, there didn't appear to be a predetermined way of walking through it. And I might have preferred that – that they were taking me through a sort of ordered thing. Maybe they were and I just didn't pick it up that easily (employee in airforce).

> You feel a slight bewilderment, a bit like a rat in a maze, not knowing quite which way to go (wood-carver).

This sense of 'bewilderment', of not being quite sure what was going on, seemed to affect visitors' own sense of their abilities to comment critically on the exhibition. A phraseology of 'deep' and 'superficial' was used by various visitors, and they suggested that they were not in a position for making a 'deep reading'. One implied reason for this was the overall nature of their visit – they were there on a day out, perhaps to celebrate a birthday or relive an previous visit, and so were not especially motivated to probe the exhibition content too deeply. For example, a barrister explained: 'We didn't actually come in with the thought of trying to find out about food. It was a case of it was there and we looked at it and it was interesting and off we went. So it's not a case of being actively interested'. He also suggested, however, that the exhibition itself did not particularly invite deep engagement: 'It doesn't go into that great depth. You sort of think "Oh well, that's that"'. For other visitors the 'busyness' of the exhibition, the constant demands to make choices, seemed to run counter to thinking too hard about anything. A research manager from Brussels explained:

> I still think there's a problem transferring information in this kind of display – because you have to make a selection. And in the end you just zonk out, you have too much. And so you look for some trivial thing that catches your eye.

He continued by explaining some of the exhibits to which he had been randomly attracted in the exhibition. Other visitors described a similar experience of being 'kept moving' or being made 'punchdrunk'.

In offering so many alternatives without a self-evident framework or narrative, then, it seemed that this exhibition did not prompt visitors into much reflection. Certainly, this is also partly a consequence of the nature of the visit itself. As we see in the next sections, some visitors do comment on the politics of the exhibition's representation of the topic. In addition, however, the counter-reflection tendency is further compounded by some visitors' views about the nature of the science, the Science Museum and sponsorship.

Science, Certainty and Common Sense

As we have seen in relation to the construction of a 'good foods, bad foods narrative', visitors tended to read Food as providing categorical 'answers' on the subject. Although this ran directly counter to a statement on one of the exhibition panels, many of the exhibits, such as the puzzles, can be said to invite the idea of single correct answers. In general, it was noticeable in visitors' accounts of the exhibition that they talked almost exclusively of the three-dimensional exhibits and only very rarely of what they had read on a panel – a point to which I shall return below. Other attempts by the Team, or more especially Jane, to highlight scientific uncertainty were also never mentioned by visitors. Moreover, only occasionally did visitors raise questions about the nature of the science and technology on display or the politics of its representation.

Indeed, in referring to science and technology in the context of the Food exhibition, Gilly observed, visitors tended to equate this with 'health and safety'. For example, on being asked whether the exhibition had changed her views in any way, a housewife replied: 'Yes, I suppose it has. Because I've realised that a lot of research does go into the food we eat – especially with the additives nowadays. It's nice to know that the food we eat is going to be safe', and a sales manager commented: 'I think that a lot of people worry about how convenience foods are packaged and prepared and I think this gives you a better, an idea of the high standards that are used in the preparation of those sort of foods'. The processing machines and the interactive sections on additives – nice clean areas (partly because of demands from sponsors such as the National Dairy Council) – were most often mentioned in such discussions.

Interestingly, when we asked visitors directly about science later in the interviews, more sceptical views emerged. No visitors agreed with the statement that 'All of today's scientific theories will be accepted in a hundred year's time'[19] although some said that they thought that the basics of many areas of science would remain. Many visitors pointed out that scientists can make mistakes (the phrase, 'They're only human', was often employed here) and some specifically indicated that commercial and political interests can affect scientific work. For example, a woman doing a degree in applied biology pointed out that 'if they [scientists] are involved in industry they may be a bit biased from the point of view of the profit of, you know, whoever they're working for'. In response to a statement that 'Science and technology are making our lives healthier, easier and more comfortable', many visitors pointed out the 'bads' as well as the 'goods' of science and gave sophisticated accounts of commercial and political dimensions of science production. For example, an economic consultant responded:

> They're *capable* of doing it. Whether they *are* is again a matter of who controls the decisions – or, and who controls the use of what science and technology is producing. I'd have my doubts about some of the commercial decisions that might be made about the applications of technology. I think they give us the – science and technology give us the capacity for those things but whether it happens isn't always the decision of the scientist. It's just either a political or a commercial decision that's often decisive.

When it came to considering the Food exhibition, however, few visitors seemed to raise such questions about its content. In some ways this was especially surprising given that, as we see in the next section, the great majority of visitors thought that Sainsbury's was the author of the exhibition. In addition to the reasons already mentioned for visitors not engaging deeply with the exhibition, there may also be some other reasons why they did not raise questions of what in media studies has been called 'manipulative intent'.[20] One reason concerns the fact that many visitors did not really regard Food as a science exhibition (a matter which we specifically raised). For example, 'It's not something that you would naturally think about being a science when you think about food' (airforce worker). For some visitors, those seeing it as primarily a historical exhibition, 'history' was contrasted with 'science' (a division made by many Museum staff too): 'I'd personally say it is more historical than scientific' (teacher). For many, however, science was contrasted with common sense and everyday knowledge, and Food for Thought was seen as more concerned with the latter. For example, in response to the question, 'Does this strike you as a scientific exhibition?' a decorator replied, 'Some of it, yes. Others – common sense'. One couple negotiated the answer as follows:

Man: Not really, no. It doesn't go into that great an analysis, its. . .
Woman: No, not substantially
Man: Science is everyday and if that's the case, then, yes
Woman: Not in the case of pure science as it were

What is evident here is a differentiation of 'types' or 'levels' of science (terms which visitors themselves employed), though also the possibility for an exhibition such as this to make visitors challenge their own ideas about it. In general, however, visitors tended to position 'real' science elsewhere – 'chemistry and physics'. This 'real science' tended to be regarded as something difficult: 'Things that you don't actually know', as a seven-year-old boy put it. An argument between one couple over whether the fact that oil and water do not mix is common sense, and therefore, as he asserted not science, or whether it is science, as she argued, because many people do not know this fact, highlighted this distinction. Science is understood as knowledge which cannot be grasped intuitively or within the framework of everyday activities. Significantly, she won the argument when he conceded that he was taught in school that oil and water do not mix.

As food generally is regarded as being concerned mostly with everyday matters, this perhaps makes visitors more likely simply to accept the knowledge with which they are presented in the Food exhibition. The strategy of presenting science through the familiar and everyday seems to have contributed to visitors not raising questions: they are lulled into a sense that they are mostly being presented with what is common sense. There is a catch-twenty-two situation for exhibitors here. If visitors do not question the everyday because they take it for granted, their perception of science as impenetrable by laypeople equally means that they are unlikely to question the science or technology with which they are presented. What other research on the public understanding of science has suggested, however, is that while lay-people rarely question scientific knowledge, they may nevertheless raise questions about trust, responsibility and social relations, just as many visitors did in response to some of our questions.[21] In other words, the kinds of framework that laypeople tend to bring to bear in raising questions about science are generally not epistemological but social. It is the likely behaviour of the persons involved and estimations of their reliability that inform lay judgements. This has some interesting implications for the public understanding of science. Many of its policies and programmes are directed towards increasing 'scientific literacy' – in other words to increasing the amount of scientific knowledge among the public. Not only does this not necessarily lead, as noted in chapter two, to the public trusting science more (which is one of the hopes of some of those involved in these programmes) but it also fails to recognise the viability of the basis on which judgements are being made. Without sufficient scientific knowledge, the public is often regarded as coming to conclusions about science on 'irrational' bases. However, we might argue that the citizenship ambitions of public understanding of science projects might be better achieved by increasing knowledge of how to judge social reliability and where to go for information on matters such as likely commercial or political interests.

Whodunit?: Authorship, Sponsorship and the Discerning Consumer

The question of trust and judgements of reliability brings us directly to the question of who visitors thought had created Food for Thought. The overwhelmingly common answer to our question, 'Who do you think wrote this exhibition?' was 'Sainsbury's', several visitors saying

'Mr Sainsbury' (and one, 'Mr Sainsbury's grandson!'), 'somebody who works for Sainsbury's', 'something to do with the Sainsbury's enterprise. I suppose their PR department', 'it was obviously someone from Sainsbury's and McDonald's and Rank Hovis – someone who wanted to promote the company'. Very few visitors regarded the exhibition as written by the Science Museum.

The main reason for identifying Sainsbury's as the author of the exhibition was the name of the gallery: 'Well, it's Sainsbury's isn't it? It's called the J.Sainsbury gallery I think. Yeah, yeah. I noticed that at the beginning. Yeah, first thought'. The content also contributed to this, visitors nearly always referring to the grocery store reconstruction and (to a lesser extent) the checkout scanner as 'Sainsbury's'. Many of the visitors who identified Sainsbury's as the exhibition's author also reckoned that this would mean that the gallery would be 'an advertisement for Sainsbury's' or 'a sort of PR for Sainsbury's'. Nevertheless, only a minority of these visitors extended this assumption to thinking about just how this might have affected the content. The following are the only sustained examples from our study:

> A woman doing an MSc in applied biology (quoted above for her sceptical view of science) was critical of the lack of attention to intensive farming and to the way that additives are presented in the exhibition: 'I think perhaps it's biased in that it tends to point out the good things about all this obnoxious things that we're having'. On being asked whether she thought that the fact that the exhibition was sponsored made any difference, she replied: 'It shouldn't but maybe that's why it's biased'.

> A man, who ran a transport business with his wife, commented: 'She thought it was more – it's quite obviously biased towards Sainsbury's. We didn't realise it when we were coming in [they had entered at Food and the Body] until we got here, that it was Sainsbury's. We thought it was more like a general idea about food. It's quite, I know that it's sponsored by Sainsbury's, that's obviously the reason why. But it's obviously, it's more like walking through a grocer's shop at Sainsbury's rather than telling you in great detail what food is all about, although it does attempt to do that.'

> A research manager said that he thought the exhibition was 'probably biased'. He added, 'probably the underlying theme would be to make supermarkets and food have a generally nice. . . The bias would be towards less controversy rather than more. You could have, I suppose, put on a

sort of anti-food one that, you know, sort of organic food and all those horrible stuff people put in'. Later in the interview he also said: 'I don't think they were addressed, though, like the mass production aspect. Yeah, I think that was the main. . . I mean most of the science and technology is designed to do that, and how do you produce volume at a cheaper price'. His wife, a schoolteacher, pointed out: 'There were big areas of modern technology that weren't shown, like meat stripping'; to which he commented: 'Yeah, well, it just wasn't, it didn't touch upon anything controversial. It was safe subjects'.

Even in this last interview, however, the respondents tended to temper their criticisms. Continuing from the above, the discussion proceeds as follows:

Man: Well, it's quite difficult to say things in public that are controversial because you get shoved out. . . It's more balanced here I think, probably less deliberately anti-food, more towards what actually happens now at the moment, and yet with the bar-code and things. . .
Woman: But Sainsbury's have a very respectable image, I mean they're very. . .
Man: Well, I have no problem with it being sponsored anyway. I think it's very American but I don't have a problem with that.
Gilly: What do you think the people who wrote this gallery want you to go away with?
Boy also present (aged twelve): Thinking that, warning you about food but telling you that it's not bad, it's just got bad points and to look out for them. But generally a good impression on food.

One point arising in the above interview is the image of Sainsbury's. Having decided that Sainsbury's is responsible for the exhibition, and even assuming that Sainsbury's are seeking to advertise themselves, visitors tend not to see this as particularly worrying. The reason that they often give for this, as above, is the respectability of Sainsbury's. For example, an economic consultant mentioned earlier told us:

Institutions like the great museums have got to look for sponsorship. I suppose that you have to choose carefully. . . but Sainsbury's is a name that is well known and does have a pretty high quality connotation. So I think it's a good name to be associated with. Because I suppose it's one of the biggest of the food companies but it has a quality connotation, a fairly honest connotation about food. Obviously a sponsor mustn't jar

> with the message. I think that there are companies in the food sector that might be thought to be pushing very hard but Sainsbury's are internationally highly recognised, so I think it's a good one.

Others also made comments similar to the following from a clerical officer visiting with her son:

> It's a name that most people know. It's a place for shopping and people have always expected a high standard from Sainsbury's [. . .] Yes, I think it's, I mean, Sainsbury's is the most, not because it's the most well-known, but it's the one that people associate the food industry with.

In addition to the sense of trust in this particular sponsor, visitors were also fairly laid-back about the role of sponsorship for several other reasons. The majority of visitors thought about sponsorship in terms of financial provision:

> All museums have cash-flow problems I'm sure. And any sponsorship you can get, providing it's, you know, used in the right way, must be a good thing. Because I take it you're always trying to improve on any particular exhibition so it must be a good thing (sales manager).

> I dare say without the sponsorship they couldn't have actually done it. Good for the Science Museum. It's very costly these days with all these sorts of things. They charge you for admission so it probably wouldn't be in the Science Museum I suppose without sponsorship (computer designer).

What they saw sponsors as getting in exchange for their money was 'advertising' and how they tended to evaluate advertising was in terms of its 'vulgarity' (National Health Service manager), or 'Americannness' (as above). It was also about making the company name as evident as possible: 'It is the Sainsbury's thing and there are a few Sainsbury's products but I didn't feel that it was too far Sainsbury's orientated [. . .] I didn't feel too much that it was "I'm Sainsbury's, aren't I good – buy me"' (trainee teacher). 'I was aware of the sponsorship but it wasn't pushed down your throat' (part-time computer worker). 'I wouldn't say they've gone over the top' (electricity meter reader). Regarding sponsorship as advertising, visitors construct any 'manipulative intent' in terms of trying to persuade them to buy Sainsbury's products:

> *Question*: Do you think the fact that it's sponsored makes any difference?
> *Man* (maths teacher): Well, I suppose it's an advertisement for Sainsbury's. Er, probably because people think. . .
> *Boy*: . . .don't mind really. . .
> *Man*: Well, food and Sainsbury's are synonymous. But I shouldn't think it has a bad effect – no. I would say it's a fairly neutral effect. I don't think people are going to suddenly rush out and buy all the Sainsbury's things because they've seen it. So that way it's not necessarily an advertisement.
> *Woman* (wood carver): Well, any exhibition of canned goods is inevitably going to carry some advertising isn't it? But I mean it's part of life really these days isn't it? I object to it in sport far more than I do here really. Brand names are the way we buy our food aren't they really? So, you know, you've got to be able to sort out what you want from them really.

What comes through in the interviews is visitors' perception of themselves as discerning or 'streetwise' consumers, aware of advertising but able to decide for themselves whether or not to buy the product. That the sponsor might shape the exhibition content in more extensive ways is either not contemplated or assumed to be limited by the involvement of science and the presence of the exhibition in the respectable location of the Science Museum. Several visitors, discussing the question of whether the fact that the gallery had been sponsored would have made a difference, said that they thought that scientists – perhaps nutritionists or food hygienists – or Science Museum staff would have been involved. One teacher told us: 'I should think that there's enough watch-dogs to make sure that the commercial side of it is carefully watched'. Another teacher: 'I know that it's sponsored by Sainsbury's but, you know, I would imagine that they would use experts'.

What we have seen in this chapter is that visitors are indeed active – sometimes too active from the Museum's point of view. They constructively appropriate the exhibition into their own cultural lists, and discuss it in relation to their own lives and interests. However, this does not guarantee that they subject the exhibition to any kind of critique. On the contrary, it is in some ways a consequence of that activity – visitors' appropriation of the exhibition into frameworks of leisure and their positioning of themselves as certain kinds of consumers – that makes them relatively unlikely to raise critical or political questions.

The way in which visitors engage with the exhibition is also cued by the exhibition itself. In the case of Food for Thought it is in some ways the very fact of the activity, the 'busyness', that is demanded of them that means that visitors do not 'read deeply' (as some put it). The constant requirement to make selections, having to interact and 'keep moving', seems to make it difficult to stop and think – though some visitors suggested that they might do so later. In many ways visitors are active consumers in the ways hoped by the exhibition makers: they are 'busy' and mostly they are having fun. Yet this is not quite the same as the active citizenship which is so often said to be an aim of public understanding of science projects. There is little sense that visitors come away from the exhibition more empowered in relationship to the subject-matter. Indeed, for some visitors it seems almost to have the opposite effect, giving them the sense of security that science, expertise and respectability are all at work in producing their food and making it safe and 'good'.

Much work on consumption has focused on illustrating audience activity. Such work is sometimes cast as morally superior to the kind of research which seeks to consider 'manipulative intent'. In the *binarist* stereotypes employed, one pays attention to 'the people' themselves in their rich variety and recognises the sophistication of, and subtle resistances in, their readings, and the other positions readers or viewers as 'cultural dopes', mere passive receptacles of producer manipulation. Here, we have seen that 'activity' is itself a more complex matter and that in some respects it is the fact that visitors must be constantly 'active' in certain ways in the exhibition that seems to make it more difficult for them to be 'active' in the sense of being critically reflective in others. Likewise, that visitors tend to see themselves as relatively aware of, and hard to influence by, 'advertising', seems to mean that they do not look for sponsor influence beyond the flashing of the sponsor name.

In considering the material from the visitor research on Food for Thought what seems particularly important is to go beyond classifications of 'active' versus 'passive' to understand more fully the ways in which visitors are likely to engage with the exhibition. These are not specific only to this exhibition. The kinds of 'cultural lists' on which a visit to this exhibition features – leisure, life-cycle, place and education – are likely to be shared, in part at least, with those for visits to other kinds of exhibitions (and, indeed, other cultural products). Research across a range of types of exhibitions could yield a fuller set of 'lists' which would come into play to greater or lesser extents. Equally, the tendency to understand this exhibition in certain ways – the search for a narrative, the expectation that the exhibition will be prescriptive and give clear-cut 'right answers' – is likely to be widely shared (especially in relation to similar media and in contexts with an authoritative national status). Further research could identify a wider repertoire of cultural framings which are likely to be employed in relation to certain kinds of exhibitions (between science and art exhibitions, for example), and this could help exhibitors to engage better with viewer responses. By 'engage with', though, I do not mean just 'try to meet the desires of' – another elision typical of this moment in popularised public culture. Rather, understanding likely presuppositions and assumptions could also provide a foundation for creating exhibitions which might draw impetus from, challenge or reflect on some of them.

Notes

1. Veron and Levasseur 1982.
2. The research was designed by Roger Silverstone, Gilly Heron and myself. It was based on a pilot study which we ran in a geology exhibition in the Natural History Museum. Gilly carried out the majority of the interviews and preliminary analysis.
3. For accounts and critiques of museum visitor research see, for example, Bicknell and Farmelo 1993; Hooper-Greenhill 1994, 1999a; Lawrence 1991 and 1993.
4. See, for example, Claeson *et al.* 1996; Hooper-Greenhill 1999; MacKay 1997; Silverstone 1994: especially ch.6.
5. See, for example, Ang 1991; McGuigan 1992; Morley 1995; Silverstone 1994: ch.6; Stevenson 1995: ch.3.
6. It is also sometimes referred to as 'the new audience studies' (see Morley 1995). Corner 1991 uses the term 'popular culture project'. He contrasts this to 'the public knowledge project', the latter being concerned with matters of public knowledge, definitional power, the politics of information, and citizenship (1991: 268).
7. Roger Silverstone is writing of television research but his point has broader relevance: 'The equation of social or individual difference and activity has been a constant theme in television research. It has been repeated to the point of banality. .. It implies that viewers (all viewers? all viewers by definition?)

construct their own meanings from their individual experiences of common texts. This notion of activity is associated with a notion of difference: different viewers create different meanings. Correlatively the idea that we may share meanings, or that the meanings that we do derive from our engagement with television are necessarily common (and in some sense determined), implies a kind of passivity' (1994: 153).

8. This has been called the problem of the disappearing text (see Silverstone 1994: 150). It has parallels with the 'disappearing science' problem noted in chapter one.

9. In their study of readers of *National Geographic* (1993) Lutz and Collins use the term 'cultural discourses' for the repertoire of ways in which readers talk about the magazine contents. They also found that social variables did not seem crucial in the deployment of these discourses (1993: 224).

10. We put up signs at the gallery entrances saying that this observation was occurring, though we nevertheless aimed to be discreet. In practice, it was generally difficult to eavesdrop.

11. That is, as broad a range as possible in terms of age and gender. We made a conscious effort to try to include non-white participants but these were not well represented in our sample, firstly because they consituted a small minority of Museum visitors and secondly because we did not continue an observation if a group was not speaking English. As the research was carried out in the summer months there were many visitors from outside the UK at the Museum. In practice, many of those we interviewed were not 'families' as such, though we did not ask specifically about their relationships to one another.

12. Only a very small minority came in through the gallery's third entrance and so we did not include this in the study.

13. In total, eighty-seven trackings were completed.

14. We also included here some questions from a national survey of scientific literacy which was being coordinated from the Science Museum at the time. Originally we had intended to compare our visitor sample with the national sample; and for this reason used questions which the organisers of the survey had found were 'good discriminators'. Our attempt was, however, interestingly unsuccessful. Rather than simply individually answering questions, visitors generally discussed them collectively and sometimes pointed out different possible interpretations of the questions or of what might be said.

15. Occupations are as visitors themselves described them. A series of dots. . . . indicates a pause, but within parentheses [. . .] it indicates that a section of the interview material has been cut here.

16. Lave 1988. She describes lists as 'structured. . . expectations about the process of shopping and what they [shoppers] will buy' (1988: 152); and the

shopping trip as 'one locus of articulation between persons-acting and the structured arena' (1988: 152).

17. Urry 1990: 10.

18. This point has been well made by Paulette McManus in her research on museum visiting: 1987, 1988.

19. This was a statement taken from the National Scientific Literacy survey. There it was intended to assess 'attitudes' to science in closed format. We, however, found it particularly interesting in terms of the discussion it prompted.

20. Richardson and Corner 1986.

21. See Irwin and Wynne 1996; Irwin et al. 1996; Wynne 1996.

Behind and Beyond the Scenes

In Kate Atkinson's *Behind the Scenes at the Museum,* Ruby relates her life story – from Conception, through Birth, through The Naming of Things, to Wisdom (her funeral) and Redemption. (All of these are chapter titles.) Alongside, or perhaps behind, and interwoven with Ruby's narration are chapter-length 'footnotes' which delve into the past tangled lives of Ruby's relatives. Through the novel, she learns, and we learn, to decipher the surface appearance of 'the museum' – her strange family. We come to understand why Ruby's mother feels about her as she does; we come to know that the slight verbal hesitation as Ruby's mother searches for her name has a history and that this tiny oral tic betrays matters of enormous significance for Ruby's own life.

One day, when I was wandering around Food for Thought, I met a curator who was working on another exhibition. He had come to look at the new gallery, to see what he liked, what he didn't like, what he would like to try to emulate, what he would avoid. Thinking ahead as much as reflecting on the gallery, he said to me:

> I suppose that once the thing is finished, you look at it and think, "How did it take so much time? How did so much work go into it?" You think, "I could have done that." But you don't see all of the work that it takes to get there. You don't see all the things you had to leave out and all the meetings and agonising over what to put in – the blood, sweat and tears. You don't see any of that stuff any more. It's like, you thought you were going to give birth to an elephant, and it's more of a mouse really.

In this book, I have told a story of the work – the blood, sweat and tears – that lies behind a finished exhibition. It is a story based on having lived through the experience of its making. But it is not the only story which could have been told. My own account could have been considerably more elephantine. In telling of exhibition-making and the workings of the Science Museum at a time of considerable change, I have been concerned to recover some of the work, difficulty and complexity of what goes on behind the scenes – some of the mess that is tidied away in the finished product. In doing so, I have also sought to try to understand why things turn out as they do, why elephants transfigure into mice rather than, say, iguanas, why some things are thought especially important to erase and others not. This has led me to pay particular attention to what seemed to shape the outcome – those, sometimes seemingly trivial or obvious events or decisions along the way which leave a later trace, like the hesitation in Ruby's mother's use of her daughter's name. I have also been concerned with the ways in which the finished, crafted and trace-strewn, cultural product is interpreted, with the ways in which the makers' dreams, hesitations and silences are themselves variously noted, diffracted and ignored by those who visit.

Specificity and Speaking Beyond

This has been the story of a particular institution – the Science Museum – and a particular gallery within it, at a particular moment in time. This particularity, this spatio-temporal location, is important, as I said at the outset. But just as a novel is not only about the particular fictional characters and plot that it narrates, an ethnography too speaks of broader themes and predicaments. Whether Food for Thought: the Sainsbury Gallery is, or is not, a 'good exhibition' (however we choose to define this), whether one likes it or not, is not especially relevant to whether it is good to 'speak from'. Largely, of course, 'speaking from' (even if it is left largely implicit) is what the ethnographer seeks to do in fashioning her narrative, though the capacity to do so is undoubtedly assisted, as Bruno Latour observes, by 'good timing'.[1] Looking at the Science Museum at a self-proclaimed moment of 'cultural revolution', and looking at an exhibition that became, uncomfortably perhaps, the vanguard of that revolution, felt like having chanced upon a time in which routine practices and long-held assumptions were being questioned. It was a time in which participants had to come up with visions and justifications for what they were doing. No longer could accomplished expertise be relied upon to deal with the demands; instead, restructuring, revisioning, rethinking, reskilling and re-presenting were called for.

This is not to say that things had been stable previously, or that nothing was assumed and nothing remained the same. The changes ushered in new assumptions, and, alongside, many museum staff clung fast to long-held and sacrosanct principles, and certain enduring ways of doing and thinking were simply not noticed. In telling the story in this book, my intention has been to try to make visible what I could of this. Below I return to some of these matters – the nearest an anthropologist can get to 'findings' – to try to speak from them a little further. But first, I want to comment briefly on this business of 'speaking from' – which some might refer to as 'generalisability' (though to my mind the 'how far is it the same elsewhere?' way in which this is usually characterised misses some of the potential and spirit of what 'speaking from' is all about).

When I started to make my first comments about Food, some in the Museum were keen to point out to me that the next exhibition to open would 'be very different indeed'. It certainly was. The George III collection of scientific instruments, presented on white plinths and in cases (a minimalism intended to 'put the objects first'), bore little similarity to Food [Figure 9.1]. The George III was not interactive or hands-on; 'fun' and 'busy' were not appropriate adjectives, and it was definitely directed at a more knowing, scholarly and adult audience than was Food.[2] 'It's Rackhams!', quipped one curator to me; Rackhams being an up-market department store, though not too up-market, and perhaps one which tries to present as more up-market than it really is (so many possible subtle value-judgements in one swiftly uttered analogy!). It was all very different from chocolate mousse-pots, McDonald's and supermarket metaphors. That the Science Museum chose to display a precious object-rich collection at this moment was not as surprising to me as some had clearly expected.

On the contrary. What I had witnessed in the Museum was a general attempt to shift the focus from the collections to the visitors. It was an attempt to move from a connoisseurship approach (in which displays are determined by developed expertise) to a forensic one (in which they have to be based on evidence of what visitors are likely to want).[3] But it was by no means uncontested or complete, or even fully realisable. As I saw when I watched the gallery planning process, for example, there was a strong object-lobby in the Museum. In part, this derived from curatorial object-love and the cultivated object-feel which even infiltrated Food. But objects were recognised as what was distinctive about the Museum, and as what made it different from other leisure or educational pursuits and from science centres. They were part of its

Figure 9.1 A different answer: the George III collection.

USP – its Unique Selling Point – as the marketing lingo of the time put it. Moreover, as we have seen, staff were abundantly aware that not to display objects was itself deeply problematic in terms of public accountability. How could they justify the continuing expense of maintaining what they had, never mind adding to the collections, if the great majority of objects were destined for the storage warehouses? In response to such concerns, the display of a historically important collection such as the George III made sense. And it did so especially in the wake of a relatively object-poor, populist interactive exhibition like Food. It was a return of the object. But it did not in and of itself signify the directions which the Museum would consistently take in future any more than did Food: this was not that kind of a time. Rather, like Food, it was one response to a set of deep-rooted dilemmas thrown up by the ongoing seismic activity.

There is one senior curator who, whenever I meet him, always says to me with a grin: 'We're restructuring again Sharon'. He does so, I think, to acknowledge on the one hand the relevance of structural change. On the other, though, he is suggesting that the restructuring which I observed and which I describe was just momentary, soon to be superseded. He is right, of course. Constant restructuring has become a feature of public organisations. There is always the hope that a new managerial structure might solve ongoing problems and accommodate the different demands and constituencies with which an organisation must deal. But alongside the structural experimentalism, there is also ample and ever-increasing evidence of the forensic approach. While attempts to recuperate some lost symbolic and literal territory for objects will be made, and while there will be the necessity of meeting new and unexpected demands too, this seems unlikely to sweep away the prioritising of the visitor. Although this may take new forms, there is no going back.

Social Drama and Hot Situations

In chapter one I noted Victor Turner's idea that 'social dramas' – 'public episodes of tensional irruption' – can be good to speak from because, as Turner writes for the Ndembu, they 'expose.. the pattern of current factional intrigue, hitherto covert and privately conducted. . . and beneath it there becomes visible the less plastic, more durable, but nevertheless gradually changing basic. . . social structure, made up of relations that have a high degree of constancy and consistency'.[4] Social dramas, Turner suggests, follow a particular processual structure: breach, crisis, redressive action and reintegration.[5] In the Science Museum in the late 1980s there was a clear sense of *breach*, signalled by the language of departure, of change, of newness and the ubiquity of the prefix 're-'. *Crisis*, Turner's analytical term for the second stage, was also characteristic of the context insofar as there was a sense of danger and suspense, of factional differences, and of a surfacing of deep dilemmas; 'crisis' was also a word locally employed and with local synonyms. *Redressive action* was also much in evidence: the restructuring, the gallery planning, the corporate plans and press statements were all part of this. But unlike in Turner's structure, these seemed to continue alongside crisis, and it was far from clear that all would settle back down into *reintegration*. On the contrary, restructuring, suspense and planning for different possible futures have continued unabated.[6]

This phenomenon of non-stop restructuring, which is characteristic of many organisations (certainly including universities) today, is typical of what Michel Callon calls 'hot situations'. These are contexts in which attempts to 'frame', or 'bracket off', events or institutions from one another are experienced as exceedingly difficult: 'reintegration' or 'closure' are not reached. Whatever 'frames' are established, there are overflows, matters which escape the boundaries established, so that 'everything becomes controversial', with the tendency for the controversies to 'lurch first one way, and then the other'.[7] In particular, 'facts and values. . . become entangled to such an extent that it is no longer possible to distinguish between two successive stages: first, the production and dissemination of information or knowledge, and second, the decision-making process itself'.[8] In other words, ideas about matters such as the public effects and usefulness of particular knowledge and information about consumption are entangled in their production and dissemination: it becomes impossible to define socially something which can serve as a 'knowledge base'.[9] No part of social life can be bracketed off as 'disinterested'; uncontroversial authority becomes increasingly difficult to find. We have seen examples of this in the case of Food, where scientists present the Team with 'facts' in a form in which they want the public to receive them, and in which the Team's own task of 'dissemination' is thoroughly shaped by notions of what the public may want and by the presence of actual as well as phantom visitors. This all makes it very difficult in hot situations to 'reach. . . agreement either on the facts or on the decisions that should be taken'.[10]

Such hot situations are, Callon suggests, 'not only becoming more commonplace, more visible and more pervasive. . .; but more importantly it is becoming exceedingly difficult to cool them down'. This is a consequence of 'the growing complexity of industrial society, a level of sophistication due in large part to the movements of the technosciences, which are causing connections and interdependencies to proliferate'.[11] Others have suggested likewise, in different language, and with different emphases.[12] So rather than returning to a relatively stable social structure as Turner imagined, what we see instead is relentless debate, drawing on existing 'givens', and perhaps with some enduring themes, about directions and possible futures. There is a search for visions, structures and frameworks capable of stemming the overflows, momentarily at least.

Framing, Containing and Transparency

Callon borrows the term 'framing' from Goffmann to describe attempts to demarcate distinct contexts, arenas or sets of interactions.[13] Framing is concerned with setting the scene so that certain connections will be made rather than others; it is about trying to direct flow and prevent overflow. This is what television producers in Silverstone's study of television science mean when they talk about 'framing' too: they hope in the first five minutes of the programme to establish a frame within which the rest of the programme will be understood – they hope to set the terms within which viewers will view.[14]

Framing can be relatively routine and taken-for-granted by social actors, as it is for the most part in Goffmann's account, or it can be a more explicit and contested matter as it is to some extent for the television producers. Making an exhibition, like making any other cultural product, is likely to involve a degree of explicit framing. What seems characteristic of the hot situation which I observed, however, was the incessant attempt to formalise framing, to make it explicit, clear and rule-governed. This was in many ways an unsurprising and even logical response to the sense of dangerous overflow, proliferation and multiple possible connections. Image management, mission statements, aims and objectives, corporate plans, and rigorous conceptual frameworks were all part of the struggle to define, to frame, in an increasingly warm climate.

One problem, however, was that the more rigorous or rigid the frame was made, the more seemed to slip outside it – or more that was important could not be accommodated. Take the Rethink, in which the Food Team revised their plans into a 'rigorous conceptual framework', consisting of a neatly organised nesting-hierarchy of explicit messages. Some of the things they had especially wanted to include could no longer fit. In itself, given the way the exhibition was proliferating, this was no bad thing. But what was lost was not only 'quirkiness' – as the Foodies generally phrased it – but also the interrogation of silences, of the unsaid or unrecognised. Frameworks became their own self-justification. As long as everything could be justified in the terms set out, and in terms of the aims and objectives neatly listed, then the job was being properly done.

Or take what would be the closest analogy to the first five minutes of a television programme: visitors' first impressions of a gallery. Here, the Team's ideas were so focused upon their own orienting messages, and upon the task of just getting the job done, that they did not fully explore how the arrangement of exhibits at the entrance would visually frame the exhibition. They did not do so partly because of a panicky sense of there being so little time (the timetable exerted its own framing effect), but also because the verbally-defined messages that had been devised excised attention to both possible non-verbal messages and to other ways in which visitors might read the gallery (beyond the targeted messages). But the Sainsbury's shop, the Sainsbury's checkout, the Sainsbury's packaging and the name of the gallery make a very clear statement to visitors: that this is a gallery created by a supermarket retailer. Certainly, there were all kinds of pragmatic and even aesthetic reasons, some of which were undoubtedly beyond the Team's control, why it turned out like this. But the point here is that the very rigorous thinking about what was included and why, was unfortunately – and in many respects understandably – not accompanied by equally rigorous attention to what was excluded and to much beyond the verbally-defined 'messages'. We might note here too that the large number of panels in the finished exhibition, that so surprised the Team members themselves, was largely a consequence of the language-based way in which 'messages' came to be conceptualised.

Also involved in this kind of framing was an attempt to make explicit or 'transparent', something deemed vital for 'accountability'. So, for example, Mr Suthers told the Team that one important reason for being explicit about the messages that the gallery intended to convey was that these could be used for evaluating visitor response to the gallery later. Now, subjecting givens to question and trying to think about why particular selections are being made is surely worthwhile. Anthropology, which entails a lot of this, generally assumes that by understanding process and being aware of what we take for granted we will be better able to do otherwise should we so wish. However, the managerialist take on making visible and explicit was not generally quite in this spirit. Rather than highlight alternatives, or make us aware of the relative nature of particular selections, it tended to be used as a means of constraining and legitimising. Success, or 'effectiveness' (the preferred term of the language of the time) was to be judged in the terms defined by the frameworks which had been set up partly with the job of evaluating this in mind. Defining a 'target audience', for example, became in part a way of defending an exhibition against criticism from others who were excluded from the frame. What tended to ensue, then, was a drive to create tight webs of self-circulating interconnections in which 'excess' and the potential for questioning the legitimacy of the framework itself were edited out. In itself, this process of trying to create internal consistency within a cultural frame is not unusual or necessarily problematic in itself. Michael Polanyi, for example, has highlighted circular forms of reasoning which serve to uphold the system and protect basic assumptions from scrutiny in a range of examples including ones from Azande witchcraft, the history of chemistry and political ideologies.[15] What is characteristic of the case here, however, is that the creation of such structures is going on before our very eyes (as it were) with a high degree of self-consciousness, clinical precision and a rhetoric of transparency and visibility. Moreover, it produces (nevertheless? consequently?) internal contradictions or 'irrationalities'.[16]

Not only was this evident in the making of the exhibition and the gallery planning, but it was also characteristic of overall managerial restructuring in the Science Museum and other organisations at the time. In a manner fully analogous with the nested-hierarchy of the exhibition 'messages', many organisations were busy concocting job specifications which would make sure that anything defined as 'redundant' to the overall mission statement or objectives identified would be made just that. Yet this had the paradoxical effect that some of the needs of the officially revered sovereign consumer could no longer be met. Thus, as the Museums and Galleries Commission reported with regard to the national museums as a whole (chapter two), and as some Science Museum staff observed, individual visitor enquiries could often not be dealt with and various educationally important programmes, such as outreach (where museums make contacts with schools), had to be reduced or curtailed. 'Effectiveness' might be increased and targets met, but only within a framework that had specified sufficiently tightly what effectiveness and targets were to be.

Enterprise, Consumer and Author Sovereignty

Many, perhaps all, staff in the Museum were well aware of this accountability fiction (which is, surely, familiar to others working in different areas of public service). Yet they also knew that to appear as a 'failing' institution could be dangerous: appearing 'effective' was vital for assuring a continued flow of funds. In the tautological neo-Darwinian language of enterprise of the time, those who failed somehow deserved to fail and the fittest survived. 'Competition' was one of the watchwords and public, perhaps especially national, institutions (especially those with any kind of scholarly aspirations) were regarded by the Thatcherite government as in particular need of being subjected to its supposed invigorations. It was clear that one function of performance indicators, if such could be devised, would be to compare institutions with one another, in order to rank them and identify some as 'ineffective'. The latter designation was cast by the government as a matter of the individual responsibility of the organisation – it was being mismanaged or showing insufficient enterprise. That it might need more funding or staff to do its job better was a line of argument likely to cast by the government as 'whingeing' (unjustified complaining) by the formerly 'molly-coddled' (protected from 'facing reality'). Museum staff continued to make such arguments, and sometimes (as in the example of the Trustees' protest, chapter two) they won victories of sorts. But, because of the ways the alternatives were presented to them and because of the harsh consequences into which these were built, they did not have limitless choice any more than did 'sovereign consumers'.

Museums did not, however, simply put into effect what was being asked of them, partly because this was scarcely feasible and the routes to achieve it were far from clear. Attempts by Museum staff to, variously, construct elaborate performance indicators which would include (rather than excise) matters such as scholarship and enlightenment, or even the introduction of charging as a means of trying to extricate themselves from government control, were in many respects admirable examples of trying to use dominant rhetoric and structures in order to strengthen rather than weaken their own hand. Even though such – in some respects daredevil – strategies risked backfiring, they also enabled some of those involved to try to bring about real and worthwhile change in museums. The desire to make things better, to make museums more open and responsive to the public, was the laudable ambition of many museum directors and staff.

In the late 1980s and 1990s, the same kind of entrepreneurial rhetoric was used in relation to both organisations and individuals. Both were conceptualised as essentially autonomous agents whose fates were determined by their own self-made choices. This was in many respects a 'strong' framing of entities: the vision was one of autochthonous units, resistant to inflows, whose directions would be determined by the selective links that they chose to make. The nation was another entity often articulated in this way. That a political programme, based on a vision of strong framing, became ascendant at a 'hot' time when stability and boundaries seemed to be, or were talked about as, waning, and fluidity and flow as increasing was not, perhaps, surprising. But just as with accountability and transparency, there was something fictive about this vision of sovereign entities. Excised from this talk of choice and independence was much that affected the choices on offer and individuals' and organisations' capacities to make them, not least the panoply of mechanisms introduced for defining and monitoring effectiveness and performance.

As we have seen, the Food for Thought exhibition in many respects played to and represented the individual as sovereign choice-maker. It could also be read as entailing some of the same fictions and excisions of the enterprise perspective. The framework within which choice was being offered was not itself made explicit and thus limits already built into the choices on offer were hard to see (as, for example, in the exclusion of primary production from the exhibition). Visitors were cast as having more agency in relation to certain matters than they surely did (as in the food poisoning case); and, despite the talk of difference, there was a tendency towards sameness in terms of the rather homogeneous way that the visitor was in fact imagined and in the final appearance of the exhibition. In relation to the latter, there was both less of a sense of variety between the different areas of the exhibition and of difference from other exhibitions than the Team had hoped – both consequences in part, I suggest, of shared cultural assumptions. The verbal-messages and panels issue was partly involved here; but so too were ambitions to speak to a generalised visitor, and the elision of fun and interactivity with citizenship.

What is clear from going behind the scenes is that the Foodies were operating with admirable and widely shared motives. What was involved was a kind of 'convergence effect' of framing, in which the Team's vision of a democratising, empowering exhibition for 'ordinary people', which they articulated to their gender and structural position within the Museum, overlapped with a different political rhetoric. In a sense, they found themselves framed: their visions and work were set in a context which gave it inflections that they had not anticipated. Yet, this was not something which anybody intentionally or unintentionally did to them, and neither were they simply structured into it. They did have an authorial voice and they did have agency, but these were not absolute. Rather, different political ambitions and perspectives were capable of sharing the same language: 'public understanding of science', 'participation', 'interactivity' and 'accountability'. As with shared symbols in other contexts, such as those discussed by Turner and mentioned earlier, the different possible political inflections rarely emerged.[17] Moreover, in the context of exhibition-making these connotations were often embedded in non-verbal matters – the layout of the exhibition, particular ways of organising, the mix of exhibits and their particular juxtaposition. The Foodies might interpret these one way – for example, that non-linearity was a good thing as it allowed visitors to 'make up their own minds' – but they were legible in other ways too. Without critical awareness of this, and without 'redressive action', the Foodies were liable to finding themselves and the fruit of their labours framed, sometimes at least, in ways which they would never have intended to inscribe. This is, I suggest, a much more common experience than is widely recognised. Moreover, Food for Thought, which was at the time in many respects an experimental exhibition, was, as I said at the outset, a learning experience for all involved (me included). I did not see the dilemmas at the time – and I was not desperately negotiating with companies and other organisations and working against a deadline to get the gallery finished. One reason for writing this book, even now, is to use this benefit of hindsight and time to reflect in order to try to raise questions which most of us, in the helter-skelter of trying to get things done, rarely have the opportunity to address.

What is also clear, then, is that there is no sovereign author: the agency to shape the outcome of the exhibition is distributed among multiple actors – non-human as well as human, conceptual as well as material. Nevertheless, it is not equally distributed. The fact that none of those involved is autonomous or overridingly powerful – not even those sometimes credited with so being (the Team, the Director, the government, the budget. . . .) – does not completely absolve responsibility for the final product. Responsibility might be distributed too, but it is not dissolved. Authorship, in the sense now of those who are formally credited with agency, is also an acceptance, and even an assertion, of responsibility.

Science and Citizenship

Food for Thought was in many respects a very successful exhibition. To dwell on its political ambiguities, silences and inflections is, therefore, perhaps, an academic exercise which has little relevance for the important business of 'the public understanding of science'. Visitors did not report major dissatisfactions with the exhibition and many said they especially liked the hands-on dimension and found it preferable to more traditional styles of museum display. The exhibition also seemed able to challenge the expectations of some visitors about science: they saw that it could be a matter of the everyday, that it could be familiar and approachable.

The ultimate ambition of public understanding of science programmes is often expressed in terms of enabling the public to participate more fully as citizens (see chapter two above). In order to do so, it is regarded as vital that the public has a better understanding of science because it is assuming an ever-greater importance in the contemporary world. So 'making science accessible' is seen as the route to providing 'understanding' and this, in turn, as a way of enabling the public to make rational choices. Although 'making accessible' might mean various things, it is often equated with making science 'fun', 'enjoyable' and 'user-friendly': cartoons are often talked about as especially good at 'getting messages across', and hands-on interactives tend to be thought of as toys. (Museum staff sometimes talk about Launch Pad as a play-pen; and Museum visitors often talk of interactives as things to 'play with'.) In Food, making science 'accessible' was also seen as about making it 'familiar' and embedding it in the safe worlds of everyday life and domesticity. All of this has a place. Yet, science is not necessarily accessible in any of these ways: it can be difficult, complicated, risky and rather unfriendly. Understanding this is part of the understanding of science too. If citizens are to be able to evaluate science and make informed choices they need to be able to understand its potential benefits *and* risks; they need to notice its presence in their everyday lives *and* its distant and global effects which may be far less visible to them.

In the making of Food we saw that differences on matters of 'fact' were very rarely at the basis of the controversial matters with which the Team struggled, and that these could not, therefore, be dealt with by 'getting the facts right'. Moreover, it was also clear that there were differences among scientists and that they did not necessarily speak with the socially good and disinterested voice that is often assumed within the public understanding of science perspective. It was far from clear, then, that members of the public would be able to make clear decisions if they were better aware of what scientists were saying. Neither would understanding scientific technicalities necessarily equip them to make choices about controversial matters involving science. Very often, the important matters that might affect public views were not about 'science itself', as it has come to be defined, but about the contexts in which it was embedded. In other words, they concerned social and environmental matters, such as consequences in particular locales and the likely interests of the parties involved. As we saw, visitors did sometimes seem to be predisposed to judge and think about science in these ways. As I suggested, then, it is to providing more sophisticated means for them to do this, and information on where to go to for the sources to make such evaluations, that public understanding of science programmes might also be directed.

One of the reasons why visitors to Food for Thought – an exhibition about a potentially highly political and controversial topic – do not ask very probing questions about either the subject-matter or the exhibition's representation is that their framings of their activity converge with those by the Team. Visitors find themselves 'busy' in the exhibition; they have fun, they are engaged in something about leisure, they recognise the familiar, and (as in their 'street-wise' approach to sponsorship) they position themselves as sophisticated sovereign consumers. Yet it is precisely this that leads them not to question deeply. The exhibition does not for the most part shake them out of their presuppositions into new perspectives and questions. Such an exhibition might, of course, be less fun and less enjoyable, though let us not assume that it would. But it is visitor 'satisfaction' and 'enjoyment' that have become overriding and sometimes exclusive indicators of what counts as success, and possibly the easiest routes to providing these do not entail raising provocative or taxing questions. This is by no means confined to this exhibition or to museums. Readers working in universities, for example, may find their own parallels. To give just one: in some university departments the quantified result of a question like, 'How enjoyable did you find the module overall?' is taken as a cumulative index of the success of a course, and, correlatively, in the equivalent of the entanglement of curatorial identities with those of exhibitions, of those teaching it. We, surely, with our relatively selected and 'captive' audiences, have even less of an excuse than do museums.

Enjoyment matters, of course. The point here is just that we shouldn't reduce everything to it or allow it to obscure other important things or its connections with other matters (such as learning, politics and objects). Museums and exhibitions are complex institutions which cannot be reduced to single functions. They are not simply fun-factories; neither are they only shrines to hallowed objects, three-dimensional text-books or citizenship training courses. And they are not supermarkets or department stores either.

Museums, and perhaps especially national museums, are invested with all kinds of public ambitions and hopes. They are expected to represent the nation and its achievements, to tell 'us' who 'we' are, to identify and conserve significant items of material culture for posterity, to engage in scholarly work on the collections, and to bring education and enlightenment to as wide a population as possible. They are also expected to provide a good day out, to let us see those specific objects which we want – for one reason or another – to see, to let us know whether something we have found is important or not, to be suitable places to celebrate a birthday or to pick up a gift for a friend. It's an important job. And it's a tall order

There have, over the years, been all kinds of predictions of the demise of the museum. It will be superseded, some have suggested, by electronic and virtual technologies – a technophiliac's dream as Charles

Saumerez Smith has put it.[18] Television is, perhaps, better able to convey a sense of context, movement and drama: so why get off the settee? Or, rather than going bodily to museums, we could visit them on-line. In the case of science museums, there have also been anxieties about science centres – hands-on interactive centres which, unhampered by 'objects', are sometimes thought better at explaining science and making it accessible than are museums.[19] Theme parks have caused qualms too: are these not just so exciting that nobody ever again will want to visit poor old museums? Or perhaps museum visiting will simply be overtaken by the growing national pastime of shopping.

It is in response to these perceived threats that museums have introduced audio-visual and computerised technologies, interactives, animated rides, ace caffs, gift shops and mail-order catalogues. That museums are alert to cultural trends, that they look for new ideas and borrow from them, seems to me to be one of their strengths. But at the same time, they shouldn't – and for the most part they don't – try to be those other places, just as they shouldn't see their role in the singular. Museums shouldn't forget the great collections of objects that they have accumulated over the years, neither should they forget their public cultural status. Museums are invested with a rather unique and special complex of cultural authority, property and expertise. Perhaps more than anything, they need to protect this against attempts to cut this down to more limited and culturally impoverished size.

Over the past decade the Science Museum has produced many new exhibitions and an impressive programme of innovative and often reflexive and interactive projects to engage the public. These have included conducting research on public views about various aspects of science, setting up public-information 'hot-lines', holding consensus conferences in which citizens come together with scientists to discuss controversial issues, hosting artists in residence, showing art-work on scientific subjects and allowing artistic and politicised interventions in existing displays, building a major new wing of the Museum dedicated to medicine, creating a new ground-floor gallery – The Making of the Modern World – to show thousands of historically important objects from the collections, mounting temporary exhibitions on controversial subjects and exhibitions in which the comments of the public become part of the exhibitions themselves, showing objects and the construction of galleries on-line, and even holding sleep-overs.[20] Some of these show the continuing dedication to objects, collections and scholarship. Others seem to signal an even more intimate relationship with the visitor and even greater opportunities for visitor activity. They also suggest changing configurations of the visitor, including more citizenly engagements, and the willingness to ask probing questions about the nature of science and science museums. Looking now from outside, rather than from behind the scenes, I am encouraged by the scope and variety of these developments. And from my time behind the scenes, I know that they will be the outcome of negotiations and struggles between extremely able and dedicated museum staff, and between museum staff and the multiple other actors involved in the production of public culture.

As I finish this book, the Science Museum announces that it will abolish admission charges. This feels like a seductive closure. But although it can serve as such for my narrative, it is not so either analytically or historically. This story has not been about the effects of admission charges (charges were but one, logical and significant but nevertheless optional, element of a bigger movement), and the abolition of charges will not jettison the Museum back to how things were in pre-admission days. We will, perhaps, see a new chapter in the life of the Museum but many of the dilemmas with which museum staff struggle – how much space to give to objects, how to understand visitors, who and what to involve in exhibition-making – will continue, and whatever happens next will also have to work with or against the changes we saw here. One of my own most lasting impressions from behind the scenes is of the dynamism, passion and commitment of many Museum staff. This may make them 'stubborn buggers' and lead to 'factional warfare' as I was warned at the beginning. But it also creates an energy in the place and makes it sufficiently complex and diverse to resist attempts to frame it too narrowly. This excess is its magic.

Notes

1. Latour 1987: 2. Geertz, comparing the analysis of the Balinese cock-fight with reading *Macbeth*, provides an insightful discussion of this business of 'saying something of something' as he puts it (1973: 448).

2. The exhibition also sought to discuss ideas about scientific knowledge as process, and indeed did so in self-conscious juxtaposition with its own presentation of science as objects. See Arnold 1996 for a discussion.

3. See Gibbons *et.al.*1994.

4. Turner 1974: 38-9.
5. Turner 1974: 33.
6. See, for example, Shelton (forthcoming).
7. Callon 1998: 260, 261.
8. Callon 1998: 260.
9. Callon 1998: 260. Callon discusses BSE (Bovine Spongiform Encephalytis – 'mad-cow disease') in an extended example.
10. Callon 1998: 261.
11. Callon 1998: 262, 261.
12. See, for example, Beck 1992, Castells 1996, Held, McGrew, Goldblatt and Perraton 1999.
13. Callon draws on Goffman (1971) in order to examine economists' attempts to define particular economic arenas. Both Callon (1998 and 1999) and Latour (1999) have recently highlighted the importance of 'framing' as a way of correcting what they see as a misunderstanding of actor network theory. The latter was never meant to imply that movement through networks was unmediated and instantaneous (Latour blames the world-wide web for this 'double-click' misapprehension). What was intended, rather, was to highlight the 'transformations' or 'deformations' involved in movements through networks: as Callon pointed out in an early paper (1986), translation entails treason. Attention should, therefore, be paid to the attempts to route and limit the movements of actors. See also Barry 2001.
14. Silverstone 1985: 108.
15. Polanyi 1982 (orig. 1958). Thomas Kuhn (1962) has also famously argued likewise. Geertz (2000: ch.7) provides an interesting anthropological evaluation of Kuhn's work.
16. Polanyi notes this phenomenon – though in other terms. 'Irrationalities' is used by Max Weber in his account of rationalization (1978) which bears strong parallels with the argument here.
17. It has been argued that one reason for the success of Thatcherism is that it was capable of colonising language in this way and thus appealing to, or becoming a means of expression of, a broader range of subjects than might have been its 'natural' constituency. See Hall 1980 and Stevenson 1995: ch.1.
18. Saumerez Smith 2000.
19. Contributions to Farmelo and Carding 1997 and Lindqvist 2000 provide discussion of this.
20. For discussion of some of these see Cossons 2000, Gammon and Mazda 2000; Joss and Durant 1995, and the Science Museum web-site: http://sciencemuseum.org.uk

Appendix: Visitor Study Questionnaire

Introduction

Hello, I am from Brunel University and we are doing a study about going to museums. Could I please ask you some questions?

A. The Exhibition

1. I am interested in the exhibition that you have just seen. Could you describe where you went and what you saw?
2. What did you think of the exhibition? Please feel free to say whatever you want.
   What did you like/like best?
   Was there anything you disliked?
3. Do you think that there was an overall theme?
   Do you think that there is a story to it?
4. What sort of people do you think this exhibition is designed for?
   Does that include you?
5. Who do you think wrote this exhibition?
   What do you think the people who made this exhibition want you to go away with?
   Did you notice that the gallery is sponsored? Who by?
   Do you think that makes any difference?
6. Does this strike you as a *scientific* exhibition?
   Were you surprised to see it in the Science Museum?
7. Is this the sort of exhibition you like?
   What sorts do you like?
8. Did the experience of visiting the exhibition change your views about the effects of science and technology on the food you eat? In what way?

9. Is there anything you still want to know about food that you could not find out about in the exhibition?

B. The Visit

1. Where have you come from today? Is that where you live? How long did it take you?
2. What prompted your visit today? Did you come especially to see this exhibition?
   What did you come to see? Did you know anything about this exhibition before you came?
   Are you particularly interested in the subject of this exhibition?
   Have you been to the Science Museum before? How often?
   Have you seen or do you plan to see any other exhibitions while you are here?
3. Do you visit museums often? When was the last time? Where was that to?
   Which museums did you visit in 1989?
4. What other sorts of things do you like to do in your free time?

C. Science

1. Now I have a question about your interest in various issues. For each of the following I would like you to tell me whether you are very interested, moderately interested or not at all interested:
   New medical discoveries
   New inventions and technologies
   New scientific discoveries
   Science fiction
2. Do you read any magazines about what is going on in science and technology? [If yes] Which do you read? Any others?
3. Turning to some television programmes [ask for each listed below] – do you watch [programme name] regularly, occasionally or never:
   TV News
   Sky at Night
   Horizon
   Tomorrow's World
   QED
   Know How
   4th Dimension
   Other science programmes (please specify)

4. I have here a list of statements. For each I would like you to tell me how much you agree or disagree with it:
   Scientists can be trusted to make the right decisions
   Science and technology are making our lives healthier, easier and more comfortable
   If scientific knowledge is explained clearly, most people will be able to understand it
   Ordinary people are not told enough about what scientists do
   All of today's scientific theories will be accepted in a hundred years time
   It is not important for me to know about science in my daily life

D. Yourself/Yourselves

Now I would like to ask you a few questions about yourself/yourselves (to help us to analyse our study)

1. Can I ask how old you are?
2. What is your occupation? (If unemployed or retired please note previous job if applicable)
3. When did you leave school? Have you done any studying since then?
4. Have you passed any exams or got a qualification in a *science* subject? [If yes] Which?

Note: For a full analysis of this see Macdonald 1993

Bibliography

Alfrey, Judith and Tim Putnam 1992 *The Industrial Heritage*, London: Routledge

Allison-Bunnell, Steven W. 1998 'Making nature "real" again: natural history exhibits and public rhetorics of science at the Smithsonian Institution in the early 1960s', in S. Macdonald (ed.) *The Politics of Display. Museums, Science, Culture*, pp.98–117, London: Routledge

Alvesson, M. 1994 *Cultural Perspectives on Organizations*, Cambridge: Cambridge University Press

Ames, Peter 1991 'Measuring museums' merits', in G. Kavanagh (ed.) *The Museums Profession: Internal and External Relations*, pp.57–68, London: Leicester University Press

Anderson, B. 1983 *Imagined Communities: Reflections on the Origin and Spread of Nationalism*, London: Verso

Ang, Ien 1991 *Desperately Seeking the Audience*, London: Routledge

Ardener, Edwin 1989 *The Voice of Prophecy and Other Essays*, edited by M. Chapman, Oxford: Blackwell

Arnold, Ken 1996 'Presenting science as product or as process: museums and the making of science', in S. Pearce (ed.) *Exploring Science in Museums*, pp.57–78, London: Athlone

Atkinson, Kate 1995 *Behind the Scenes at the Museum*, London: Transworld Publishers

Audit Commission 1989 *Managing Services Effectively – Performance Review*, Management Papers 5, London: HMSO

Bal, Mieke 1996 *Double Exposures. The Subject of Cultural Analysis*, London and New York: Routledge

Barry, Andrew 1998 'On interactivity: consumers, citizens and culture', in S. Macdonald (ed.) *The Politics of Display. Museums, Science, Culture*, pp.98–117, London: Routledge

—— 2001 *Political Machines. Governing a Technological Society*, London: Athlone

Bauman, Zygmunt 1989 *Legislators and Interpreters*, Cambridge: Polity
Beaney, Michael (forthcoming) *Analysis*, Teddington: Acumen
Beck, Ulrich 1992 *Risk Society: Towards a New Modernity*, London: Sage
Becker, Howard 1982 *Art Worlds*, Berkeley: University of California Press
Bedini, Silvio 1965 'The evolution of science museums', *Technology and Culture*, 6, pp.1–29
Beer, Samuel 1982 *Britain Against Itself: The Political Contradictions of Collectivism*, London: Faber and Faber
Begeron, L. 1993 'The new generation of museums: technical, industrial and "ecomuseums"', in B. Schroeder-Gudehus (ed.) *Industrial Society and its Museums, 1880–1990: Social Aspirations and Cutural Politics*, pp.91–5, Chur, Switzerland: Harwood Academic, Paris: Cité des Sciences et de l'Industrie
Benedict, B. 1983 *The Anthropology of World's Fairs*, London: Scolar Press
Bennett, Tony 1995 *The Birth of the Museum*, London: Routledge
—— 1998 'Speaking to the eyes: museums, legibility and the social order', in S. Macdonald (ed.) *The Politics of Display. Museums, Science, Culture*, pp.25–35, London: Routledge
Berland, Jody 1992 'Angels dancing: cultural technologies and the production of space', in L. Grossberg, C. Nelson and P. Treichler (eds) *Cultural Studies*, pp.38–50, London: Routledge
Bicknell, Sandra and Graeme Farmelo 1993 *Museum Visitor Studies in the 90s*, London: Science Museum
Born, Georgina 1995 *Rationalizing Culture. IRCAM, Boulez, and the Institutionalization of the Musical Avant-Garde*, Berkeley: University of California Press
Bouquet, Mary 1995 'Exhibiting knowledge: the trees of Dubois, Haeckel, Jesse and Rivers at the Pithecanthropus centennial exhibition', in M. Strathern (ed.) *Shifting Contexts: Transformations in Anthropological Knowledge*, pp.31–55, London: Routledge
—— (ed.) 2001 *Academic Anthropology and the Museum. Back to the Future*, Oxford: Berghahn
Bourdieu, Pierre 1984 (1979) *Distinction. A Social Critique of the Judgement of Taste*, London: Routledge
—— and Alain Darbel (with Dominique Schnapper) 1991 (1969) *The Love of Art: European Art Museums and their Public*, Cambridge: Polity
Bowker, Geoffrey C. and Susan Leigh Star 1999 *Sorting Things Out: Classification and its Consequences*, Cambridge, Mass.: MIT Press
Boylan, Patrick (ed.) 1992 *Museums 2000. Politics, People, Professionals and Profit*, London: Routledge

Bud, Robert 1988 'The myth and the machine: seeing science through museum eyes', in G. Fyfe and J. Law (eds) *Picturing Power. Visual Depiction and Social Relations*, pp.134–59, London: Routledge

—— 1993 'The museum, meaning, and history: the case of chemistry', in S.H. Mauskopf (ed.) *Chemical Sciences in the Modern World*, pp.277–94, Philadelphia: University of Pennsylvania Press

—— 1995 'Science, meaning and myth in the museum', *Public Understanding of Science*, 4.1, pp.1–16

—— Martin Cave and S. Hanney 1991 'Measuring a museum's output', *Museums Journal*, January 1991, pp.29–31

Burnett, Andrew and John Reeve (eds) 2001 *Behind the Scenes at the British Museum,* London: British Museum Publications

Burke, Seán 1995 *Authorship: from Plato to the Postmodern,* Edinburgh: Edinburgh University Press

Burrett, F.G. 1982 *Rayner Scrutiny of the Departmental Museums: Science Museum and Victoria and Albert Museum* (unpublished)

Butler, Stella 1992 *Science and Technology Museums*, Leicester: Leicester University Press

Callon, Michel 1986 'Some elements of a sociology of translation: domestification of the scallops and fishermen of St Brieuc Bay', in J. Law (ed.) *Power, Action, Belief: a New Sociology of Knowledge?*, pp.196–233, London: Routledge and Kegan Paul

—— 1998 'An essay on framing and overflowing: economic externalities revisited by sociology', in M. Callon (ed.) *The Laws of the Markets*, pp.244–69, Oxford: Blackwell

—— 1999 'Actor network theory: the market test', in J. Law and J. Hassard (eds) *Actor Network Theory and After*, pp.181– 95.

—— John Law and Arie Rip (eds) 1986 *Mapping the Dynamics of Science and Technology: Sociology of Science in the Real World*, London: Macmillan

Campbell, Colin 1987 *The Romantic Ethic and the Spirit of Modern Consumerism*, Oxford: Blackwell

Cannon-Brookes, Peter 1989 'Refurbishing the East Hall of the Science Museum, London', *International Journal of Museum Management and Curatorship*, 8, pp.69–76

Carrier, James G. (ed.) 1997 *Meanings of the Market: the Free Market in Western Culture*, Oxford: Berg

—— 1998 'Introduction', in J.G. Carrier and D. Miller (eds) *Virtualism: A New Political Economy*, pp.1–24, Oxford: Berg

Carter, James 1999 'How old is this text?', in E. Hooper-Greenhill (ed.) *The Educational Role of the Museum* (2nd ed.), pp.211–14, London: Routledge

Castells, Manuel 1996 *The Rise of the Network Society*, Oxford: Blackwell

Caulton, Timothy J. 1998 *Hands-on Exhibitions: Managing Interactive Museums and Science Centres*, London: Routledge

Claeson, Bjorn, Emily Martin, Wendy Richardson, Monica Schloch-Spana and Karen-Sue Taussig 1996 'Scientific literacy, what it is, why it's important, and why scientists think we don't have it. The case of immunology and the immune system', in L. Nader (ed.) *Naked Science. Anthropological Inquiry into Boundaries, Power and Knowledge*, pp.101–16, London: Routledge

Clifford, J. 1997 *Routes. Travel and Translation in the Late Twentieth Century*, Cambridge, Mass.: Harvard University Press

Cohen, Anthony P. 1985 *The Symbolic Construction of Community*, London: Routledge

—— 1992 'The personal right to identity: a polemic on the self in the enterprise culture', in P. Heelas and P. Morris (eds) *The Values of the Enterprise Culture. The Moral Debate*, pp.179–93, London: Routledge

Conn, Steven 1998 *Museums and American Intellectual Life, 1876–1926*, Chicago: Chicago University Press

Coombes, Annie E. 1994 *Reinventing Africa: Material Culture and Popular Imagination in Late-Victorian and Edwardian England*, New Haven: Yale University Press.

Corner, John 1991 'Meaning, genre and context: the problematics of "public knowledge" in the new audience studies', in J. Curran and M. Gurevitch (eds) *Mass Media and Society*, pp.267–84, London: Edward Arnold

—— and Sylvia Harvey 1991 'Introduction: Great Britain Limited', in J. Corner and S. Harvey (eds) *Enterprise and Heritage. Crosscurrents of National Culture*, pp.1–20, London: Routledge

—— 1991a 'Mediating tradition and modernity: the heritage/enterprise couplet', in J. Corner and S. Harvey (eds) *Enterprise and Heritage. Crosscurrents of National Culture*, pp.45–75, London: Routledge

Cossons, Neil (ed.) 1985 *The Management of Change in Museums*, London: National Maritime Museum

—— 1987 'Dangers of a dinosaur mentality', *The Listener*, 16 April 1987, pp.18–20

—— 1988 'Our museums must blow off the dust', *Sunday Times*, May 1 1998

—— 1989 'Plural funding and the heritage', in D. Uzzell (ed.) *Heritage Interpretation Volume 2: the Visitor Experience*, pp.16–22, London: Bellhaven Press

—— 1991 'Class, culture and collections', in G. Kavanagh (ed.) *The Museums Profession: Internal and External Relations*, pp.13–24, Leicester: Leicester University Press

—— 1991a 'Scholarship or self-indulgence?', *RSA Journal*, Vol.CXXXIX no.5415, pp.184–91

—— 1992 'Rambling reflections of a museum man', in P. Boylan (ed.) *Museums 2000. Politics, People, Professionals and Profit*, pp.123–47, London: Routledge

—— 2000 'Museums in the new millennium', in S. Lindqvist (ed.) *Museums of Modern Science*, pp.3–16, Canton, MA: Science History Publications

Crook, J.M. 1972 *The British Museum*, London: Penguin

Danilov, Victor J. 1982 *Science and Technology Centers*, Cambridge, Mass.: MIT Press

—— 1991 *America's Science Museums*, New York: Greenwood Press

Davis, John 1992 'Tense in ethnography: some practical considerations', in J. Okely and H. Callaway (eds) *Anthropology and Autobiography*, pp.205–20, London: Routledge

Davis, Susan G. 1997 *Spectacular Nature. Corporate Culture and the Sea World Experience*, Berkeley: University of California Press

Day, Lance 1987 'A short history of the Science Museum', *Science Museum Review 1987*, London: Science Museum

Delaney, Carol 1991 *The Seed and the Soil*, Berkeley: University of California Press

Derrida, Jacques 1995 'The Exhorbitant. Question of Method', in S. Burke (ed.) *Authorship: from Plato to the Postmodern*, pp.117–24, Edinburgh: Edinburgh University Press

Dias, Nélia 1998 'The visibility of difference: nineteenth-century French anthropological collections', in S. Macdonald (ed.) *The Politics of Display. Museums, Science, Culture*, pp.36–52, London: Routledge

Downey, Gary Lee 1998 *The Machine in Me. An Anthropologist sits among the Computer Engineers*, London: Routledge

du Gay, Paul 1997 'Introduction', in P. du Gay (ed.) *Production of Culture/ Cultures of Production*, pp.1–10, Milton Keynes: Open University and London: Sage

Duncan, Carol 1995 *Civilising Rituals. Inside Public Art Museums*, London: Routledge

Durant, John 1992 'Introduction', in J. Durant (ed.) *Museums and the Public Understanding of Science*, pp.7–11, London: Science Museum, in association with the Committee on the Public Understanding of Science

Edwards, Jeanette 2002 'Bits and bytes of information', in N. Rapport (ed.) *British Subjects: an Anthropology of Britain*, Oxford: Berg
Elsner, John and Roger Cardinal (eds) 1994 *The Cultures of Collecting*, London: Reaktion Books
Farmelo, Graham and Janet Carding (eds) 1997 *Here and Now: Contemporary Science and Technology in Museums and Science Centres*, London: Science Museum
Feist, Andrew and Robert Hutchinson (eds) 1989 *Cultural Trends 1989*, 4, London: Policy Studies Institute
—— 1989a *Cultural Trends 1989*, 1, London: Policy Studies Institute
—— 1990 *Cultural Trends 1990*, 5, London: Policy Studies Institute
Follett, David 1978 *The Rise of the Science Museum under Henry Lyons*, London: Science Museum
Forgan, Sophie 1994 'The architecture of display: museums, universities and objects in nineteenth-century Britain', *History of Science*, 32.2, pp.139–62.
—— 1996 '"A nightmare of incomprehensible machines": science and technology museums in the 19th and 20th centuries', in M. Pointon (ed.) *Museums and late-Twentieth-Century Culture*, pp.46–68, Manchester: Manchester University Press
Forsythe, Diana 1992 'Blaming the user in medical informatics: the cultural nature of scientific practice', *Knowledge and Society: the Anthropology of Science and Technology*, Vol.9, pp.95–111
Foucault, Michel 1995 '[from] What is an author?', in S. Burke (ed.) *Authorship: from Plato to the Postmodern*, pp.233–46, Manchester: Manchester University Press
Fowler, Peter J. 1992 *The Past in Contemporary Society: Then, Now*, London: Routledge
Fox, Robert 1992 'Research and curatorship in the national science museums: a reflexion on threats and opportunities', *Impact of Science on Society*, no.159, pp.263–71
Fyfe, Gordon 1996 'A Trojan Horse at the Tate: theorizing the museum as agency and structure', in S. Macdonald and G. Fyfe (eds) *Theorizing Museums*, pp.203–228, Oxford: Blackwell
—— 2000 *Art, Power and Modernity*, London: Leicester University Press
Gammon, Ben and Xerxes Mazda 2000 'The power of the pencil: renegotiating the museum-visitor relationship through discussion exhibits', in S. Lindqvist (ed.) *Museums of Modern Science*, pp.159–168, Canton, MA: Science History Publications
Geertz, Clifford 1973 'Deep play: notes on the Balinese cock-fight', in C. Geertz *The Interpretation of Cultures*, pp.412–53, New York: Basic Books

—— 2000 *Available Light. Anthropological Reflections on Philosophical Topics*, Princeton, NJ: Princeton University Press

Gellner, David and Eric Hirsch (eds) 2001 *Inside Organizations: Anthropologists at Work*, Oxford: Berg

Gibbons, Michael *et al.* 1994 *The New Production of Knowledge*, London: Sage

Giddens, Anthony 1990 *The Consequences of Modernity*, Cambridge: Polity.

—— 1991 *Modernity and Self-Identity*, Cambridge: Polity

Goffman, Erving 1969 [1959] *The Presentation of Self in Everyday Life*, Harmondsworth: Penguin

—— 1971 *Frame Analysis: an Essay on the Organization of Experience*, Chicago: Northeastern University Press

González, Roberto J., Laura Nader and C. Jay Ou 1999 'Towards an ethnography of museums: new directions from the museum experience', *focaal. tidschrift voor antropologie*, 34, pp.107–117

Greenhalgh, Paul 1988 *Ephemeral Vistas: The Expositions Universelles, Great Exhibitions and World's Fairs, 1851–1939*, Manchester: Manchester University Press

Grint, Keith 1995 *Management: A Sociological Introduction*, Cambridge: Polity

Gucht, Daniel 1991 'Art at risk in the hands of the museum: from the museum to the private collection', *International Sociology*, 6.3, pp.361–72

Gusterson, Hugh 1996 *Nuclear Rites. A Weapons Laboratory at the End of the Cold War*, Berkeley: University of California Press

Hall, Stuart 1980 'Encoding/Decoding, in S. Hall *et al.* (eds) *Culture, Media, Language*, pp.128–38, London: Hutchinson

—— (ed.) 1997 *Representation. Cultural Representations and Signifying Practices*, London: Sage

Handler, Richard and Eric Gable 1997 *The New History in an Old Museum. Creating the Past at Colonial Williamsburg*, Durham: Duke University Press

Hanna, Max 1989 *Sightseeing in 1988*, London: British Tourist Authority/English Tourist Board

Haraway, Donna 1989 'Teddy bear patriarchy: taxidermy in the Garden of Eden, New York City, 1908–1936', in *Primate Visions: Gender, Race and Nature in the World of Modern Science*, London: Routledge

—— *Modest_Witness@Second_Millennium.FemaleMan©_Meets_OncoMouse™*, London: Routledge

Harvey, David 1989 *The Condition of Postmodernity*, Oxford: Blackwell

Harvey, Penelope 1996 *Hybrids of Modernity: Anthropology, the Nation-state and the Universal Exhibition*, London: Routledge
—— (forthcoming) 'Memorialising the future: the Museum of Science and Industry in Manchester', in M. Bouquet and N. Porto (eds) *The Museum as Ritual Site*, Oxford: Berghahn
Heady, Patrick 1984 *Visiting Museums*, London: HMSO
Heelas, Paul and Paul Morris (eds) 1992 *The Values of the Enterprise Culture. The Moral Debate*, London: Routledge
Hein, Hilde 1990 *The Exploratorium: The Museum as Laboratory*, Washington: Smithsonian Institution
Held, David, Anthony McGrew, David Goldblatt and Jonathan Perraton 1999 *Global Transformations. Politics, Economics and Culture*, Oxford: Blackwell
Hendry, Joy 2000 *The Orient Strikes Back. A Global View of Cultural Display*, Oxford: Berg
Herzfeld, Michael 1992 *The Social Production of Indifference: Exploring the Symbolic Roots of Western Bureaucracy*, Oxford: Berg
Hewison, Robert 1988 *The Heritage Industry*, London: Methuen
—— 1991 'Commerce and culture', in J. Corner and S. Harvey (eds) *Enterprise and Heritage. Crosscurrents of National Culture*, pp.162–77, London: Routledge
Hooper-Greenhill, Eilean 1992 *Museums and the Shaping of Knowledge*, London: Routledge
—— 1994 *Museums and their Visitors*, London: Routledge
—— (ed.) 1999 *Museum, Media, Message* (2nd ed.), London: Routledge
—— (ed.) 1999a *The Educational Role of the Museum* (2nd ed.), London: Routledge
Hoskins, Janet 1998 *Biographical Objects. How Things tell the Stories of People's Lives*, London: Routledge
Howell, Signe 1997 'Cultural studies and social anthropology: contesting or complementary discourses?', in S. Nugent and C. Shore (eds) *Anthropology and Cultural Studies*, pp.103–25, London: Pluto Press
Hudson, Kenneth 1975 *A Social History of Museums*, London: Macmillan
Huyssen, Andreas 1995 *Twilight Memories. Marking Time in a Culture of Amnesia*, London: Routledge
Irwin, Alan and Brian Wynne (eds) 1996 *Misunderstanding Science? The Public Reconstruction of Science and Technology*, Cambridge: Cambridge University Press
—— 1996a 'Introduction', in A. Irwin and B. Wynne (eds) *Misunderstanding Science? The Public Reconstruction of Science and Technology*, pp.1–17, Cambridge: Cambridge University Press

Jordanova, Ludmilla 1989 'Objects of Knowledge: a Historical Perspective on Museums', in P. Vergo (ed.) *The New Museology*, pp.22–40, London: Reaktion Books

Joss, Simon and John Durant (eds) 1995 *Public Participation in Science: the Role of the Consensus Conferences in Europe*, London: Science Museum

Karp, Ivan 1991 'Culture and representation', in I. Karp and S. Lavine (eds) (1991) *Exhibiting Cultures: the Poetics and Politics of Museum Display*, pp.11–24, Washington: Smithsonian Institution.

—— Christine M. Kreamer, and Steven Lavine (eds) 1992 *Museums and Communities: the Politics of Public Culture*, Washington: Smithsonian Institution

Kawashima, Nobuko 1997 *Museum Management in a Time of Change. Impacts of Cultural Policy on Museums in Britain, 1979–1997*, Warwick: University of Warwick Centre for the Study of Cultural Policy

Kidder, Tracey 1982 (1981) *The Soul of a New Machine*, London: Allen Lane

Kirby, Sue 1988 'Policy and politics: charges, sponsorship, and bias', in R. Lumley (ed.) *The Museum Time-Machine*, pp.89–101, London: Comedia

Kirschenblatt-Gimblett, Barbara 1998 *Destination Culture. Tourism, Museums, and Heritage*, Berkeley: University of California Press

Kohn, Marek 1989 'Can the Science Museum keep up?', *Telegraph Weekend Magazine*, 4 March 1989, pp.40–47

Kuhn, Thomas 1962 *The Structure of Scientific Revolutions*, Chicago: Chicago University Press

La Fontaine, Jean 1985 *Initiation. Ritual Drama and Secret Knowledge across the World*, Harmondsworth: Penguin

Lash, Scott and John Urry 1987 *The End of Organized Capitalism*, Cambridge: Polity

—— 1994 *Economies of Signs and Space*, London: Sage

Latour, Bruno 1987 *Science in Action: How to Follow Scientists and Engineers through Society*, Cambridge, MA: Harvard University Press

—— 1996 *Aramis, or the Love of Technology*, Cambridge, MA: Harvard University Press

—— 1999 'On recalling ANT', in J. Law and J. Hassard (eds) *Actor Network Theory and After*, pp.15–25, Oxford: Blackwell

—— and Steve Woolgar 1979 *Laboratory Life: the Social Construction of Scientific Facts*, London: Sage

Lave, Jean 1988 *Cognition in Practice. Mind, Mathematics and Culture in Everyday Life*, Cambridge: Cambridge University Press

Lavine, Steven D. and Ivan Karp 1991 'Introduction: Museums and Multiculturalism', in I. Karp and S.D. Lavine (eds) *Exhibiting Cultures*, pp.1- 9, Washington: Smithsonian Institution

Law, John 1991 'Introduction: monsters, machines and sociotechnical relations', in J. Law (ed.) *A Sociology of Monsters: Essays on Power, Technology and Domination*, pp.1–23, London: Routledge.

—— 1994 *Organizing Modernity: Social Ordering and Social Theory*, Oxford: Blackwell

—— and John Hassard (eds) 1999 *Actor Network Theory and After*, Oxford: Blackwell

Lawrence, Ghislaine 1991 'Rats, street gangs and culture: evaluation in museums', in G. Kavanagh (ed.) *Museum Languages: Objects and Texts*, pp.11–32, London: Leicester University Press

—— 1993 'Remembering rats, considering culture: perspectives on museum evaluation', in S. Bicknell and G. Farmelo (eds) *Museum Visitor Studies in the 90s*, pp.117–24, London: Science Museum

Levidow, Les and Bob Young 1984 'Exhibiting nuclear power: the Science Museum cover-up', *Radical Science* 14, pp.52–79

Lewenstein, Bruce V. 1992 'The meaning of "public understanding of science" in the United States after World War II', *Public Understanding of Science*, 1, pp.45–68.

Lidchi, Henrietta 1997 'The poetics and politics of exhibiting other cultures', in S. Hall (ed.) *Representation. Cultural Representations and Signifying Practices*, pp.151–208, London: Sage

Lindqvist, Svante (ed.) 2000 *Museums of Modern Science*, Canton, MA: Science History Publications

Lindqvist, T. 1993 'An Olympic stadium of technology: Deutches Museum and Sweden's Tekniska Museet', in B. Schroeder-Gudehus (ed.) *Industrial Society and its Museums, 1880–1990: Social Aspirations and Cultural Politics*, pp.37–54, Chur, Switzerland: Harwood Academic/ Paris: Cité des Sciences et de l'Industrie

Lowenthal, David 1998 *The Heritage Crusade and the Spoils of History*, Cambridge: Cambridge University Press

Lumley, Robert 1988 'Introduction', in R. Lumley (ed.) *The Museum Time-Machine*, pp.1–23, London: Comedia

Lutz, Catherine A. and Jane L. Collins 1993 *Reading National Geographic*, Chicago: University of Chicago Press

Macdonald, Sharon 1993 *Museum Visiting: A Science Museum Case Study*, Working Paper no.1, Keele: Keele University Department of Sociology and Social Anthropology

—— 1996 'Theorizing museums: an introduction', in S. Macdonald and G. Fyfe (eds) *Theorizing Museums: Representing Identity and Diversity in a Changing World*, pp.1–18, Oxford: Blackwell
—— 1997 'The museum as mirror: ethnographic reflections', in A. James, J. Hockey and A. Dawson (eds) *After Writing Culture. Epistemology and Praxis in Contemporary Anthropology*, pp.155–75, London: Routledge
—— (ed.) 1998 *The Politics of Display. Museums, Science, Culture*, London: Routledge
—— 1998a 'Supermarket science? Consumers and the "public understanding of science"', in S. Macdonald (ed.) *The Politics of Display. Museums, Science, Culture*, pp.118–38, London: Routledge
—— 2001 'Ethnography in the Science Museum, London', in D. Gellner and E. Hirsch (eds) *Inside Organizations: Anthropologists at Work*, pp.77–96, Oxford: Berg
—— 2002 'On old things: the fetishization of past everyday life', in N. Rapport (ed.) *British Subjects: an Anthropology of Britain*, pp.115–37, Oxford: Berg
—— and Roger Silverstone 1990 'Rewriting the museums' fictions: taxonomies, stories and readers', *Cultural Studies* 4.2, pp.176–91
—— and Roger Silverstone 1992 'Science on display: the representation of scientific controversy in museum exhibitions', *Public Understanding of Science*, 1.1, pp.69–87
McGuigan, Jim 1992 *Cultural Populism*, London: Routledge
—— 1996 *Culture and the Public Sphere*, London: Routledge
MacKay, Hugh (ed.) 1997 *Consumption and Everyday Life*, London: Sage and Milton Keynes: Open University Press
McManus, Paulette 1987 '"It's the company you keep": The social determination of learning related behaviour in a science museum', *International Journal of Museum Management and Curatorship* 6. pp.263–70
—— 1988 'Good companions: more on the determination of learning-related behaviour in a science museum', *International Journal of Museum Management and Curatorship*, 7. pp.37–44
—— 1989 *A Survey of Science Museum Visitors on Food and Nutrition Topics*, unpublished report commissioned by the Public Services Division of the Science Museum
Macnaghten, Phil and John Urry 1998 *Contested Natures*, London: Sage
Marcus, George E. 1998 *Ethnography through Thick and Thin*, Princeton: Princeton University Press
Marquand, David 1992 'The enterprise culture: old wine in new bottles?', in P. Heelas and P. Morris (eds) *The Values of the Enterprise Culture. The Moral Debate*, pp.61–72, London: Routledge

Martin, Emily 1994 *Flexible Bodies: Tracking Immunity in American Culture from the Days of Polio to the Age of AIDS*, Boston: Beacon Press
—— 1996 'Managing Americans. Policy changes in the meanings of work and the self', in C. Shore and S. Wright (eds) *Anthropology of Policy*, London: Routledge
Mayr, Ott *et al.* 1990 *The Deutsches Museum*, London: Scala
Merriman, Nick 1989 'Museum visiting as a cultural phenomenon', in P. Vergo (ed.) *The New Museology*, pp.149–71, London: Reaktion Books
—— 1991 *Beyond the Glass Case: the Past, the Heritage and the Public in Britain*, London: Leicester University Press
Miles, Roger *et al.* 1988 *The Design of Educational Exhibits* (2nd ed.), London: Unwin Hyman
Miles, Roger and Alan Tout 1992 'Exhibitions and the public understanding of science', in J. Durant (ed.) *Museums and the Public Understanding of Science*, pp.27–33, London: Science Museum in association with the Committee on the Public Understanding of Science
Miller, Daniel 1997 *Capitalism. An Ethnographic Approach*, Oxford, New York: Berg
—— 1998 'Conclusion: a theory of virtualism', in James Carrier and Daniel Miller (eds) *Virtualism. A New Political Economy*, Oxford: Berg, pp.187–215
Moore, Kevin 1997 *Museums and Popular Culture*, London: Leicester University Press
Morley, David 1995 'Theories of consumption in the media', in D. Miller (ed.) *Acknowledging Consumption*, pp.296–328, London: Routledge
Museums and Galleries Commission 1988 *The National Museums. The National Museums and Galleries of the United Kingdom*, London: HMSO
—— 1997 *To Charge or not to Charge? Full Report*, undertaken by Glasgow Caledonian University, London: Museums and Galleries Commission
Natural History Museum 1990 *Corporate Plan 1990–95*, London: Natural History Museum
Newhouse, Victoria 1998 *Towards a New Museum*, New York: The Monacelli Press
Office of Arts and Libraries 1991 *Reports on the Development of Performance Indicators for the National Museums and Galleries*, London: Office of Arts and Libraries
O'Hanlon, Michael 1993 *Paradise: Portraying the New Guinea Highlands*, London: British Museum
Outram, Dorinda 1996 'New spaces in natural history', in N. Jardine, J.A. Secord and E.C. Spary (eds) *Cultures of Natural History*, pp.249–65, Cambridge: Cambridge University Press

Parker, Martin 2000 *Organizational Culture and Identity*, London: Sage
Pearce, Susan (ed.) 1993 *Museums and the Appropriation of Culture*, London: Athlone
—— 1995 *On Collecting: an Investigation into Collecting in the European Tradition*, London: Routledge
—— (ed.) 1996 *Exploring Science in Museums*, London and Atlantic Highlands, NJ: Athlone
—— (ed.) 1997 *Experiencing Material Culture in the Western World*, London: Leicester University Press
—— (ed.) 1998 *Collecting in Contemporary Practice*, London: Sage
Physik, John 1982 *The Victoria and Albert Museum: the History of its Building*, London: Victoria and Albert Museum
Pickstone, John 1994 'Museological science? The place of the analytical/comparative in nineteenth-century Science, Technology and Medicine', *History of Science*, 32.2, pp.111–38.
Pizzey, Steve (ed.) 1987 *Interactive Science and Technology Centres*, London: Science Projects Publishing
Polanyi, Michael 1982 'The stability of scientific theories against experience', in M.Marwick (ed.) *Witchcraft and Sorcery*, pp.452–59, Harmondsworth: Penguin
Porter, Gaby 1988 'Putting your house in order: representations of women and domestic life', in R. Lumley (ed.) *The Museum Time-Machine*, pp.102–27, London: Routledge
Power, Michael 1994 *The Audit Explosion*, London: Demos
—— 1997 *The Audit Society*, Oxford: Oxford University Press
Prösler, Martin 1996 'Museums and globalization', in S. Macdonald and G. Fyfe (eds) *Theorizing Museums*, pp.21–44, Oxford: Blackwell.
Rabinow, Paul 1996 *Making PCR: A Story of Biotechnology*, Chicago: Chicago University Press
Richardson, Kay and John Corner 1986 'Reading reception: mediation and transparency in viewers' reception of a TV programme', *Media, Culture and Society*, 8.4, pp.9–29
Ritzer, George 1996 *The McDonaldization of Society* (2nd. ed.), Thousand Oaks, CA: Pine Forge Press
Robbins, Bruce 1993 'Introduction: the public as phantom', in B. Robbins (ed.) *The Phantom Public Sphere*, pp.vii–xxvi, Minneapolis: University of Minnesota Press
Roche, Maurice 1992 *Rethinking Citizenship. Welfare, Ideology and Change in Modern Society*, Cambridge: Polity
—— 2000 *Mega-Events and Modernity. Olympics and Expos in the Growth of Global Culture*, London: Routledge

Rogoff, Irit 1998 'Studying visual culture', in N. Mirzoeff (ed.) *Visual Culture Reader*, pp.14–26, London: Routledge
Rose, Nikolas 1990 *Governing the Soul. The Shaping of the Private Self*, London: Routledge
—— 1992 'Governing the enterprising self', in P. Heelas and P. Morris (eds) *The Values of the Enterprise Cutlure. The Moral Debate*, pp.141–64, London: Routledge
Royal Society 1985 *The Public Understanding of Science*, London: Royal Society
Sabbagh, Karl 2000 *Power into Art*, London: Penguin
Salaman, Graeme 1997 'Culturing production', in P. du Gay (ed.) *Production of Culture/Cultures of Production*, pp.235–72, Milton Keynes: Open University and London: Sage
Samuel, Raphael 1995 *Theatres of Memory*, London: Verso
Saumerez Smith, Charles 1989 'Museums, artefacts and meanings', in P. Vergo (ed.) *The New Museology*, pp.6–21, London: Reaktion Books
—— 2000 *The Future of Museums*. The third Andrew Martindale lecture given at the University of East Anglia (unpublished)
Schneider, Andrea 1998 *Creating the Musée d'Orsay. The Politics of Culture in France*, Pennsylvania: Pennsylvania State University Press
Schroeder-Gudehus, Brigitte (ed.) 1993 *Industrial Society and its Museums, 1880–1990: Social Aspirations and Cutural Politics*, Chur, Switzerland: Harwood Academic/Paris: Cité des Sciences et de l'Industrie
Shapin, Steven 1994 *A Social History of Truth: Civility and Science in Seventeenth-Century England*, Chicago: Chicago University Press.
Sheets-Pyenson, Susan 1989 *Cathedrals of Science: the Development of Colonial Natural History Museums during the late Nineteenth Century*, Montreal: McGill University Press
Shelton, Anthony (forthcoming) 'New pilgrims: post conservative museology and the re-definition of the object', in M. Bouquet and N. Porto (eds) *The Museum as Ritual Site*, Oxford: Berghahn
Sherman, Daniel J. 1989 *Worthy Monuments. Art Museums and the Politics of Culture in Nineteenth-Century France*, Cambridge, MA: Harvard University Press
—— and Irit Rogoff 1994 'Introduction: frameworks for critical analysis', in D.J. Sherman and I. Rogoff (eds) *Museum Culture. Histories, Discourses, Spectacles*, pp.ix–xx, London: Routledge
Silverstone, Roger 1985 *Framing Science: the Making of a BBC Documentary*, London: British Film Institute
—— 1988 'Museums and the media: a theoretical and methodological exploration', *International Journal of Museum Managment and Curatorship*, 7, pp.231–42

—— 1989 'Heritage as media: some implications for research', in D. Uzzell (ed.) *Heritage Interpretation Volume 2: the Visitor Experience*, London: Frances Pinter

—— 1991 'Communicating science to the public', *Science, Technology and Human Values*, 16.1, pp.69–89

—— 1992 'The medium is the museum: on objects and logics in times and spaces', in J. Durant (ed.) *Museums and the Public Understanding of Science*, pp.34–42, London: Science Museum in association with the Committee on the Public Understanding of Science

—— 1994 *Television and Everyday Life*, London: Routledge

—— 1999 *Why Study the Media?*, London: Sage

Simmons, Ian 1996 'A conflict of cultures: hands-on science centres in UK museums', in S.Pearce (ed.) *Exploring Science in Museums*, pp.79–94, London: Athlone

Star, Susan Leigh 1991 'Power, technology and the phenomenology of conventions: on being allergic to onions', in J. Law (ed.) *A Sociology of Monsters. Essays on Power, Technology and Domination*, pp.26–56, London: Routledge

—— and James R. Griesemer 1989 'Institutional ecology, "translations" and boundary objects: amateurs and professionals in Berkeley's Museum of Vertebrate Zoology, 1907–39', *Social Studies of Science*, Vol.19, pp.387–420

Stearn, W.T. 1981 *The Natural History Museum at South Kensington: a History of the British Museum (Natural History) 1753–1980*, London: Heinemann

Stevenson, Nick 1995 *Understanding Media Cultures. Social Theory and Mass Communication*, London: Sage

Stone, Peter and Brian Molyneux (eds) 1994 *The Presented Past. Heritage, Museums and Education*, London: Routledge

Strathern, Marilyn 1987 'The limits of auto-anthropology', in A. Jackson (ed.) *Anthropology at Home*, pp.16–37, London: Tavistock

—— 1992 'Enterprising kinship: consumer choice and the new reproductive technologies', in P. Heelas and P. Morris (eds) *The Values of the Enterprise culture. The Moral Debate*, pp.165–78, London: Routledge

—— 1992a *After Nature. English Kinship in the late Twentieth-Century*, Cambridge: Cambridge University Press

—— 1992b *Reproducing the Future*, Manchester: Manchester University Press

—— 1995 'Foreword', in M. Strathern (ed.) *Shifting Contexts. Transformations in Anthropological Knowledge*, London: Routledge

—— (ed.) 2000 *Audit Cultures. Anthropological Studies in Accountability, Ethics and the Academy*, London: Routledge

Swade, Doron 1989 'Mouseproof pedals and the curator's dilemma', *Science Museum Review 1989*, pp.50–52, London: Science Museum

Tait, Simon 1989 *Palaces of Discovery. The Changing World of Britain's Museums*, London: Quiller Press

Taylor, Charles 1985 *Sources of the Self. The Making of the Modern Identity*, Cambridge: Cambridge University Press

Thomas, Nicholas 1999 'Becoming undisciplined: anthropology and cultural studies', in H.L. Moore (ed.) *Anthropological Theory Today*, Cambridge: Polity, pp.262–79

Traweek, Sharon 1988 *Beamtimes and Lifetimes: the World of High Energy Physicists*, Cambridge, MA: Harvard University Press

Turner, Victor 1967 *The Forest of Symbols: Aspects of Ndembu Ritual*, Ithaca, NY: Cornell University Press

—— 1974 *Dramas, Fields and Metaphors: Symbolic Action in Human Society*, Ithaca, NY: Cornell University Press

Urry, John 1990 *The Tourist Gaze*, London: Sage

—— 1996 'How societies remember the past', in S.Macdonald and G. Fyfe (eds) *Theorizing Museums*, pp.45–65, Oxford: Blackwell

Van Gennep, Arnold 1960 (1909) *Rites of Passage*, London: Routledge & Kegan Paul

Van Maanen, John 2001 'Afterword: Natives "R" Us: Some notes on the ethnography of organizations', in D. Gellner and E. Hirsch (eds) *Inside Organizations: Anthropologists at Work*, pp.233–61, Oxford: Berg

Veron, Eliseo and Martine Levasseur 1982 *Ethnographie de l'Exposition*, Paris: Bibiotheque Publique d'Information

Wallis, Brian 1994 'Selling nations: international exhibitions and cultural diplomacy', in D.J. Sherman and I. Rogoff (eds) *Museum Culture. Histories, Discourses, Spectacles*, pp.265–81, London: Routledge

Walsh, Kevin 1992 *The Representation of the Past: Museums and Heritage in the Post-Modern World*, London: Routledge

Weber, Max 1978 (1921) *Economy and Society*, G. Roth and C. Wittich (eds), Berkeley: University of California Press

Whitehead, P. 1981 *The British Museum (Natural History)*, London: Scala

Willis, Paul 1997 'TIES: Theoretically Informed Ethnographic Study', in S. Nugent and C. Shore (eds) *Anthropology and Cultural Studies*, pp.182–92. London: Pluto Press

Wilson, David 1989 *The British Museum: Purpose and Policies*, London: British Museum Publications

Wittlin, Alma 1949 *The Museum: its History and its Tasks in Education*, London: Routledge and Kegan Paul

Woolgar, Steve 1991 'Configuring the User: the case of usability trials', in John Law (ed.) *A Sociology of Monsters. Essays on Power, Domination and Technology*, pp.57–99, London: Routledge

Wright, Patrick 1985 *On Living in an Old Country – The National Past in Contemporary Britain*, London: Verso

Wright, Susan (ed.) 1994 *The Anthropology of Organizations*, London: Routledge

Wulff, Helena 1998 *Ballet across Borders. Career and Culture in the World of Dancers*, Oxford: Berg

Wynne, Brian 1991 'Knowledges in context', *Science, Technology and Human Values*, 16, pp.111–21

—— 1995 'Public understanding of science', in S. Jasanoff, G.E. Markle, J.C. Peterson and T. Pinch (eds) *Handbook of Science and Technology Studies*, pp.457–79, London and Beverly Hills: Sage

—— 1996 'Misunderstood misunderstandings: social identities and the public uptake of science', in A. Irwin and B. Wynne (eds) *Misunderstanding Science? The Public Reconstruction of Science and Technology*, pp.19–46, Cambridge: Cambridge University Press.

Yanni, Carla 1999 *Nature's Museums: Victorian Science and the Architecture of Display*, London: Athlone

Young, Lord (of Graffham) 1992 'Enterprise regained', in P. Heelas and P. Morris (eds) *The Values of the Enterprise Culture. The Moral Debate*, pp.29–35, London: Routledge

Zabusky, Stacia E. 1995 *Launching Europe. An Ethnography of European Cooperation in Space Science*, Princeton: Princeton University Press

Ziman, John 1991 'Public understanding of science', *Science, Technology and Human Values*, 15, pp.99–105

Index